Systems Development Without Pain:

a user's guide to modeling organizational patterns

Systems Development Without Pain:

a user's guide to modeling organizational patterns

by Paul T. Ward

Foreword by Edward Yourdon

Yourdon Press
1501 Broadway
New York, New York 10036

Library of Congress Cataloging in Publication Data

Ward, Paul T.
    Systems development without pain.

    Includes index.
    1. System design.   2. Electronic data processing.
I. Title.
QA76.9.S88W37   1984   001.64   83-27368
ISBN 0-917072-40-5

Printed in the United States of America

Library of Congress Catalog Number 83-27368

ISBN: 0-917072-40-5

This book was set in Times Roman by YOURDON Press, 1501 Broadway,
New York, N.Y., using a PDP-11/70 running under the UNIX® operating system.*

---

*UNIX is a registered trademark of Bell Laboratories.

Acknowledgments

The ideas for this book developed slowly, and I was immeasurably aided during these years by discussions with my colleagues at YOURDON inc. I especially wish to acknowledge the contributions of Steve McMenamin, John Palmer, Steve Mellor, Gary Schuldt, Sandi Rapps, Ira Morrow, and Tom DeMarco.

I am also indebted to those who read the initial drafts of this manuscript and who offered helpful suggestions: Dell Campbell, Bea Goldman, Agnes Ward, and Thomas Ward. Special thanks go to Pamela M. Plate, who not only read the completed manuscript, but also served as a counselor and a friend during the writing. Much of the book's organization is due to her valuable suggestions.

Finally, I thank Wendy Eakin of Yourdon Press for encouragement, assistance, and patience. I also wish to acknowledge Yourdon Press staff members Susan Moran, Gerry Fahey, Jacob Lasky, Dennis Ladd, and Janice Wormington for their assistance during the book's final weeks of production.

To Gladys

Contents

Preface

Computers, like all the fruits of human invention, have been both a blessing and a burden. In nearly twenty years of working with automated systems, I have become increasingly convinced of the computer's potential for humanizing the work environment. I have also become increasingly frustrated because this potential is so often unrealized. Too many people whose daily work could have been made easier by systems tailored to their needs have instead been saddled with ill-fitting systems that have made their work harder. The benefits of automated technology will be fully realized only when the end users of computer systems are able to communicate their needs effectively. I have written this book to present a set of effective communication techniques to the general reader.

The methods described in this book have all been successfully and extensively used in systems development. However, the underlying unity of these methods has often been masked by inconsistent and confusing computer jargon. Furthermore, the accessibility of these methods to the non-computer expert has been limited, since the methods have primarily been presented in courses and books for the data processing professional.

In writing this book I have attempted to remove these barriers, and I believe that any reasonably intelligent reader can learn to use the techniques presented. However, I do not wish to mislead you into believing that the learning process will be effortless. In order to use these methods effectively, you must learn to see the everyday patterns of your work environment in a completely different way. This will require patience in thinking through the examples given and in allowing me to gradually develop complex topics. If you are serious about applying the techniques, you will almost certainly need to reread sections of this book several times.

However, if you are willing to expend the effort, not only will you increase your ability to communicate systems development needs, but you will also develop a set of general-purpose thinking tools with much broader applications. Since our daily lives are permeated with patterns of activities and information, the ability to perceive and comprehend these patterns can be a valuable personal asset.

New York City   P.T.W.
November 1983

Foreword

The banker, the businessman, the marketing manager, and the myriad other end users in a typical organization are finding it more and more important to know something about computers. This has been true for several years, but it becomes more apparent every day as we see terminals and personal computers on the desk of every professional worker and every manager of every organization.

End users generally want to learn only as much as necessary to effectively use a computer to get their work done. The question is, What should the users learn about computers? Is it sufficient to become "computer literate"? Should they learn BASIC or Fortran? Should they learn to use word-processing packages like Wordstar® or spreadsheet programs like VisiCalc®?

All of these may be interesting and relevant to the user, but Paul Ward's book, *Systems Development Without Pain,* does not attempt to teach any of these things. Why? Because the individual terminal or individual personal computer on the user's desk only becomes interesting when it is connected to other terminals and other personal computers — that is, when it becomes part of a larger *system.* There is no doubt that a businessman with a spreadsheet program on his personal computer will argue that he is better off than he was ten years ago with his pencil-and-paper calculations — but it requires only a small amount of mechanical training to teach him how to use that program.

Developing a system, though, is an entirely different matter. In a typical business organization, a system consists of a number of individuals (or departments or divisions) who receive data from the outside world and who process, compute, and transform that data before sending it back to the outside world or to others in the organization. Tracing the flow of data through the organization can be a difficult, time-consuming process, but it is an important step if one is to properly model a business system within an organization. And it is an activity in which users must be intimately involved, since they — and not the data processing specialists — have the detailed knowledge of the organization from which such models can be built.

It has recently become fashionable to talk about user-friendly programming languages that allow users to implement systems entirely on their own, without any assistance from data processing experts. Such languages are an important improvement over earlier software technology, but it remains true that *you can't implement a system in ANY language if you don't know what that system is supposed to do.* A simple, one-person system can be implemented in an ad hoc fashion using user-friendly programming languages; but a complex system that involves multiple users, multiple sources of data from the outside world, and multiple stores of data *must* be properly modeled before it can be implemented. To draw an analogy: A skilled carpenter could conceivably build a simple, one-room shack without first drawing some plans; he might even be able to construct a three-bedroom house if he were given prefabricated components. But if he were designing a small village, then the problems of construction would pale before the problems of "requirements analysis."

The business of modeling is what Paul Ward's book is all about. It is a book that can and should be read by computer programmers, systems analysts, project managers, and other computer specialists — for they are almost always involved in model building in the early stages of a computer project. But more than anything else, *Systems Development Without Pain* is intended for *users* of computer systems. It is written in simple terms, without any unnecessary technical jargon; yet it is not a simple book, for it guides the reader through a process of developing business models that is more formal and more rigorous than would have been thought possible a few years ago. To draw another analogy: Educators began to realize some time ago that high-school and college-level concepts of algebra and even calculus could be, and should be, introduced to children at an early age. Any parent who remembers struggling through high-school algebra, and who now watches his or her child effortlessly learning the same concepts in elementary school, realizes how much work must have gone into translating high-school material into grade-school material. Clearly, Paul's book too translates technical material in such a way as to make it fully accessible to nontechnical people.

The process of building YOURDON inc. during the past ten years has brought a number of rewards; one of the most satisfying has been watching important technological ideas grow and evolve. Ideas about system modeling that began as an informal discussion between YOURDON consultants at a lunch table in 1975 have been refined, formalized, and passed on to succeeding generations of technical people — and the resulting technology has made an important contribution to the EDP industry's ability to build reliable, adaptable computer systems. Paul Ward is an excellent case in point: He joined YOURDON in January of 1981 and immediately began applying his many years of practical experience in the field to our then-extant technology of structured analysis and structured design. Now, three years later, he has written a book that adds greatly to the ideas set forth in Victor Weinberg's *Structured Analysis* (New York: Yourdon Press, 1978) and Tom DeMarco's *Structured Analysis and System Specification* (New York: Yourdon Press, 1978).

If you are a nontechnical computer user, I think you will find *Systems Development Without Pain* to be one of the most important books you've ever read about computers. In any case, I can guarantee it will be one of the most enjoyable books you will ever read about computers.

New York City
December 1983

Edward Yourdon

Systems Development Without Pain:

a user's guide to modeling organizational patterns

Part 1
Introduction

The six chapters that make up Part I provide background material so that the reader can more easily understand the approach to developing computer systems described in detail in the rest of the book.

The first two chapters examine the general nature of systems development problems. Chapter 1 shows that the development of automated systems isn't working efficiently in many organizations, and finds that the cause of this phenomenon is human communication problems. A close examination of the human communication process reveals some requirements for effective communication of complex subject matter. Chapter 2 discusses these requirements, which revolve around the building of models.

The next three chapters focus on the specifics of model building and of systems. Chapter 3 describes various types of models, shows that a sensitivity to model characteristics is required for effective model building, and explains the relevant characteristics. Chapter 4 explores the general features of all systems since such information is necessary before a model of a system can be built. Chapter 5 discusses the identification of aspects of systems that must be modeled (through a combination of a knowledge of models and an understanding of systems) and gives preliminary examples of system models.

Finally, Chapter 6 outlines a systems development approach called A Systems Modeling Language (ASML). This approach, described in the remainder of the book, requires building a series of models, each of which has a specific organization.

1

The Trouble with Computers Today

1.1 Frustrated expectations

Computers have been around for quite a while now, and there are a lot of them. As a result, the Gee Whiz! reaction to the latest achievements of automated technology has begun to die down. The generation currently approaching adolescence, raised with computerized toys, will come to accept the new technology as unblinkingly as preceding generations accepted jet aircraft or automobiles. Both wide-eyed astonishment and casual acceptance tend to direct attention away from an undramatic but important fact: Within the large organizations where most of us spend our work lives, the track record of computer systems has been mediocre. In other words, the *consumers* (people within the organizations who use the systems to get their work done) aren't getting their money's worth.

In order to justify such a sweeping statement, I will have to convince you that

- there are reasonable standards by which to measure the success of computer systems;

- many systems in many organizations have fallen short of these standards;

- it is possible to pinpoint the reasons for these shortcomings; and

- it is possible to improve the situation.

The first three points will be dealt with in this chapter; the last point will occupy the remainder of the book.

I can't usefully discuss the situation by pointing to dramatic successes (the use of computers for manned excursions into space, for example) or dramatic failures (such as the missing data within the U.S. Social Security Administration). The issue here is one of averages, not one of extremes.

A better approach involves comparing computer systems development with similar types of human endeavor. I contend that building systems is an engineering activity. Indeed, systems development professionals often describe what they do as "software engineering." Therefore, let's look at another common engineering activity, the construction of houses. There are two obvious ways in which a construction project can fall short. The first is a failure to complete the project. An abandoned, half-built house represents a waste of materials and labor, and is of no use to anyone. A second type of failure is a completed project that is unsatisfactory to its tenants. (Imagine a home with a doorway between the kitchen and the dining room so low that adults must crouch while going through it.)

Now put yourself in the position of an investor in a housing development. What percentage of uncompleted houses would you accept before concluding that something is amiss? What percentage of houses with significant structural defects would you tolerate?

Whether or not you share ownership in your organization, you have invested in it — in the form of your valuable time. In addition to your salary, your return on investment comes in the form of resources (such as automated systems) to assist you in your work. Like any investor, you can critically examine the value of these resources. I maintain that most of you, if you applied standards of this kind to systems development in your organizations, would find significant shortcomings.

Of course, organizations are understandably reluctant to acknowledge their systems' failures. The employee who points out that the new automated system takes longer and makes more mistakes than the old manual one is about as popular as the boy crying, "The emperor has no clothes!" The new technology is so glamorous and takes so much time and money to install that surely the effort is justified.

A classic case of a so-called technological advance involved the substitution of magnetic tape for punched cards. Most computer-readable information in the 1950s and early 1960s was stored on eighty-column punched cards, which had many disadvantages from a technical point of view. The cards were bulky and easily damaged, and reading them into the computer was (relatively) slow and somewhat error-prone.

Despite these disadvantages, users found punched cards to be extremely attractive. Most cards contained printing as well as punches, and were thus human-readable as well as machine-readable. The information on the cards was accessible without the intervention of computers or computer specialists. Consider a file consisting of time cards, each showing the details of an employee's work hours within a certain time period. A clerk wishing to extract data for selected employees could shuffle through the file, find the appropriate cards, and copy the data onto a sheet of paper. Changing an incorrect time card simply involved extracting it, punching a replacement, and inserting the new card. Both of these procedures were accessible to a non-computer-expert, making simple, nonstandard operations possible without the intervention of the data processing staff.

Now consider the effect of loading this time card file onto a magnetic tape. The tape as a storage medium is more durable than the file of time cards and takes considerably less space, and the information can be transferred to and from the computer quickly and with few errors. That's the good news. The bad news is that the information is no longer directly human-readable. Extracting data now will require scanning voluminous printouts. Changing a single time card involves reading the entire tape into the computer and writing it back out. Both of the preceding tasks require the intervention of data processing specialists. The net result of the technological improvement has been to make the data less accessible to its users.

I want to be careful here not to overstate my case. Magnetic tape technology *has* improved many systems and benefited many organizations. But not all of the claimed improvements and benefits will stand up under critical analysis.

However reluctant to acknowledge it, organizations have obviously been conscious of the shortcomings of their computer systems. Each new generation of hardware and software has been touted by its creators and eagerly awaited by its purchasers as a solution. Surely the promise of the new technology would be realized when faster processing units were installed, when more data could be stored and retrieved quickly, when interactive video terminals became widely available, and so on. On the software side, the story has been the same. Teleprocessing systems, database management systems, and networking systems in succession have been expected to set things right. Sometimes a maturing technology has allowed successful implementations. Too often, however, throwing technology at a problem has failed to improve the situation.

The latest chapter in this story of frustrated expectations concerns the dramatic increase in the accessibility of computers to the average person. Three streams that have converged to create the phenomenon are the availability of computer education, the explosion of microprocessor technology, and the sophistication of available software. Most people born during the 1950s and 1960s learned something about computers in college or high school. Many children born during the 1970s and later are learning a good deal more about computers, and they are learning it in elementary school or even before. Personal computers are being sold by the hundreds of thousands. Today, anyone with one hundred U.S. dollars to spend can own a computer. In a few years, this will probably seem inordinately expensive. The new personal computers are also quite user-friendly, allowing people to use prewritten software packages with only a little training. Newer programming languages, for the more powerful personal computers and for larger systems, allow nonspecialists to enter and implement their own program logic fairly easily. Word-processing hardware and software and other office automation products also promise easy access to the benefits of the electronic age.

Prior to the advent of these newer technologies, data processing specialists controlled access to computer resources within organizations. Computer services departments have thus often been blamed for failures of automated systems to live up to expectations. The blame is frequently justified, for individual departments often have failed to serve their organizations well, and have concealed their failures behind a smoke screen of jargon. In many enterprises, users have been understandably frustrated by balky systems and multiyear development backlogs. These problems have arisen even in situations in which the competence of the computer specialists has been unquestioned.

The entry of computer technology into the consumer marketplace has caused virtual explosions in many of these enterprises. Personal computers have appeared overnight in the offices of professional workers and middle managers. In most cases, the data processing professionals have not been consulted; in some cases, they have been openly defied, giving rise to the fantasy of platoons of small-computer users executing an end run on the data processing department and breaking through to some technological nirvana.

1.2 The tragedy of the commons

The introduction of personal computers has had many positive effects. Certainly, computer literacy and access to automated technology are beneficial to individuals. The average manager has many local, small-scale needs for computer power that are well met by personal computers or by self-created programs implemented on a larger system. Electronic spread sheets and personal data files help managers make better decisions. Telephone data-transmission links allow the personal computer user to access public data banks of general and specialized knowledge. Waiting years for a programmer to do for you what you could do for yourself in a few hours is patently ridiculous.

The obvious positive results of this development have tended to obscure its failure to resolve the basic problem. The proliferation of personal computers within an organization has the potential for creating what biologist Garrett Hardin has dubbed the tragedy of the commons.* It is possible for a community of individuals to pursue goals that are beneficial at a personal level but that are injurious to the community as a whole. No individual farmer who buys extra cattle to graze on a common pasture intends to destroy the pasture's usefulness. But a group of farmers acting thus can "graze out" a pasture and ultimately make grazing impossible. In a similar way, the local successes of small-scale computer technology can cause problems to an enterprise.

An organization functions effectively by coordinating the actions of the individuals who carry out its work. This coordination is carried out primarily by exchanging information. Many routine activities (and nearly all nonroutine ones) require the correlation of information from a variety of sources both inside and outside the organization. Some of this information is used as soon as it becomes available; some must be stored for use at a later time. Stored data is thus a valuable resource of an organization. Its value depends on its relevance, accuracy, and accessibility. The automated systems of an organization serve as storage containers and communication channels for its information.

Suppose Mary Jones serves as collector (and also as user) of information on products of her enterprise's competitors. She stores this information and receives reports on its status by using a centralized automated system. The centralized system in turn serves as a source of information for other employees concerned with the competition (Figure 1.1). Ms. Jones may not be aware of all the uses of the information she collects.

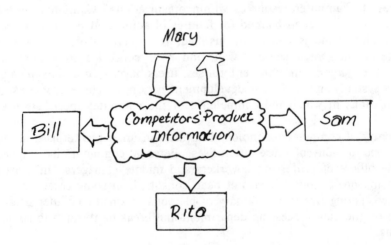

Figure 1.1. A centralized system.

*G. Hardin, "The Tragedy of the Commons," *Science,* Vol. 162, No. 12 (December 1968), pp. 1243-51.

Let's say that Mary is dissatisfied with the performance of her system. Receiving no data processing department response to her requests for improvements, she acquires a personal computer and creates a highly satisfactory local storage and retrieval scheme for herself. There now exists a danger that she will become less attentive to the quality of the information stored in the central system, since it no longer serves her immediate needs. A decrease in quality will hurt anyone else in the organization who uses that system as a source of information (Figure 1.2).

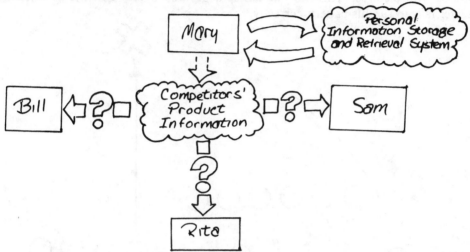

Figure 1.2. Effect of personal computer introduction.

The personal system is very useful to one person (Mary), but may have effects that are detrimental to the organization as a whole — effects that may take a long time to be noticed. It's not practical to prevent Mary from getting a personal computer. While the potential problems are not very visible, Mary's career prospects are very visible, and may depend on her being more enterprising than Joe down the hall. Can she trust Joe not to get a personal computer?

I want to emphasize that the primary issue here is not centralized versus decentralized technology, but rather organizational coordination. It is technologically feasible to create a network of small computers that share programs and data. In the case of Mary Jones, however, letting others in the organization have access to her personal storage and retrieval system won't necessarily correct the situation. Since the scheme was created to serve Mary's personal needs, it may render the stored information inconvenient or even impossible for others to use. A comprehensive solution would require identifying everyone else who uses the data and devising methods to translate the information from the local storage scheme into a form usable by others.

The point of all this does not depend on postulating a tragedy of the commons outcome. Let's assume that employees are farsighted enough not to become information hoarders who damage larger-scale coordination. Let's also assume that the new technology helps these employees to become more productive, and that it thus is visibly beneficial to their organizations. The fundamental problem, that automated technology is not being used as effectively as possible to serve the larger-scale needs of organizations, will still remain.

1.3 Organizational patterns

As I indicated above, organizations operate by coordinating the activities of their members. An organization can be described in terms of *patterns of activities* (Figure 1.3) and *patterns of stored data* (Figure 1.4). In team sports, the patterns of activities take on a visible and striking form. The offensive and defensive patterns used in football are familiar to millions of people. They are given descriptive names and can be illustrated with pictures. An avid fan can spot deviations very quickly, as when a pass receiver fails to run his pattern correctly.

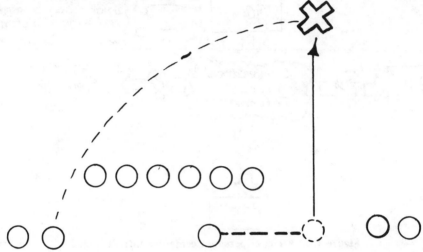

Figure 1.3. An activity pattern.

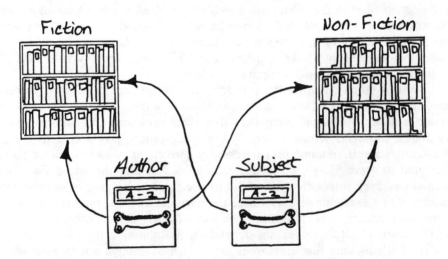

Figure 1.4. A stored data pattern.

There are also patterns of activities in enterprises such as banks and insurance companies. Imagine a customer handing off a deposit to a teller, who fades back, updates the account balance, and passes the transaction down field to a clerk who incorporates it into a statement. This pattern is not visually striking, but is no less real for its abstract quality. Like a football pattern, it can be named and described pictorially.

Perhaps the clearest example of a visible pattern of stored data is a library. Books are carefully arranged by subject matter, and there is an elaborate series of indices that interrelate the books by subject, by author, and by first word of title, for example. The stored data of a tax collection agency or a manufacturing company may not have a pattern that is clear to the eye, but there is a pattern nevertheless and it may be described graphically. Picture a shelf of customer records and a shelf of product records, with a card catalog itemizing which customers have bought which products.

Sometimes managers within organizations are clearly aware of these patterns, and consciously organize their personnel so as to maintain effective patterns. There are many situations, however, in which patterns develop gradually as an organization grows. In these cases, no single individual is clearly aware of the large-scale patterns, and they persist independently of day-to-day management activities. The survival of an organization, of course, depends on the durability and adaptability of these patterns. A robust organization can replace individuals and maintain its patterns. A weaker organization may have patterns that are easily disrupted or that conflict with one another.

When I use the term "system," I refer to some pattern of an organization. Systems exist at various levels, and an entire enterprise may be thought of as a single large system or pattern consisting of many levels of smaller systems or patterns. Systems typically involve both activities and stored data, and may be carried out by people, or computers, or both. An automated system is simply the incorporation of some organizational pattern into computer logic. For the purposes of our discussion, it is unimportant whether the pattern existed previously in a manual form or a different automated form or is wholly or partially new.

To incorporate an organizational pattern successfully into a computer system, one must have access to skilled implementers, adequate technology, and good quality control procedures. Most importantly, the organizational pattern must be mirrored accurately in the computer's stored instructions and data. Systems development thus necessarily involves subject matter specialists, or users (who know the details of the patterns, although that knowledge may not be well organized), and implementers (who incorporate the pattern into the new system).

Early automated systems incorporated relatively local, small-scale patterns, typically relating to financial transactions. A typical system might have read a deck of time cards, another deck of employee deduction cards, and then printed paychecks and a check register. These systems were easy to think about and describe. Not much coordination was necessary because of the small scale. These early implementations had a good success rate, since the small scale eased communications between users and implementers. The systems were well understood, and the users played relatively passive roles as sources of information. As hardware grew more powerful, larger systems were attempted. The organizational patterns to be mirrored were larger in scale, coordination became more important, and the success rate of implementations declined. The methods described in this book were born out of the concern over this decline.

1.4 Failures of traditional systems development

The shortcomings of automated systems have a human cause, not a technological one. Large systems fail because the organizational patterns are not faithfully mirrored in the implementation. The people involved in systems development, both users and implementers, don't understand the patterns clearly enough. Even worse, they don't realize that they don't understand them. Yet if the pattern, the larger-scale coordination, isn't accurately reflected, the implemented system will not work well. It will be at best error-prone and at worst unworkable. However powerful the available technology, it cannot effectively support the purposes of the enterprise under these conditions.

Systems development is the discovery and articulation, or clear expression, of the patterns of activity and patterns of data of an enterprise. The narrower meaning of the term "articulation," referring to a jointed anatomical structure, is very appropriate here. The individual data or activity units can be examined separately, but the functioning of the whole can be understood only through the interconnections. Systems development must integrate the understandings of individual people — who may have fragmentary or fuzzy views of organizational patterns — into a unified whole. This book describes a new method for developing systems, called A Systems Modeling Language (ASML). The new method is necessary because traditional development methods simply aren't powerful enough to articulate large organizational patterns effectively.

1.5 Need for new methods

This book has two major themes: that new methods are necessary to effectively incorporate large-scale organizational patterns into automated systems; and that users, as consumers of the finished product, must become involved in the application of the methods in order to get full value from their systems. The importance of both these themes arises from the size and complexity of the automated systems being developed by today's enterprises. Early automated systems were small enough that the tools and techniques used to describe them weren't a major issue. What's more, they were small enough that a computer expert could learn all about them with only casual assistance from the user community. When systems are complex, powerful methods of description are needed, and the methods must be understood by the people who are grounded in the subject matter of the system. Systems analysts whose primary background is in data processing clearly have significant roles to play in systems development. However, when analytical ability and knowledge of subject matter reside with two distinct groups of people, systems development doesn't work nearly as well. The accurate description of organizational patterns can best be done by users who understand the development techniques.

What will be the effect of an enterprise's use of ASML? First, the effect will be gradual; existing systems that are unsatisfactory can't be replaced overnight. The first fruits of the effort are likely to be newly developed automated systems that are more usable than their predecessors. In the longer run, there will be consequences beyond the success of individual systems:

- There will be an increased appreciation within the organization of the importance of large-scale systems issues to organizational survival. For example, ASML will facilitate the discovery of weak patterns, which may then be corrected before being incorporated into computer logic.

- The chronic backlog of the data processing department will be reduced as some of the burden of systems development is shifted to the users.

- The available technology (large central computers, minicomputers, personal computers, and office automation and data communication devices) will fall into place in the service of the appropriate levels of organizational activity.

1.6 Summary

Technology has been oversold as a solution to problems of all kinds. Nevertheless, it has an important role to play when placed in proper perspective. The ideas and procedures presented in this book *do* offer a *technology* to computer system users. It happens to be in the form of an intellectual discipline rather than in the form of computer hardware and software.

Ultimately, the benefits of using ASML will extend beyond the area of automated systems development. Any organization can be viewed as a single large system, containing patterns of activities and data at various levels. As more and more of these patterns are studied, the effect should be a consciousness of the enterprise itself. Such consciousness may be very beneficial in keeping organizational patterns effective and allowing them to adapt to a changing environment.

Of course, some of what goes on in any organization (the most interesting part) involves creative thought and judgment and so transcends any pattern. Current automated systems can't step out of the pattern in any significant way, and thus creative activities can't be automated. However, activities requiring human judgment typically depend on routine patterns as sources of information. If done intelligently, automation of routine patterns needn't dehumanize an organization. Consciousness of the routine patterns can make clear when it's necessary to step outside of these patterns. Efficient automated systems can provide information for, and leave time for, more properly human activities.

Contrary to the title of this chapter, the trouble is not with computers but with the way we use them. In the next chapter, I'll begin to explore some methods for dealing with the trouble.

2

The Communications Gap

If knowledge of automated technology isn't the essential element in systems development, then what is? In this chapter, I argue that the essential element is an understanding of the human communication processes involved.

2.1 A party game

Most people have played the party game called telegraph. The rules are fairly simple: Players stand in a circle, and one person is chosen to start things off. The starter is given a message (written on a piece of paper). The message is then passed around the circle by being whispered from person to person. Eventually, of course, the message gets back to the starter. The fun of the game lies in what happens to the message during its passage around the circle, as shown in Figure 2.1 on the next page.* If there are a reasonable number of people in the circle, the message that returns to the starter is usually considerably different from the original message.

2.2 Systems development as a telegraph game

A phenomenon very similar to the one observed in telegraph is noticeable in many systems development efforts, but its effects are not considered to be overly funny. Let's consider a game of telegraph consisting of only three players; they are given the titles requester, designer, and builder. The requester starts things off by passing a message to the designer. The message is called the essential model [1]; its content will be described later. The designer, in turn, passes a message called the implementation model to the builder. Finally, the builder passes a message called the completed system back to the requester who started the whole thing off.

The names given to the players represent not individual people but *roles* that are part of the systems development process. The requester is a composite of all the people who have some part in deciding what a proposed system needs to do. This group of

---

*W. Safire, *On Language* (New York: New York Times Books, 1980), pp. 166-72. The section entitled "Mondegreens" contains the "Lady Mondegreen" example represented in Figure 2.1, among other delightful examples of messages distorted between sender and receiver.

people includes users, a term which usually implies familiarity with the subject matter of the system to be built. Members of the accounting department, for example, are considered the users of an accounts payable system. However, the requester group often includes, and sometimes is dominated by, data processing professionals with the title of systems analyst. Ideally, the systems analysts act as facilitators, using their abilities to gather and organize information to assure an adequate description of the users' needs. In some cases, however, the analysts simply make educated guesses about user needs and get their conclusions rubber-stamped by some user manager.

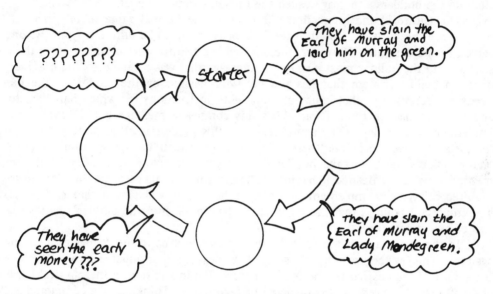

Figure 2.1. Playing the telegraph game.

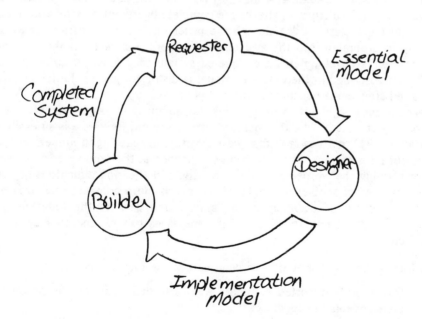

Figure 2.2. The systems development game.

However well or badly the process is carried out, the result is the communication of a complex message to the designer. Figure 2.2 merely shows the net result of a complex series of interactions within the requester group and between the requesters and the designers. What I have called the essential model is more commonly called a functional specification or a statement of requirements.

The designers, although almost certainly dominated by data processing specialists, normally include users, since the choice of hardware and software technology will affect the costs and the user interfaces of the system. The job of the designers is to pass along to the builders a message called the implementation model.

The nature of the interaction differs from the normal game of telegraph at this point, since the message passed to the builder is meant to be different from the one received by the designer. However, the analogy is a fruitful one to pursue since the message sent to the builder must *contain* the message that was received by the designer. In order to build a system that has the behavior desired by the requester, the builder needs a description of that behavior along with instructions for which hardware to use and how to organize the software. It's this composite message that I have called the implementation model. (The actual result of this process is often quite different from the idealized model presented here. Typically, the functional specification contains implementation details, and the builder doesn't get a complete description of the implementation or of the desired behavior of the system. In this case, the builder guesses at required behavior or implementation details; he or she is playing designer or requester. The important point is that the information has to get into the builder's hands regardless of how it gets there.)

In the final stage in the process, the builder returns to the requester a completed system. This system can be considered a message that must embody the desired behavior and the desired technological organization in addition to the physical hardware and software, a concept that is depicted in Figure 2.3. Thinking of a completed system as containing a message of some sort may not be common, but it makes a lot of sense. When a sweater is knitted from a pattern, the completed garment may be said to consist of the yarn and the pattern. Even though the paper on which the pattern is written is not physically incorporated into the sweater, the pattern is present in the sweater. In the game of systems development, a completed system that does not embody the pattern of behavior described in the essential model is distorted, just as the telegraph message is distorted after being whispered around the circle.

We gain some insight into why systems development messages are often so distorted by looking at exactly why the message passed around the circle is so easily mangled. Fundamentally, the reason is that we human beings are highly imperfect senders and receivers of information. The distortion can happen at the sending end (whispering too softly or garbling the words) or at the receiving end (hearing difficulties or inattention). The same set of problems applies to the much more complex messages passed from the requester to the designer to the builder and back to the requester in the course of systems development. Each of the messages can be distorted by any of a number of factors:

- Information that should have been part of the message is lost.

- Information is distorted in such a way as to make part of the message understandable but incorrect.

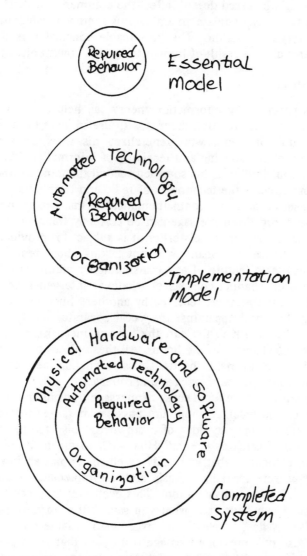

Figure 2.3. Evolution of the systems development message.

- Information is distorted in such a way as to make part of the message indecipherable.

- In a longer message, one part of the message is distorted so that two portions contradict each other.

In the systems development situation, the problem is magnified because at each stage of the process information is added to the message *that is dependent on correct receipt of the previous message.* Even if the essential model is sent and received correctly, errors can be introduced into the automated technology organization part of the message by the designer or the builder. If the essential model is in error to start with, the problem is compounded since the technological organization has to be compatible with the essential model.

The fact that systems development messages are normally transmitted in written form instead of being whispered doesn't affect the argument. A written message can be missing a vital sentence, can contain an ambiguous sentence, can contain two sentences that are contradictory, and so on. The inescapable conclusion is that many systems development failures are the result of human-to-human communication problems.

2.3 Information theory

The insights provided by information theory can help us send messages that are clearly understood. One information theorist with useful ideas for us was the American mathematician Claude Shannon, who generalized his work on secret codes into a mathematical theory of the sending and receiving of information.* Shannon's most important theoretical contribution is his so-called second theorem. Although its most immediate applications involve the technology of radio and telephone transmissions, it has a much broader significance. In nonmathematical terms, Shannon's second theorem states that a properly organized message can be correctly transmitted along a transmission channel no matter how much distortion it is subject to, provided that the channel is not overloaded. Notice that Shannon is not talking about removing the distortion. Distortion is an inevitable feature of any transmission medium. In the telegraph party game, the transmission channel consists of whatever intervenes between the message held in one mind and the message received by another: Such interventions include the nerves controlling the vocal apparatus, the vocal apparatus itself, the air carrying the sound waves from the mouth to the ear, the hearing mechanism, and the nerves connecting the hearing mechanism to the brain. All these pieces of the channel have limitations. The trick is not to make the transmission channel perfect, but *to arrange the message so that distortions can be recognized and corrected.*

Shannon noted that the effectiveness of message transmission is intimately related to the *uncertainty* of the receiver about the possible messages that could be received. Suppose that we are at opposite sides of a crowded, noisy room, and that you shout something to me that I catch as " −ee." How am I to fill in the distorted part of the word so that I can recognize what you said? Well, if it's not an international crowd, I can assume that you were speaking English, and can immediately eliminate the German words "die" or "sie" from consideration. This decreases my uncertainty and increases the probability that I can figure out what you said, although not by much. The word could still be "tree," "flee," "plea," or any other of a large set of possibilities. Suppose I knew, because of a previous message from you, that you were going to give me a number between one and ten. This reduces my uncertainty considerably, and allows me to identify the word as "three" with a high level of confidence.

Notice the correct identification of the word was actually the result of receiving a compound message; part one was "a number is coming" and part two was " −ee." In order to reduce my uncertainty, you had to add some *redundancy* to the message, to make it longer than it needed to be if it wasn't subject to distortion. Another way to add redundancy, of course, is simply to repeat the message a number of times, but the art of effectively sending messages involves picking just the right kind of redundancy.

---

*For more on Shannon's work, see J. Campbell's *Grammatical Man* (New York: Simon & Schuster, 1982).

The remainder of this chapter describes some of the ways that the complex messages sent and received during systems development can be organized to allow the detection and correction of distortions.

2.4 Human channel capacities

To pursue the information theory perspective of this chapter, let's examine the abilities of humans as receivers of information. It's easy to overload the channels that a human being has for accepting messages. If a person tries to listen to two people speaking at the same time, he usually must block out one of them or he will understand neither. Clearly, in creating the complex message that describes the desired behavior of a system, the channel capacity of the receiver of this message must be considered.

One of the common deficiencies of systems development messages is that they don't use the most effective communication channels available. I'd like to try a little experiment by sending you some information across two different channels. Ready to receive? Here comes the first message:

The knot is composed of three wraps situated one below the other along the axis of the post. The wraps enclose a segment of the rope used to form the knot, which lies parallel to the axis of the post. This segment loops around the bottom wrap and ascends vertically on the outside of the wraps to form the beginning of the top wrap.

Got that? Now look at Figure 2.4: It sends the same message on another channel. You may object that I've used the same channel (your eyes) for both messages, but there is an obvious difference. Although both messages went *through* your eyes, the nerve circuits that form part of the receiving channel were quite different for the narrative description than for the picture. Extensive research on the function of the brain has revealed that the left hemisphere of the brain processes written messages, while the right hemisphere processes pictures [2].

If you think about your experience with the two messages about the knot, it should be clear that while you had to build a conception of the knot slowly and painfully from the words, the picture gave it to you all at once. As shown in Figure 2.5, the right hemisphere of the brain provides an information channel that is better at receiving certain kinds of information, provided that the message is organized so that it can be received by that channel. The ability of the right side of the brain to grasp patterns all at once is not unlimited; a picture that is too complex will overload this channel, and can be grasped only by examining one section at a time. Experiments suggest that a picture with many more than a half-dozen distinguishable elements can't be grasped as a unit. Nevertheless, the right brain/left brain separation of our information receiving capabilities means that complex information can be communicated more effectively by pictures [3]. It may not be clear to you at this point how pictures can be used to communicate desired system behavior, but you should at least be aware of the potential; the topic will be explored in the following chapters.

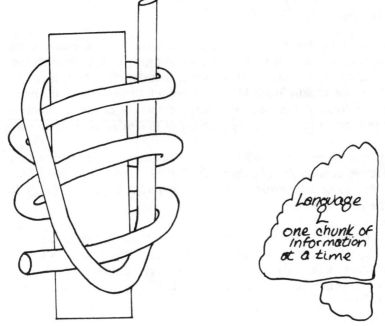

Figure 2.4. A graphic message.

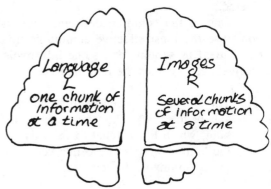

Figure 2.5. Right brain and left brain functions.

2.5 Partitioning the message

When information is transmitted across a noisy channel, my ability to make sense of it is increased if I have some idea of the nature of the message. (Remember the word "−ee" shouted across the noisy room.) Let's explore this idea in more depth. Suppose you and I both have electric typewriters, connected by a circuit so that when I type something on my typewriter it also appears on yours. The circuit, however, is subject to electrical noise, so that errors can creep in during transmission between the typewriters. The most common type of error is the addition, dropping, or changing of a single character within a word.

I'm now going to send you a message. I'll give you the advance information that the content will be a list of words that are either names of men or names of trees, and that I won't use any words that might fall in both categories. Ready? Here's the list:

JOHN   MAPLE   ARTHUR   SBRUCE   WILLOW   SAMUEL

The problem, of course, is making sense out of the fourth entry in the list. Is it BRUCE with an S added to its beginning, or SPRUCE with the P replaced by a B? Since there's no redundancy in the message, that is, no extra information to help you identify and correct problems, one guess is as good as the other. Here's another version of the message, with some redundancy added:

LENGTH: 32   JOHN   MAPLE   ARTHUR   SBRUCE   WILLOW   SAMUEL

If you count the letters in the message (not including the length entry), you'll find there is one too many, allowing you to conclude that the word should be BRUCE. Adding some measurement of a message to the message itself is a common trick used by communications technologists to detect transmission errors. Although effective, this is a laborious and very artificial method of checking messages. It would be nice if there were something more closely related to the meaning of the message that could be used to determine correctness. Now here's a final version:

> START OF TREES
> MAPLE
> WILLOW
> START OF MEN
> JOHN
> ARTHUR
> SBRUCE

This one seems to fill the bill. Not only does the added redundancy permit the correction of errors, but the organization of the message is related to the organization of the subject matter. This particular type of redundancy is referred to as a *partitioning* of the message.

The connection between these simple messages and the real-life job of systems development may not seem obvious at this point, but bear with me a bit longer. Imagine that you are one of the requesters of a system that will automate the matching of teachers with students within an adult education program. Here's part of a description of the required behavior of this system:

> The information must include teacher name, teacher address, and subject.

Since this message is to be passed to the designers and the builders, any error in it will cause a failure of the completed system to perform as desired. The most likely error in this kind of statement is the omission of a required piece of data or the inclusion of an unnecessary one. Is this statement correct or not? Clearly, a reasonable answer to this question requires more information about the context of the statement: Does the description refer to the total collection of stored information about a teacher, or to the information required to do the matching? If it refers to the latter, does making a match involve the teacher's living near the student? It is the process of partitioning that provides this context, that focuses your attention on some subdivision of the subject matter so that you can bring your critical faculties to bear.

I'm not suggesting that traditional systems development methods ignored partitioning; they used it, of course. However, a complex description of system behavior can be partitioned in a variety of ways, some of which make it much harder than others to identify and correct errors. Careful attention to partitioning is essential to effective systems development, and the topic will be explored in depth later.

2.6 Use of appropriate vocabulary

However useful pictures are in conveying messages during systems development, words are clearly of extreme importance in the process. An appropriate choice of vocabulary can significantly ease the task of creating and verifying the models passed from requester to designer to builder.

Suppose I were to say to you, Contract your deltoids so as to bring the long axes of your radius and ulna to an approximate perpendicular to your vertebral column. Depending on your background, you might struggle to remember some long-ago anatomy or physiology lecture, rush to a dictionary, ignore me, or lift your arm as I asked you to do. Whatever your response, you undoubtedly would think my utterance foolish. I would have managed to make the message unnaturally difficult for you to receive and understand. The difficulty, of course, results from the selection of an inappropriate vocabulary.

The concept of an appropriate vocabulary plays a critical role in the transmission of information during systems development. What, do you suppose, is the natural vocabulary to use to describe a payroll system? If you are going to describe what the system does, the words you might use include salary, federal withholding amount, deduct, overtime, and so on. On the other hand, if you are describing the automated implementation of a payroll system, words such as data entry transaction, screen display, and disk file might make sense.

Is it reasonable to use words drawn from both these vocabularies? It is reasonable in the implementation model, since this model contains both the required behavior and the technological organization. In fact, the implementation model describes a *fitting* of the technology to the required behavior. On the other hand, using an implementation vocabulary in the essential model is counterproductive. At best, it indicates an unnecessary addition of implementation details, which makes the model larger than necessary, harder to partition effectively, and more difficult for users to review. At worst, it embodies a decision made by misguided users that since the system is to be incorporated into a computer, they had better use computerese in describing it. In the latter case, the damage is often fatal, since the resulting model has perfectly good natural vocabulary terms replaced by vague data processing expressions like "edit the input." Such a model is not terribly useful as an implementation guide, since the creators don't know enough about automated technology to be specific about implementation details. What's more, it can't be effectively reviewed as a statement of desired system behavior because of the inappropriate vocabulary. The message simply will not be effectively transmitted.

2.7 Making the models predictive

In the game of telegraph, the fact that the original message was written on paper serves to quiet skeptics who don't believe it could have been so badly distorted. Keeping this in mind, consider the following scenario.

I (the developer) hand you (the user) a system, complete with a keyboard and display screen. You decide to try out the system by typing in some information through the keyboard and reading the responses on the screen. Your tentative smile is rapidly replaced by a deepening frown. You finally turn to me in exasperation and blurt out, "But this isn't what I wanted the system to do!" At which point I snarl, "Oh, yeah? Prove it!"

Completely nonplussed by my hostility, you calmly open the folder you've brought with you and search for a little while. You then triumphantly announce, "It says right here in the essential model that when the system gets an X it should produce a Y. I've just given it an X and I got back a Z. Gotcha!"

This little fantasy illustrates the most important characteristic of the essential and implementation models. It's not sufficient to state that they must be *complete,* since that's not specific enough. The models must be *predictive;* they must contain enough information to serve as a standard against which the behavior of the completed system can be judged. These ideas will be explored further in the next chapter.

2.8 Summary

The way to bridge the communications gap that so often plagues systems development is to send effective messages along the human communication channels involved in the process. The characteristics of these messages can be discovered by an examination of what it takes to communicate effectively across a noisy channel. Some of these characteristics are that the messages

- use graphics where possible to convey complex, pattern-type information;

- are partitioned, containing just enough controlled redundancy to facilitate understanding and critical review;

- use the vocabulary that is appropriate to each stage of the process; and

- are predictive so that they can be used as an objective basis for measuring the acceptability of the completed system.

In the next chapter, I explain in more detail how to build a model that conveys a complex message.

Chapter 2: References

1. J. Palmer and S. McMenamin, *Essential Systems Analysis* (New York: Yourdon Press, 1984).

   The authors introduce and explore in detail the idea of the essential model.

2. C. Sagan, *The Dragons of Eden* (New York: Random House, 1977), pp. 152-86.

   The chapter entitled "Lovers and Madmen" is a fascinating exposition of the research that led to man's understanding of left brain and right brain processes.

3. B. Edwards, *Drawing on the Right Side of the Brain* (Los Angeles: J.P. Tarcher, Inc., 1979).

   Betty Edwards shows not only that the right side of the brain can grasp graphic messages better, but also that by deliberately cultivating this mode of perception you can communicate better using graphics.

3

Building Models

The key to making effective use of computers in an organization is clear communication about organizational patterns. The only practical way to accomplish this is by building *models* of the patterns. Good systems developers must thus be good model builders. Because of this, I need to explain some things about models before we proceed.

3.1 Modeling physical objects

The most familiar examples of models are three-dimensional miniatures of physical objects. Nearly all of us spent some time as children playing with dollhouses or model airplanes. These toys serve to illustrate a basic characteristic of all models; namely, we can use the model to learn things about the original. Staring at the inside of a dollhouse, a child learns about typical arrangements of rooms and interconnections between areas of a house. Lying on a bed while "flying" a model plane, he or she learns how aircraft look from various points of view. Of course, the possibilities for learning go far beyond appearance and arrangements of parts. An appropriately constructed model actually can be used to predict the behavior of the original. Some model planes can really be flown, and will react to variations in wind direction as a real aircraft would. Toy furniture can be arranged in a dollhouse to predict whether placing a sofa and two chairs along a wall will be practical or esthetically pleasing.

The predictive aspect of model building makes three-dimensional models far more than children's toys. Building a new type of aircraft, automobile, or bridge requires an immense investment of time, materials, and money. The engineers responsible for constructing these items invariably build scale models and subject them to the stresses that the full-size product is expected to encounter. Performance problems can be discovered and corrected in the model with far less expense than in the finished product.

So what does all this have to do with systems development? A lot! Successful development involves building a *predictive model* of the desired system. Another way to think of this is that you can get *answers about the system* by asking *questions of the model*. A realistic-acting airplane model, as I mentioned earlier, is predictive in this sense. Suppose I want to know what will happen if an airplane flies into a crosswind with its nose up at a forty-five degree angle. I can "ask" this question by finding a suitable breeze (or by turning on a fan) and launching the model with the appropriate direction and orientation. The model will "answer" the question by behaving in a certain way. Similarly, a predictive model of a system must be able to answer questions like, If I provide such-and-such an input with so-and-so stored data, how will the system behave? Note that the model must provide *specific* answers to questions. A model that answers questions with generalities is not a useful model. (The fact that systems development documents are often called "specifications" implies that they should provide specific answers. Unfortunately, many specifications are not at all specific.) The model can also be thought of as a set of acceptance criteria for the completed system. The finished product will not be satisfactory to the customer unless it behaves as predicted by the model.

It's appealing to imagine building a three-dimensional miniature of something like an accounts payable system, with tiny desks, filing cabinets, computer terminals, and so on. Unfortunately, this model isn't predictive in a useful way; it won't answer the significant questions we need to ask about this kind of system. Instead, we must turn to a less captivating but more useful model, one that can be built with a pencil and a sheet of paper.

3.2 Paper-and-pencil models

An obvious type of paper-and-pencil modeling job is the production of an accurate drawing of a three-dimensional object. It is very difficult for the modern reader to appreciate the seriousness of this problem. Artists struggled with it for thousands of years. It was finally completely solved in the fifteenth century by some of the most brilliant minds of the Italian Renaissance.

Imagine that you are standing at one end of a large room, looking at the floor, which is composed of square tiles. How do you draw a picture of what you see? Since you can perceive that all the tiles are the same size, one obvious solution is to draw something like that presented in Figure 3.1.

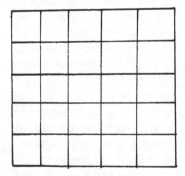

Figure 3.1. Tiled floor.

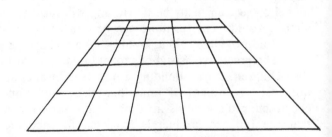

Figure 3.2. Tiled floor in perspective.

This representation is one that primitive artists used for many, many years. The problem, of course, is that you don't really "see" all the tiles as being the same size. You *know* they're all the same size, but the more distant tiles make a smaller image on your retina than do the near tiles. The correct way to draw what you see (that is, the way a camera would record the image from that point of view) is shown in Figure 3.2.

The fact that this seems so obvious is due both to the pioneering work of Renaissance scholars and also to the invention of photography.*

The crux of the problem is that the original has a different number of dimensions from the model. The three-dimensional original must be compressed or projected into the two-dimensional model. Models with a different dimensionality than the original have problems of completeness. Imagine that there is an object sitting on the tile floor, as in Figure 3.3. There is no way you can tell from this drawing what the far side of this object looks like. More generally, no single drawing can show all the details of a three-dimensional scene. When the real situation has more dimensions than the model, multiple models must be created. Thus, an architect routinely creates a floor plan and various elevations of a proposed building. The various models in this case must be coordinated, with common reference points so that the viewer can match them.

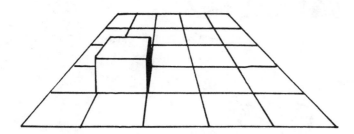

Figure 3.3. Tiled floor with object.

A drawing is certainly predictive in the sense that you can learn about the object portrayed by studying the drawing. However, let's look at a paper-and-pencil model that is predictive in a much more specific way. Figure 3.4 is a map of some of the imaginary lands depicted in Tolkien's *The Lord of the Rings*. This map can answer very specific questions, such as, How can I get from South Ithilien to the Dark Tower? (Answer: Go north to the crossing of the road from Anorien, east through the mountains, then northeast), or Where will I end up if I go southeast from the Sea of Nurnen? (I'll let you figure out the answer to that one.)

Some board games are like maps. They have named locations and routes to be traveled between the locations, but in addition there are rules governing the moves. In the game shown in Figure 3.5, a player who lands on Tight Spot while it is occupied by another player must return to his or her starting space.

Let me take the concept a step further and describe to you a rather fanciful paper-and-pencil model, which I'll call Playing Stagecoach; it is shown in Figure 3.6.

---

*For more information on the development during the Renaissance of the technique for modeling a three-dimensional object on a two-dimensional medium, see M. Kemp's *Leonardo Da Vinci* (Cambridge, Mass.: Harvard University Press, 1981), pp. 26-34.

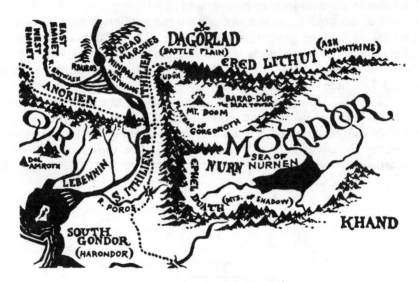

Figure 3.4. Middle Earth.*

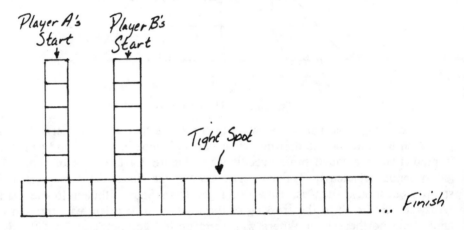

Figure 3.5. A board game.

This model has some features that are characteristic of a game (although there's no particular objective) and some features of a map. Use of the roads in this imaginary land is restricted to certain kinds of vehicles and occupants. The rules specify that a Land-Rover Party must consist of at least four people in a four-wheel-drive vehicle, and a Stagecoach Party must consist of no more than two people in a horse-drawn vehicle. When a Land-Rover Party reaches the Etadpu Bridge, it must stop, and any passenger whose hair color matches the hair color of a guest at the Erots Hotel must

---

*I've reproduced the frontispiece art from Volume One of J.R.R. Tolkien's *The Lord of the Rings* (New York: Ballantine Books, 1965), originally published in *The Lord of the Rings* by J.R.R. Tolkien. Copyright © 1965 by J.R.R. Tolkien. Reprinted by permission of Houghton Mifflin Company.

dismount and check in; the driver is exempt. The driver and any remaining passengers (this party is now renamed a Depleted Land-Rover Party) then move on. When a Stagecoach Party reaches the Eveirter Pass, it must stop, and any guest at the Erots Hotel whose last name matches the last name of a passenger must check out and join the party. The (possibly larger) group then continues on as an Augmented Stagecoach Party.

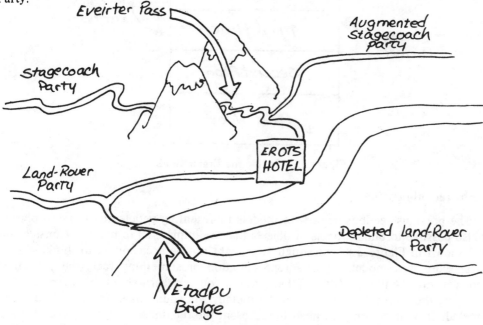

Figure 3.6. Playing Stagecoach.

To use this model in a predictive way, we have to set the scene. Let's say that the following guests are staying at the Erots Hotel:

- Kathleen O'Leary (red hair)
- Egbert Entwhistle (grey hair)

Now suppose a Land-Rover Party arrives and is composed of

- Gloria Fernandez (driver)
- Sean O'Brien (red hair)
- Patrick O'Brien (red hair)
- Lucy Chen (black hair)

The rules say that the O'Briens must check into the Erots Hotel, and that Ms Fernandez and Ms Chen must resume travel. Using the revised guest list for the Erots Hotel, tell me what happens if a Stagecoach Party composed of Sally Entwhistle and Nora O'Brien arrives.

Right about now, you are probably asking yourself what all this has to do with organizational patterns, stored data, and systems development, but allow me the author's prerogative of being a bit mysterious. I *will* offer you a hint: Certain organizational patterns look a lot like the Playing Stagecoach game. But let me be mysterious for a while longer. Figure 3.7 shows some game-playing relationships among the guests at the Erots Hotel; relationships of *this* kind are also important in organizations.

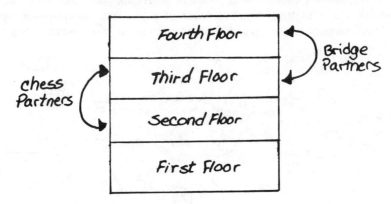

Figure 3.7. Inside the Erots Hotel.

3.3 Abstract dimensions

The previous sections dealt with models representing people and physical objects. It is also possible to build models of objects that are immaterial in nature. Consider the model shown in Figure 3.8. Although you might not be accustomed to thinking so, a musical score is a model. It is a representation of something real (the pattern of sounds constituting the melody). What's more, you can learn about the piece of music by studying the score; it predicts what the melody will sound like. In order to describe the melody in visible form, we need to represent the relationship of one piece of melody to the others. We describe the pitch of a musical note as high or low. The pitch of a note in this model is shown by writing it in a higher or lower position on the staff. The pitch is thus one dimension of the melody. The other dimension is time, shown by the left-to-right sequence and also by the shapes of the individual notes.

Figure 3.8. A musical score.

As we switched from a three-dimensional miniature to a drawing to a musical score, the idea of dimension also underwent a change. A model can be said to be isomorphic (from the Greek words meaning "same form") with the object being modeled. In the case of a miniature, three-dimensional replica of a physical object, the isomorphism is very literal and very obvious. Your eyes can perceive the sameness of contour between the model and the original. Except for the difference in scale, the dimensions of the two are exactly the same. A drawing of a three-dimensional object, on the other hand, compresses three dimensions into two. The eye can perceive the sameness of contour between the drawing and the object, but some information about the object is lost. It takes a collection of drawings, representing different perspectives, to capture the three-dimensional object completely. The isomorphism between the set of drawings and the object is there, but it is slightly more abstract.

Properties become still more abstract in the case of the musical score. As a matter of fact, there is still some visual resemblance between the musical score and the sound: If you watch a pianist playing, the right-and-left pattern of the fingers striking the keys corresponds closely to the up-and-down placement of the notes on the score. Nevertheless, it takes some intellectual effort to "see" the pitch of a note as a dimension of the piece of music.

Let's consider a still more abstract model, one that represents stock market activity over a period of time. The vertical dimension in Figure 3.9 depicts the average trading price of a group of stocks. The concept of dimension here is removed from the visible activity of stock trading, which typically involves the exchange of documents and the entry of data into computers. In addition, the model omits a great mass of detail so that a pattern can emerge.

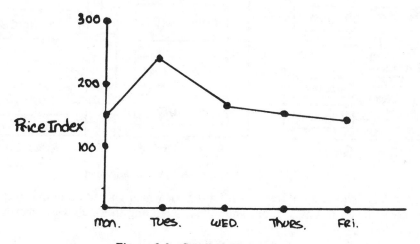

Figure 3.9. Stock market graph.

The implication for systems development is that it takes careful thought to identify the appropriate dimensions for our models of activity and stored data patterns. The properties that are important may be several levels of abstraction removed from the visible details. The dimensions of a model may seem obvious after we've had a chance to study it, but it probably took a great deal of experimentation and many false starts before someone realized, for example, that pitch and time were the right dimensions for a musical model.

3.4 Partitioning of models

Now assume I want to build a model of the internals of an automobile. Since this model will be rather complex, it will be advantageous to divide it into sections so that people using the model can study it a section at a time. That way, they won't be overwhelmed with details as they would if everything were thrown together. How should the model be divided? What factors should determine my packaging? Before we develop answers to these questions, let's look at a list of the parts of the automobile whose interconnections will be described in the model:

- battery
- headlights
- carburetor
- ignition switch
- distributor
- spark plugs

- light switch
- fuel line
- fuel tank
- taillights
- cylinders

One obvious way to create the model is to divide or partition it in terms of geography, by placing parts together on the model if they are physically close to each other in the automobile. As you can see from Figure 3.10, there are many connections among the three portions of the model.

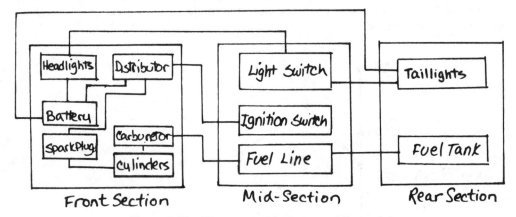

Figure 3.10. The geographical automobile model.

Figure 3.11 shows a different partitioning, in which all parts relating to the flow of gasoline are grouped in one section, and all parts relating to the flow of electricity are in another section.

If you compare Figure 3.11 with the previous figure, you should notice two interesting aspects. First, the two models are visually different in that there are substantially fewer connections between sections in Figure 3.11 than were depicted in Figure 3.10. Second, the section names of the flow-oriented model have more to do with automotive technology than do the section names in the geographical model.

This tells us something about the nature of partitioning that will be useful to us in systems development, where the question of how to partition a large model also arises. During the systems development process, as in the automobile model, there may be various approaches to dividing things. Questions of how to connect sections of the model and how to name pieces of the model will recur.

Note the difference between the question of dimensions and the question of partitioning. Dimensionality has to do with the number of varieties of information (for example, length, width, height) that must be dealt with. Partitioning, on the other hand, has to do with the complexity of the thing being modeled. Even a model with very few dimensions can be complex enough so that it must be separated into sections for clarity of presentation.

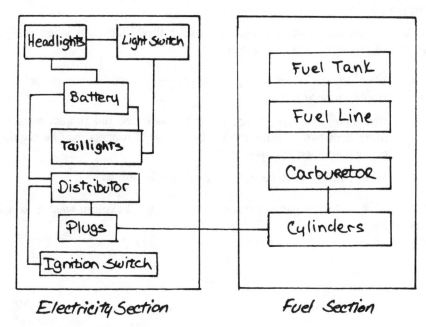

Figure 3.11. The flow-oriented automobile model.

3.5 Narrative models

I can't leave the subject of models without addressing a time-honored and very prevalent type of model, a model that consists entirely of words. All of us who have ever taken English composition or creative writing classes have had some experience with word models, and most people who have been involved with systems development have had additional exposure to them. After all, many systems specifications are built as word models.

The use of narrative text is common, but is it an effective tool? In my view, there is nothing wrong with a word model, as long as what we're describing is reasonably simple. Words, when used carefully, can describe things completely and precisely. However, when the amount of material to be described is relatively large, our capacity for absorbing detail diminishes; the details must be organized into groups, the groups into still larger groups, and so on. Pictures are simply much more effective than words at portraying such an organization.

If you still doubt that pictures describe masses of information more effectively than does narrative text, compare the ability of graphic versus word models to *predict* behavior by preparing a graphic model and a narrative model of the same subject matter. Give the graphic model to one person and the narrative model to a second, and then ask each person a set of questions about details of the subject that has been modeled. I predict that the answers from the person with the graphic model will win hands down in terms of speed and accuracy. The question of whether a model is predictive is not simply theoretical. A model that cannot be conveniently and rapidly used to answer questions is not, in any practical sense of the word, predictive.

3.6 Summary

The aspiring model builder should consider three questions when confronted with a new type of problem. These questions are,

- What are the relevant dimensions to be included in the model (for example, time or size)?

- How many dimensions are needed to describe the subject matter? (If more than two or three are needed, a *set* of models may be required to provide an adequate description.)

- What strategy is to be used to partition the model?

Now that we've looked at various types of models, we'll explore *what is to be modeled* in the next chapter.

4

What Is a System?

In order to learn more about what aspects of systems need to be modeled, let's look at a *specific* system. Through this system, or case study, I can present general observations about the characteristics of systems [1], while introducing you to a system that we'll use for a variety of examples throughout Part II of the book.

4.1 Introducing Carol

Carol, now in her mid-thirties, had been an energetic and well-liked teacher in the New York City school system until she fell victim to a funding crisis. Unable to find a teaching position in her field, she obtained a job with an advertising agency.

This turned out to be a good choice: Carol had a natural flair for marketing and soon rose to hold a well-paid and responsible position at the agency. Nevertheless, Carol missed the electricity that flowed between teacher and student, which had characterized her former job. Perhaps largely for this reason, Carol kept in contact with her colleagues, and recognized that whether or not they were teachers, her friends tended to be people for whom learning was a way of life.

Just before Easter one year, Carol gave a party. One of her guests brought a friend, a man who had recently emigrated from the Ukraine and who presented Carol with a beautifully hand-painted Easter egg. In talking with this man, Carol learned that he had been a well-known folk artist in his native land, and that he had painted the egg himself. The egg, which received considerable attention during the party, was admired by two of Carol's friends. Carol overheard one of them remark that she'd give anything to learn to paint like that and promptly introduced her friends to the Ukrainian. Because the man was looking for some extra income, a deal was made on the spot and a Ukrainian egg-painting seminar flourished in Brooklyn Heights for several months.

At the same party, Carol talked with a former colleague who made beautiful and unusual jewelry from hard-to-find materials. Carol bought a piece of jewelry from the woman, and wore it to the office a few weeks later. It provoked much admiration from her coworkers, one of whom confided that he'd always wanted to learn to make jewelry. Carol's ears perked up, but it was a very busy week for her and she never followed up on the man's statement.

Comment

All systems start from some sort of external opportunity or danger. Thus, all systems have an economic basis, with "economic" being defined in the broadest sense of the word. Systems exist because there are jobs and tasks that need tending to, and because it's worth somebody's while to tend to them. For example, payroll systems exist because there are people who are willing to exchange their efforts for money. In such cases, it's worthwhile for the employer to operate a system, since workers wouldn't stay long if they didn't get paid regularly. A payroll system has an economic justification in a very obvious sense. However, a system that distributes food to hungry children in underdeveloped countries may be thought of in the same way. Clearly, there is something that needs tending to. It is also worthwhile for someone to operate the system, for reasons that may have to do with personal satisfaction or social responsibility rather than personal gain.

Getting specific

In Carol's case, the thing that needs tending to is clear: There are people who want to learn things, and other people willing to teach them. Carol's motivation for playing matchmaker appears to be (at least at this early stage) the personal satisfaction she gets. However, there's one important factor that prevents me from calling what Carol does a system. Her response to the need isn't predictable. *In the Easter egg case, she helped her friends link up. When presented with a similar opportunity in the case of the jewelry, she did not.*

4.2 An idea grows

Over the next few months, Carol played matchmaker for a number of other friends by linking up people who had something unusual to teach with people who wanted to learn about it. One Saturday, as she was recovering from a particularly high-pressured week at the office, an idea occurred to her: The world seemed to be full of potential teachers and potential students, wandering around with no effective way to contact each other. What a wonderful idea for a business! It would work somewhat like a real estate brokerage. People who had something unusual to teach would list their specialties with Carol. She would then locate potential students, find what they wanted to learn, and organize classes by matching their needs with her teacher listings. Like a real estate broker, she would collect a fee (from the students, the teachers, or both) for a successful match.

Starting that very day, Carol began spending a lot of time on the telephone. She canvassed her network of friends and acquaintances and took notes on what they'd like to teach or learn. She made a few immediate match-ups. More importantly, however, she began an extensive file of students in search of teachers and vice versa. Naturally, the word spread about what was going on, as Carol's friends told *their* friends. Carol was soon receiving calls from people she didn't know, requesting that they be listed.

As the months went by, Carol spent more and more time on her avocation. She also began to make an appreciable amount of income on the fees collected for linkups. Inevitably, her interest in advertising work paled. Finally, Carol took the big step: She left the agency and incorporated as The Ad Hoc College of Uncommon Knowledge, an organization that came to be known as The Un-College.

Comment

When behavior patterns become predictable, it's reasonable to describe them as systems.

Getting specific

The Un-College is a full-fledged system. Carol's response to the need is now "systematic," or predictable. Although it may not be written down, a relatively stable set of rules exists for determining how potential teachers or students should be treated. A planned, predictable response is at the core of the system. A payroll system that was unpredictable (say, that gave out paychecks one week and vouchers for a free ice cream cone the next) would clearly be unacceptable to those who used it.

Note

The concept of a system has nothing intrinsically to do with computer technology. Any planned response to a need or opportunity is a system, whether carried out by people, machines, or some combination of the two.

4.3 An organization grows

Let's look in on The Un-College once again: It has expanded to two locations. The main office (on New York's Upper West Side near Lincoln Center) is staffed by Carol and her assistant Bob. It is at this location that students are signed up, matches are made, invoices are sent out, and payments are processed. The Un-College's general administrative tasks (such as accounting and taxes) are also handled in the main office, where two filing cabinets, groaning at the seams, are kept. Carol has thought of computerizing some of this operation, but hasn't quite gotten to it yet.

The remainder of The Un-College's business takes place in a small office in the West Village, where Carol's assistant Alice works. Alice accepts teacher sign-ups, and makes calls to both teachers and students informing them of matches. Of course, she has to communicate with the uptown office to do this. Once a day she makes a call to Carol, tells her about the latest teacher sign-ups, and gets the match-up lists. Alice actually spends only a fraction of her time working on Un-College business. The rest of her time is spent taking orders for a small clothing mail-order house. This is a very useful arrangement for Carol. It takes some of the work off Bob's and her shoulders, provides full-time coverage and a separate telephone line for teacher sign-ups, and is much cheaper than hiring another full-time employee.

Comment

One important thing about systems is that they can be transferred.

Getting specific

Part of the work that Carol was originally doing is now being done by Bob and Alice. If Carol couldn't explain to someone else how she did her match-ups, it wouldn't be a system in any way that would interest us. The essence of the systems development process is communication about the patterns involved. It is this transferability that is ultimately responsible for our ability to automate organizational patterns.

Notice that there are quite a few things happening now that weren't happening when Carol started her system. For example, account ledgers are kept, and tax forms are filled out. The original needs for which the system was created are still being met, but the enlarged system must respond to some new needs (such as "The tax people need revenue reports"). Such needs are certainly derivative and secondary to the basic purpose of the system. Nevertheless, they are quite real and have to be taken into account in any description of The Un-College.

Experiment

Let's imagine that we can erect a kind of customs barrier around the uptown office of The Un-College. The barrier will intercept any information entering or leaving the office: mail, telephone calls, hand-delivered documents, and so on. If we watch for a while, we will see student sign-ups crossing the barrier on the way in, invoices crossing on the way out, teacher sign-ups from Alice coming in, and so on. You can think of the system as living inside this imaginary barrier, and dealing with the outside world by means of data traffic.

Let's look once again at that last piece of traffic, the incoming teacher sign-ups. This is different from other traffic, since it comes from another piece of The Un-College rather than from the outside world. Or does it? When you come right down to it, from the point of view of a particular system, the outside world is anything we say it is! Alice's need to submit teacher sign-ups is as good a need as any other. The fact that the uptown office is only a piece of The Un-College doesn't make it any less of a system.

In a similar way, what Alice does could be considered a system in its own right. Let's put a similar customs barrier around her office and watch what happens. Here comes a teacher sign-up. There goes a report on new teachers to Carol's office. Here comes a mail order for clothing . . . whoops! Something has gone wrong here. Clearly, Alice's handling of mail orders has no relevance to The Un-College. This tells us something important about the boundaries of systems. Although it's useful to picture a boundary around a system, such boundaries aren't geographical. They exist only as mental images, and so we're free to imagine a barrier around Alice's office that doesn't allow us to see the mail orders.

Since the nature of a system boundary is not specific to a place, let's imagine a larger boundary that encompasses both Carol's office and the non-mail-order aspects of Alice's office. What's inside this boundary is all of The Un-College. From this point of view, Carol's office and Alice's office are subsystems. We can extend this idea by drawing a boundary inside Carol's office that encloses only tax-related activities. This, too, is a system in its own right, responding to its own external needs, even if it's only a fraction of The Un-College's overall activity. This idea of "wheels within wheels within wheels" is very useful for picturing systems. The smaller subsystems, such as the tax-handling one, may deal with needs that have no obvious relationship to the overall purpose of the system.

4.4 Inside The Un-College

As time went on, and business grew, Carol became more concerned with getting organized. With only three people in the organization and frequent telephone or face-to-face contact, this was not a problem. Misunderstandings or difficulties could be ironed out on an ad hoc day-to-day basis. However, as the volume of business increased, it became necessary to hire extra help. Because the new people couldn't be expected to learn the routine without some formal training, Bob and Carol started spending time (late evenings, when the phone was quiet) writing an instruction manual for new employees.

The first thing they documented was a procedure for taking phone calls. There were a lot of things to know, for example, when a potential student called. Certain kinds of information were always required, and other kinds were required only in special circumstances. (For example, people who wanted to learn something requiring vigorous physical activity had to be asked about medical problems.) Also, under certain circumstances, The Un-College would refuse to accept a potential student. Carol was fairly liberal, but occasionally a student would come along with a request that, if granted, would have gotten everyone involved thrown in jail. (One of the milder ones was the fellow who wanted a workshop class in building tactical nuclear weapons.)

Another issue had to do with the organization of files. This issue was fairly complex, since a student could request instruction in more than one subject, a teacher could offer to teach more than one subject, and so on. Things had to be cross-referenced very carefully in order to make the system work.

As Bob and Carol developed the training manual, they discovered that a number of tasks were hard to describe. They also discovered some differences in their individual procedures. They compared notes to settle on a single approach. While working out these details, Bob and Carol wondered whether some of the procedures and files might be computerized. Clearly, certain tasks, like deciding whether a requested subject was illegal or immoral, required human judgment, but others were obviously repetitive, routine aspects of the work.

Bob and Carol were ambivalent about computerization, since they were venturing into unknown territory. It was clear to both of them, however, that if the organization kept growing, computers were an inevitable part of their future.

Comment

In looking at the needs to which the system responds, and in drawing boundaries around a system and watching information enter and leave, we've been looking at systems from the outside. Although this perspective is important, it's also necessary to look at the inside of a system.

Getting specific

When Bob and Carol began writing their instruction manual, they were building a model of the inside of The Un-College, although they may not have thought of it in those terms. They were trying to reduce the complexities of their system to a form that they could communicate to other people. What they found themselves describing were patterns of activities (such as the rules for signing up potential students) and patterns of stored data (file organization). Carol and Bob seem to be having trouble with this task. Since they haven't had the benefit of reading this book, they're trying to describe the patterns by using narrative text rather than by using a graphic model. Don't worry; they'll learn.

Although they aren't thinking in these terms, Bob and Carol are also encountering the distinction between the essentials of a system and its implementation. The basic rules of The Un-College are determined by just two things: the needs to which it responds and the purposes of the organization. It would be simpler if we could say that the basic rules were determined only by needs, but it's not quite true. There are some subtle interactions between the two; for example, some students have needs of which the organization doesn't approve and thus refuses to fill. Even with this complication, the basic situation is easy enough to understand. Give me a description of the needs that a system meets, and an understanding of its basic purpose, and I can create a reasonable, workable set of activity and stored data patterns.

The situation changes when Bob and Carol bring up the subject of computerization. They're not talking about the basic rules of the organization any more. A file system, for example, could be created either by using paper forms and filing cabinets or by storing data in a computer's memory. The pattern is the same; what is different is not the needs being responded to, or the purpose of the organization, but the use of technology. I'm certainly not suggesting that technology is unimportant; it might influence the efficiency of the organization, its potential for growth, or its profitability. However, none of these issues is an essentials issue (as described in Section 2.2); they are examples of implementation. The difference manifests itself in the type of expertise *required to solve problems. The essential view of The Un-College has to do with matching people who want to teach and people who want to learn. The implementation view has to do, for instance, with which computers are available and what their capabilities and costs are. While obviously important, expertise in automating a system is far removed from Bob's and Carol's basic skills and from the needs and purposes of the organization.*

4.5 Summary

Here are the major points about systems that I've made in this chapter:

- Systems arise as responses to something in the outside world that can be thought of as external, that is, a need or opportunity that should be tended.

- Systems also have a specific purpose; the precise nature of a response to an external event is flavored by this purpose.

- Systems have to make predictable responses; they follow a prescribed set of rules for responding to external events.

- Systems are transferable; the rules by which they operate must be capable of being described so that people can communicate about them.

- Systems can be characterized in terms of a boundary, which separates them from their environment and through which information passes. This boundary, however, is not geographical in nature.

- The inside of a system consists of patterns of activities and patterns of stored data, which are the machinery for responding to external events in terms of the system's purpose.

• The basic rules of a system are independent of the technology used to make the system work. The basic rules constitute the essential view of a system, and the technology constitutes the implementation view. Technology consists both of manual and automated patterns of activities and of data storage.

In the next chapter, we will explore systems' dimensions, and will build some preliminary models.

Chapter 4: Reference

1.   J. Palmer and S. McMenamin, *Essential Systems Analysis* (New York: Yourdon Press, 1984).

      This book introduces the basics of the characterization of systems described in this chapter.

5

Systems Development as Model Building

If you've stuck with me this far, you've noticed that I've done a lot of jumping around, talking about consumers' rights and party games and all sorts of things. In order to make it worth your while to continue reading, I owe it to you to pull the scattered threads together to form a consistent picture. However, I don't apologize for jumping around. I think it was necessary to give you enough information to understand ASML. I *could* have started out by saying, In order to do systems development, step one is to draw a picture of XYZ, step two is to check ABC, and so on, but that approach makes the *why* of the process just so much magic.

The tools and techniques described in this and the following chapters work very effectively, but only if they are used intelligently. If you understand the nature of the process clearly enough, you can devise your own tools and techniques (although I hope to spare you that time and trouble). On the other hand, all the tools and techniques in the world won't prevent you from getting off track if you're painting by numbers. So in this chapter, I show how the diverse threads of the preceding chapters form a single, coherent picture.

5.1 Where we've been and where we're going

First, let me repeat the points I have made in the preceding chapters. In Chapter 1, I suggested that you, as a consumer, may not be getting your money's worth out of the resources your organization expends on computers. If the result of spending millions on systems development is a collection of balky systems that make life harder rather than easier for the end users, the organization might just as well spend its money on employee raises, medical benefits, or something truly beneficial. Throwing technology at the problem won't solve it, since the problem has to do with a failure in communications. In particular, buying truck loads full of personal computers may well produce small-scale gains at the expense of larger-scale coordination. In other words, just as in any other consumers' rights movement, the only effective strategy is to get involved in the process of deciding what's to be produced, that is, in the systems development process.

In Chapter 2, I told you that getting involved requires that you understand the human communication problems that are the main cause of faulty systems. These problems are illustrated by the telegraph party game. Similar human communication failures lead to distortion of the information that must be passed from person to person during systems development. Understanding these problems leads to the building of models of systems that are organized to make recognizing and correcting errors easier. Such models must be graphic, partitioned, appropriate in vocabulary, and predictive.

In Chapter 3, I presented models and dimension. Models of organizational patterns must be created with pencil and paper. They can't represent the pattern in the direct way that a drawing represents a physical object, but must be somewhat abstract, and must be created by someone who is aware of the dimensions of the patterns being represented.

My primary point in Chapter 4 was that you must explore a system's basic nature if you are to discover the dimensions of systems (patterns). To facilitate this exploration, I introduced The Ad Hoc College of Uncommon Knowledge, an imaginary organization whose fortunes we'll be following in Part II. Using this organization as an example, I pointed out some basic things about systems: Systems consist of planned responses to needs in the outside world. They aren't trapped in the minds of their creators, so they can be shared and discussed with other people, and incorporated into computers. They can be thought of as having an outside and an inside. The outside is marked by an imaginary boundary through which they communicate with the world, and the inside contains the patterns of activities and data that respond to the needs. Finally, you can picture them according to their basic operation (the essential view) or in terms of who does what (the implementation view).

With this summary as background, I use the balance of this chapter to describe the dimensions of systems. I'll do this by proving the need for multiple models (since a complex original should not be described by a single model), and by giving some basic examples of the models (which I'll explore in detail later in the book).

5.2 The dimensions of systems

In this section, I list the properties and qualities of systems. In this list, I differentiate between identifying (naming) something (for example, "a message from mother"), describing the details of that thing (for example, "Mother wrote that the cat died"), and identifying the medium that carries the thing (for example, a telegram). The properties of systems are

1. names of people, organizations, computers, and so on that are outside a particular system and that communicate with the system by sending data to it or receiving data from it

2. names of chunks of data that cross the system boundary, either going in or coming out

3. details of chunks of data that enter and leave the system

4. media by which data enters and leaves a system

5. needs in the outside world to which the system responds

6. names of responses that the system makes to various needs in the world outside

7. details of particular responses

8. identities of people (or perhaps simply their job titles), names of departments, model numbers of computers, all of which carry out the responses to the outside needs

9. names of types of data that the system must store in order to carry out its responses

10. details of various types of stored data

11. connections between responses and types of stored data needed to make the responses

12. connections among various categories of stored data

13. media on which data in the system is stored

14. connections between storage media and people and machines who use stored data to respond to external needs

This is quite a formidable list. It may not be necessary to convince you that there's too much here to be included in a single model, but it's worth spelling out. Suppose you were to teach an anatomy course, and had to provide your students with learning aids to help them understand the human body. It seems clear that, first, you would want to give them models, and second, that a single model labeled Everything You Ever Wanted to Know About the Human Body would not be the best choice. It seems so natural to think about a model of the skeleton, a model of the circulatory system, a model of the digestive system, and so on. Although organizational patterns aren't nearly as complex as the human body, the number of aspects to be considered is quite formidable; multiple models are clearly needed. I hope it's also clear that some careful thought needs to go into which dimensions get assigned to which models. Imagine the poor anatomy student confronted with a model of all the blood vessels, organs, and bones whose names begin with P. Rather than spell out my proposed method of organization in detail, I'll show it to you first and discuss it later. Actually, I gave away most of the secret back in Chapter 1. The main strategy is to separate patterns of activities from patterns of stored data.

5.3 Modeling processes

Back in the early days, when Bob and Carol were the only employees of The Ad Hoc College of Uncommon Knowledge, they kept a daily log of their activities.* A typical day's entries are reproduced on the next page.

Before going to work on this example, I'll give you more details. Signing up students entailed recording basic information on a student form, ensuring that the student's choice of subject wasn't illegal or immoral, and informing the student whether his or her sign-up was accepted. The procedure varied a little, of course, depending on how the sign-ups came in. On the telephone, the student could be prompted for the

---

*In fact, one additional person needs to be introduced: Ted is Carol's cousin, who filled in while she went shopping.

required information, and informed of the acceptance or rejection verbally. This worked essentially the same way whether the initial call was answered in person or by the answering machine. When the student left a message on the machine, an information gathering call was initiated by an Un-College employee. When the student applied by mail, missing information was solicited by return mail if the student couldn't be reached by phone. In some cases, the student would be informed of acceptance or rejection by mail.

TIME	ACTIVITY
8:30 a.m. to 10:30 a.m.	Bob signs up students from mail registrations Carol signs up students by phone
10:30 a.m. to 12:30 p.m.	Bob signs up students by phone Carol matches students with teachers
12:30 p.m. to 2:00 p.m.	Lunch (answering machine on)
2:00 p.m. to 4:00 p.m.	Bob signs up students by responding to answering machine messages Ted signs up students via the telephone
4:00 p.m. to 5:30 p.m.	Bob matches students with teachers

After the forms for the accepted students were completed and placed in a basket, an attempt was made to match each student with an available teacher. Sometimes, this attempt was made immediately: If the person doing the matching was not busy, he or she simply took the student form from the basket as soon as it was completed. The procedure for matching involved searching the file of teachers for someone willing to teach the student's subject. If a match was found, both the student and teacher forms would be annotated and notes would be sent to both student and teacher. Whether a match was actually made, the student form would be filed at the end of the procedure.

Now that we have all the basic information, let's build a model. The most obvious kind of model is a drawing; however, I'll use as a starting point the drawing's more modern cousin, the photograph. In fact, I'll be even more sophisticated and use time-lapse photography. (I'm sure you've seen photographs of a busy street after dark. By making multiple exposures on a single piece of film, the photographer causes the cars to appear as streams of lights.) Imagine that a camera is set up in front of Carol's desk at 8:30 a.m. and that the automatic timing mechanism is on. A single photograph might catch Carol lifting the phone receiver, as does the drawing in Figure 5.1.

Figure 5.1. Carol picks up the phone.

However, for a group of exposures superimposed on a single negative, Carol's movements will form a central blurred area, the movements of the phone receiver will form a track, and the movements of the completed forms to the basket will form another track. The superimposed action is represented in Figure 5.2.

Figure 5.2. Time-lapse image of Carol.

Now let's suppose that during exactly the same time period, a similar camera apparatus is set up in front of Bob's desk. Bob has a basket for completed forms in the same spot on his desk as Carol has on hers, but in place of the phone receiver, he has an In/Out mail basket. (He doesn't use the phone during this period.) Assume that a time-lapse photograph of Bob like the one taken of Carol is obtained and then *the two photographs are superimposed.* Figure 5.3 shows that the motions of the phone cradle and of the mail to and from the basket have merged into a single stream, and of course the superimposition of the central figures makes it impossible to tell who's performing the activity. To avoid insulting your intelligence by excessively spelling out details, I'll simply state that adding a picture of Ted's activities to the collage won't change the result appreciably.

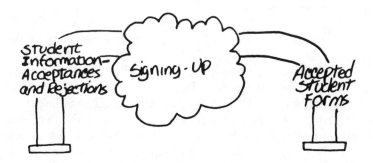

Figure 5.3. Bob's and Carol's signing-up activities superimposed.

Note that our strategy has been to track an activity no matter who's performing it. If the same strategy is followed for the matching activity, and then the two composite images are set side by side so the completed forms baskets overlap, something like Figure 5.4 results. (Those of you who are literal-minded will note that I've reversed right and left when convenient.)

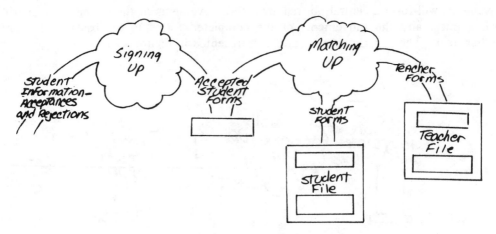

Figure 5.4. Combined signing-up and matching-up activities.

At this point, let's take a closer look at Figure 5.4. The time-lapse procedure has dropped details of the individual sign-ups and match-ups, making the day-to-day activities abstract. In addition, superimposing photographs of different people has made abstract the details of who does what. Finally, by superimposing phone and written inputs, we've dropped details of the media that carry the data. Now let's compare the model with the list of system dimensions from the previous section. The model describes

- chunks of data that cross the system boundary (2)
- system responses (6)
- types of stored data (9)
- connections between stored data and responses (11)
- storage media (13)

The model covers roughly one-third of the significant dimensions of this area of The Un-College's business.

So far, I've examined the consequences of *de-emphasizing* the people involved. Now let's try emphasizing the people. Instead of superimposing photos of different people performing one activity, I'll superimpose the details of different activities carried out by the same person. Arranging the results side by side produces Figure 5.5.

The dimensions described by Figure 5.5 and Figure 5.4 overlap somewhat. Chunks of data (2), types of stored information (9), and storage media (13) are covered by both. However, the responses (6), and thus the connections between the stored data and the responses (11), certainly aren't obvious. To compensate for this, the model contains additional information about the people who carry out the responses (8) and about the connections between the people and the storage media (14); for example, both Bob and Carol use the files but Ted does not. Both models seem to cover about the same percentage of the dimensions, although different selections. Notice that neither model covers sources and destinations of data outside the system, nor any of the things I labeled as details (of the responses, of the composition of the chunks of data, and so on). Separate models will be used for these, and they will be covered in a later chapter.

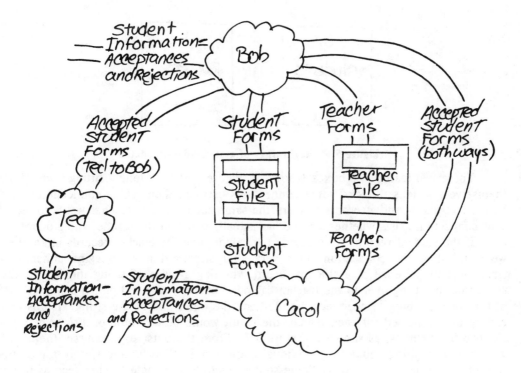

Figure 5.5. Processes grouped by persons.

Meanwhile, a comparison of Figure 5.4 with Figure 5.5 reveals a number of differences:

- Figure 5.4 emphasizes *what* is done, while Figure 5.5 emphasizes *who* does it.

- Figure 5.5 has more complicated interconnections than Figure 5.4.

- Figure 5.5 is more likely to change than Figure 5.4 if changes are made to the system.

I will return to this comparison of types of process models later in the chapter. But for now, it's time to discuss the modeling of stored data.

5.4 Modeling stored data

In the process models described in the last section, stored data was depicted by pictures of filing cabinets, and streams of data were shown flowing between the storage areas and the processes. This time let's start with a model containing just the stored data about the students and teachers. I won't draw them as filing cabinets, but simply as featureless boxes labeled with the type of data contained.

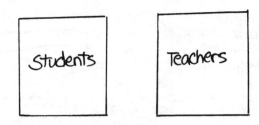

Figure 5.6. Beginnings of a stored data model.

These two featureless boxes (shown in Figure 5.6) look lonely sitting there all by themselves, so let's think of some connections between them. One connection would be the fact that a student wants to learn the same subject that a teacher wants to teach. This connection exists whether anyone has actually matched the teacher and student.

If the student records were in one file cabinet and the teacher records in another, we could show the connections in a very straightforward way. Imagine punching a small hole in the edge of a student record, knotting a piece of string through it, and stretching the string over to the teacher cabinet. There, you could punch a similar hole in the corresponding teacher record and attach the other end of the string. If this procedure were repeated for each match, the result would be a bundle of strings between the two file cabinets, as shown in Figure 5.7. From the outside, of course, there's no way to tell anything about the individual connections. The bundle simply represents the total of all the connections. Some student records and some teacher records would have no strings attached to them, indicating that there was no teacher or no student with a matching subject.

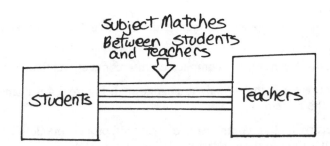

Figure 5.7. Student-teacher connections.

There's another possible kind of connection in this model. Think of tying pieces of string among all the student records that match on a particular subject. These strings, of course, would be invisible from outside the model, since they would be internal to the student box.

Before looking at another kind of model of stored data, compare Figure 5.7 with the list of dimensions. It shows the categories of stored data (9) and the connections between these categories (11). It does not show details of the stored data (10). For the details, as in the corresponding situation for the process model, a separate model will be used.

Now I'll let you in on a little trick I pulled on you. In discussing the process model in the last section, I assumed (and let you assume) that all teacher records were in one file cabinet and all student records in another. But that isn't the case! Carol started out using 3" × 5" file cards for student records and 8½" × 11" forms for teacher records. She purchased a small two-drawer cabinet for the student records and a big one for the teacher records. After keeping records for a while, she decided that she needed more information about students than about teachers, and switched record sizes. The result? You guessed it. The small cabinet has one drawer of old student records and one drawer of new teacher records; the large cabinet, the reverse. Notice that this doesn't change Figure 5.7 at all if we think of the boxes as *categories* of data, rather than as specific locations. If we were to build a model of where the data is, however, it would look like Figure 5.8.

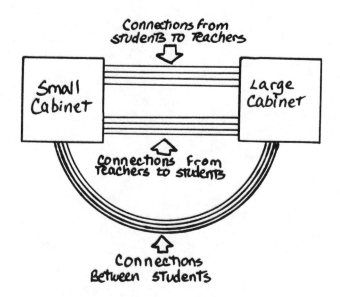

Figure 5.8. Data locations and connections.

The differences between Figures 5.7 and 5.8 bear strong resemblances to the differences between Figures 5.4 and 5.5:

- Figure 5.8 emphasizes *where* the data is; Figure 5.7 emphasizes *what* it is.

- Figure 5.8 has more complicated connections than Figure 5.7 (either more bundles of string or a single, messier bundle).

- Figure 5.8 is liable to change if changes are made to the system; Figure 5.7 is not. (Notice what would happen to each of the models if we replaced the filing cabinets with computer files.)

5.5 Summary

In this chapter, we have explored

- the dimensions of systems;
- the basics of modeling an activity pattern; and
- the basics of modeling a stored data pattern.

In the following chapter, the outline of a more formal approach to modeling will be presented.

6

The ASML Modeling Process

Now that all the groundwork has been laid, let's take a look at the overall organization of the ASML systems development discipline. First, look back at Figure 2.3, which pictures the development of a system rather like the layers of an onion; each successive stage embodies the information from the previous stage. Table 6.1 contains the same information in a slightly different form. In the table, systems development is shown as a sequence of activities, which results in the evolution of a completed system from a model. First, a description of the system's required behavior is created; this is the essential model. It is derived from an understanding of the basic purpose of the system to be built. The essential model uses the vocabulary of the system's subject matter, and describes those things the system would need to do to fulfill its purpose regardless of how it was implemented.

Table 6.1
Evolution of a System

	Activity	Comment	
Subject Matter of ASML {	build essential model	describe required behavior of system	Direction of Evolution
	build implementation model	describe automated technology organization that embodies required behavior	
	build system	embody implementation model in hardware and software	

The implementation model is created from the essential model by adding to the essential model details of how available technology is to be used to make the system behave as required. For example, assume that the essential model says the system will produce a certain type of output data. The implementation model might add that the output data will be displayed on a screen, with a paper copy available upon request. The implementation model thus *evolves* from the essential model through the addition

53

of details. Its vocabulary is drawn both from the system's subject matter and from the implementation technology. Thus, a chunk of data that an essential model calls a savings withdrawal may end up being called a savings withdrawal message packet if it's sent electronically from one computer to another.

The final construction stage described in Table 6.1 is the creation of the system from the implementation model. This stage is outside the scope of ASML, which is a model building discipline. ASML is designed to create the most accurate, most complete possible guide for the system builder, but does not address system building per se.

Table 6.2
The ASML Models

	Stage	Comment
Essential Model	environmental model	description of environment in which system operates
	behavior model	description of behavior in response to (external) events in environment
Implementation Model	processor configuration model	description of processor layout that will carry out required behavior
	software configuration model	description of organization of processes and data within each processor
	code organization model	description of organization of computer instructions within each process

(Right-side brackets: "Book's Main Subject Matter" for environmental and behavior models; "Book's Secondary Topics" for software configuration and code organization models.)

Table 6.2 gives a more detailed view of the essential model and the implementation model. The essential model is actually built in two stages. The environmental model is built first: It describes the purpose of the system, the connections between the system and the outside world, and the events occurring in the outside world to which the system must respond. The behavior model is derived from the environmental model, and describes what the system must do to accomplish its purpose in response to events that occur in its environment.

The implementation model is also built in stages; in this case, however, only the first of the three stages is of central concern to the subject of this book. The other two stages are summarized in Chapter 19. Table 6.3 shows why this book concentrates on the first implementation model stage, emphasizing that the software configuration and code organization models concern the details of automated technology. Their purpose is to guide the creation of computer instructions, which are organized for ease of implementation and maintainability. The choice of one scheme over another for organizing computer instructions has no observable effect on the behavior of the completed system, and thus needn't be the concern of the users. On the other hand, the details of the processor configuration model have a decidedly observable effect. The choice between using a single computer or a network of computers to implement a system may affect the cost of the system dramatically, and choosing to display output on screens rather than to print it may significantly affect ease of use. Since these implementation details are also vital to automated technology experts, building this stage of the model must be a joint venture of the user and data processing communities.

Table 6.3
ASML Model Characteristics

	Phase	Required Scope of Involvement	Effect of Model Details
Essential Model	environmental model	subject matter experts (users)	observable
	behavior model		
Implementation Model	processor configuration model		
	software configuration model	automated technology experts	non-observable
	code organization model		

Table 6.4
Structure of ASML Model

	Process Model	Data Model
Schematic Section	process schema	data schema
Detail Section	process description	data description

Table 6.4 shows the internal organization of one of the ASML models (all five of the models in Table 6.3 have essentially the same four-part layout). The overall model is divided into the process model and the data model. Each of these models has two sections, a schematic section and a detail section. In the process model, the process schema shows the overall organization of the work of the system, and the process

description provides the details of each individual process. In the data model, the data schema shows the overall organization of the system's stored data, and the data description provides the details of the stored data categories and linkages, and also of the data produced and used by the processes.

The remainder of the book will be devoted to explaining what the pieces of the ASML model are, and how the various stages of the model are created.

Part II
Modeling Tools

The Part II chapter layout, shown below, corresponds to the organization of the ASML model shown in Table 6.4.

Chapter 11	
Chapter 7 Process Schemas	Chapter 8 Data Schemas
Chapter 10 Process Descriptions	Chapter 9 Data Descriptions
Leveling and Balancing	

There is a chapter for each section of the model, and a chapter showing how all the sections fit together. As a unit, Chapters 7 and 8 describe the building of the schematic level of the model, with Chapter 7 focusing on modeling processes and Chapter 8 on modeling data. Chapter 9 describes the building of a detailed model in the context of data definition and data composition, while Chapter 10 provides guidelines for modeling process details. Finally, Chapter 11 explains the procedures for organizing the complete model for presentation and for assuring its correctness.

The basic model structure introduced in these five chapters will be used to build both stages of the essential model, and also to build the implementation model. Since the main focus of this book is on the essential model, most of the examples in Chapters 7 through 11 illustrate essential modeling, although a few examples of implementation models are also presented.

7

Process Schemas

You've already seen the fundamental idea behind building a process model. In this chapter, I'll lay out the details, give some more examples, and deal with how to tell whether a process schema you've built is a good model.

7.1 Basics of the model

The process schema describes a situation in which something comes in, is modified, and then the modified something goes out [1]. To illustrate this, let's look at an example of great historical importance, namely the rhyme "Four-and-twenty blackbirds baked in a pie." Here, something comes in (the blackbirds), something happens (baking), and something goes out (the pie). To create the process schema, the words are replaced with the picture shown in Figure 7.1.

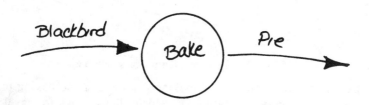

Figure 7.1. A simple process schema.

Aha! Just a minute! Maybe it isn't so simple after all, since something has been changed. The "four-and-twenty" has disappeared. The point is that modelers deliberately choose to show only certain details on a model. Details like how many blackbirds get baked into one pie don't show up. The model does not show everything about blackbird pie making, just a layout of the basic pattern. The quantity of blackbirds and other details, such as how long to bake and at what temperature, will show up elsewhere; they won't be forgotten.

Although some things should be left out of the model, others must be included, and in this case there's been a terrible omission. A pie composed solely of blackbirds would clearly fall apart long before it was set before the king. It obviously needs a crust. If we do assume that it *has* a crust, then the crust must have been created by magic inside the Bake part of the model. To rectify this situation, we must add something else, namely, the dough. Figure 7.2 illustrates a situation which, although not described in great detail, is at least correct.

Figure 7.2. A corrected process schema.

This scheme is correct, but essentially trivial and boring. If process schemas could describe only simple situations like this, they wouldn't be worth much. Fortunately, more complicated patterns can be described by linking processes together. Figure 7.3 extends the model to cover the making of the dough.

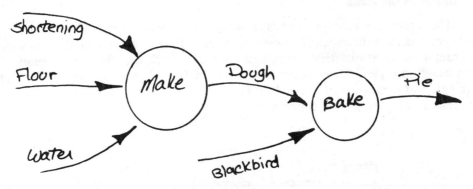

Figure 7.3. An expanded process schema.

Notice that the dough connects the making process and the baking process. Connections such as this one serve as pathways, which allow things to travel through the model. A lump of shortening comes in to the Make process, is incorporated into the dough, and finally becomes part of the (crust of the) pie. Although the shortening might not be recognizable at the other end of the process, it has traveled all the way through and forms a portion of the output. Both the Make process and the Bake process have *transformed* the shortening in some way. Most of the processes examined in this book will be transformations of one thing into another.

Now I'll extend the model by showing that something happens to the pie (it is eaten) and that something comes out (well, I'll be polite and say, flesh, blood, and bones).

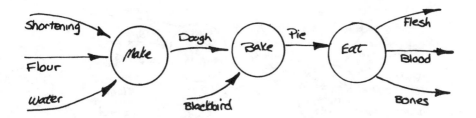

Figure 7.4. Extending the model.

Figure 7.4 isn't entirely satisfactory, for the simple reason that if the king ate the pie immediately after the baking process, he'd have second-degree burns in his royal mouth. This is the only place in the model so far where there's been a need to wait. The dough can be made as soon as the shortening, flour, and water are available; the same holds true for the baking process when dough and blackbirds are present. However, time delays are important enough to show in the model. Figure 7.5 shows that the pie must cool before it is eaten, but the figure also has been extended to indicate one more item in the king's diet: curds and whey.

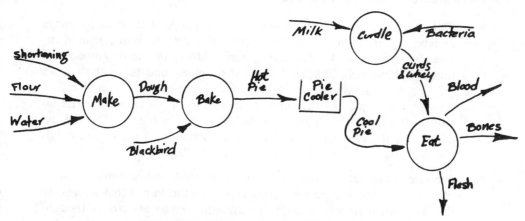

Figure 7.5. Process schema with time delay.

Since any system is created to respond to needs in the outside world, it's worth asking what needs this system answers. A reasonable, general answer might be that an efficient monarchical government requires a well-fed king. But it's possible to be more specific. As a matter of fact, the system responds to two different needs that occur at two different times. The first need is that the raw materials for the king's dinner need processing and the second need is that it's time for the king to eat.

Before we leave this imaginary realm completely, let's take a look at a different picture of the same system. In this model (Figure 7.6), the focus is on *who* does things rather than on *what* is done.

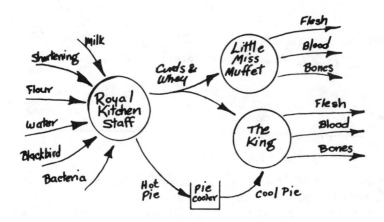

Figure 7.6. Who does what?

Now I'll be a little more formal, and introduce you to flows, processes, and stores, all of which are pieces of the process schema:

- *Flows* are the arrows with labels on them. Think of them as pathways or pipelines through which things enter the system, move around inside the system, and leave the system. Most commonly, models of this kind have *data* flowing through their pipes, and the pathways are referred to as dataflows. However, other kinds of things can also flow through a system, like the food in the blackbird pie example. The labels on the arrows name the various flows. The name can describe the content of the flow (for example, Royal Promotion List) or the medium that carries the flow (such as, Scroll with Royal Seal).

- *Processes* (also called activities, transformations, minisystems, or bubbles) are the labeled circles. They represent the things that happen to the flows on their way through the system. A process can be thought of as a diagram of an imperative sentence (for example, Bake the blackbirds into a pie), or as an agent that performs work (for example, a water wheel or grinding wheel). The label on the process names what happens to the flow, or gives the name of the person or organization that makes it happen, or the name of the place where it happens. Even in the case in which the process is labeled Royal Kitchen Staff or something along those lines, the model is really indicating that the process represents some part of the work done by the Royal Kitchen Staff. It certainly doesn't mean that *everything* the staff does is represented by the process.

- *Stores* (or time delays) are three-sided labeled figures. They represent flows that pause on their journey through the system; think of them as storage tanks or buckets. The label may refer either to what's stored (for example, Last Year's Petitions to the King) or to the storage medium (such as the Little Jewel-Encrusted Chest).

The process schema represents the work done by a system by picturing it as a network of processes connected by flows and stores.

7.2 Process schema details

In order to look at the process schema in more depth, let's return to The Ad Hoc College of Uncommon Knowledge. Following is a refinement of the description given earlier for one piece of the operation:

> *When student sign-ups come in, they are evaluated for completeness of information and suitability of topic. Sign-ups that are accepted are temporarily stored, and later matched against the teacher file. If there is a match, both the teacher record and the student sign-up are updated to indicate this. Whether or not there is a match, the information from the student sign-up is permanently stored in the student file. Students and teachers who have been matched up are notified.*
>
> *When teacher sign-ups come in, they are also evaluated for completeness and suitability of topic. Teacher sign-ups that are accepted are temporarily stored, and later matched against the student file. If there is a match, both the student record and the teacher sign-up are updated. Whether or not there is a match, the information from the teacher sign-up is permanently stored in the teacher file. Teachers and students who have been matched up are notified.*

This rather dull piece of text is certainly a model of The Un-College matching operation, but systems of this nature are more clearly described by pictures than in words. Figure 7.7 presents the basic layout of the system in a more succinct, accessible way than does the narrative description.

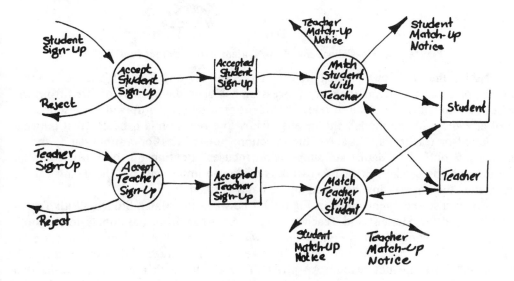

Figure 7.7. Un-College matching system.

The incoming data on the diagram is "lumped" to avoid excessive complexity. Although I know that the student submits his or her name, address, desired subject, and so on, I call the whole collection by the single name of Student Sign-up rather than overload the diagram with all these details. This lumping can be carried out to whatever extent is useful. For example, I could combine Student Sign-up and Teacher Sign-up into a single flow called Client Sign-up, although there's no advantage to be gained in this particular case. Lumping is not restricted to flows. There could be a single data store in this model called Client, instead of the separate Student and Teacher data stores. Finally, the Accept Student Sign-up and Match Student With Teacher processes could be combined into a single process called Serve Student, and something similar could be done for the Teacher processes. Incorporating all these changes produces Figure 7.8. It's still the same system; only the level of detail has changed.

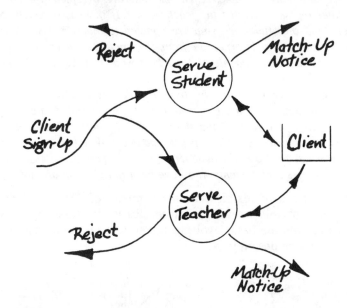

Figure 7.8. Un-College matching system with different lumping.

Notice the two flows labeled Reject in Figures 7.7 and 7.8. This is not a mere lumping of details; some of the error processing has been deliberately omitted from the model. Although the *decision* to reject a student or teacher sign-up will be described in detail elsewhere in the model, the details of how the rejection is handled (that is, what the student or teacher is told about the rejection, possibilities for resubmission, and so on) are left out. This deliberate suppression focuses attention on the normal flow of data through the model. Error processing is of course important, but the details can be added after the normal flow has been studied and verified.

Notice also the connections in Figure 7.7 between the Match Student With Teacher bubble and the Student and Teacher stores. An arrow from the bubble to the store means that the contents of the store are *changed* by the process. This connection ignores the fact that data normally must be taken out of storage if it is to be changed, and models only the net result. An arrow from the store to the bubble means that some data from the store is incorporated into the output of the process. A double-headed arrow means that both things happen.

Now, go back to Figure 7.7 for a minute and think about whether it describes *what* happens, or whether it describes *by whom* or *where* things are done. I think you'll agree it's mostly a *what* model. The distinction isn't an absolute one. There are models that mostly describe what happens (the essentials), models that mostly describe by whom and where things are done (the implementation), and models that are somewhere in between. By packaging The Un-College model from the last two figures in a different way, we come up with the model shown in Figure 7.9.

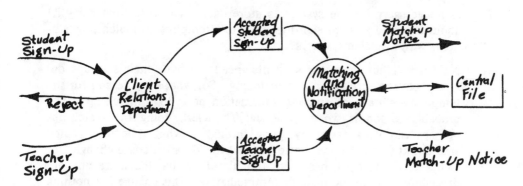

Figure 7.9. Implementation model of The Un-College matching system.

Obviously, this model shows a later stage in the history of The Un-College than has been presented so far, since there were no departments in the original. The important point, though, is that this is the same system as was pictured in Figures 7.7 and 7.8. It's just been rearranged to emphasize where things are done.

Packaging processes to emphasize work locations and adding other implementation details is reasonable if the model builder's purpose is to describe the implementation. However, it is not desirable to let implementation details slip in accidentally, since they make the model more complicated. The essential model is the simplest model possible; an implementation model has to contain information about what's done, plus information about who does the work or where it's done. One can determine whether a process schema contains implementation details by looking at each flow, store, and process, and by asking whether it is necessary for the system to have that feature in order to fulfill its purpose or to respond to outside needs. Let's try this out on the model shown in Figure 7.7:

Q: Is it necessary for the system to have the input dataflow called Student Sign-up?

A: Yes. The student's need to get matched up with a teacher can't be met without information about the student.

Q: Is it necessary for the system to perform the Accept Student Sign-up process (that is, filter out incomplete and undesirable sign-ups)?

A: Yes. The system can't successfully match students with teachers unless student data is complete. Furthermore, the purpose of the system requires that illegal and immoral subject choices be rejected.

Q: Is it necessary for the system to store student information (that is, to put it in the Student data store) if a match can't be made immediately?

A: Yes. Imagine that a student signs up to learn Siberian fly tying on June 1, and that a teacher signs up to teach Siberian fly tying on June 15. Since the system has no control over the timing of these events, the best it can do is to store the student's data to permit a match-up at a later date. Otherwise, it couldn't fulfill the student's need.

Q: Is it necessary for the system to store data (that is, to time delay it) about accepted student sign-ups prior to attempting to match new students with available teachers?

A: No! It will not serve the students' needs to have their sign-ups delayed between acceptance and matching. So, what's the reason for the temporary storage of student information prior to a match-up? The probable reason is work efficiency: The clerk doing the match-ups perhaps can work faster by going through a whole pile of accepted sign-ups at once. Notice, however, that the situation could change (for example, if the clerk has more free time) so that the more efficient procedure is to do the matching immediately. This change has nothing to do with the purpose of the system or the external events to which it responds. The time delay between acceptance and matching is part of a particular implementation and is not part of the essential model of the system. Thus, Figure 7.10 is closer to representing an essential model than is Figure 7.7.

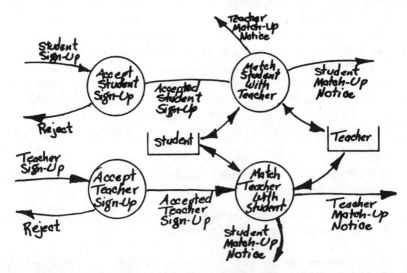

Figure 7.10. The Un-College matching system without implementation details.

The dataflow called Accepted Student Sign-up in Figure 7.10 conveys the information that the output from the Accept Student Sign-up process is needed by the Match Student With Teacher process. It also conveys that there is no need for a time delay; that is, the matching is to be done as soon as possible after the acceptance.

This may seem a small issue, but it's precisely problems of this sort that plague the systems development process. Imagine that the student and teacher sign-up process has been partially automated, and that the users ask the system builders, Why do you hold all the accepted sign-ups until the end of the day before matching them? The answer? "Well, there was a delay of that kind in the original manual system!" Whether the system builders should have been smart enough to know better is beside the point. Users have an ideal opportunity to tell the system builders what *is* required by building a process schema.

7.3 Kinds of flows

The flows on most process schemas carry data; but, as the four-and-twenty black-birds example at the beginning of the chapter demonstrated, models of this kind may also be useful in describing the flow of materials. Let's move for a moment from The Ad Hoc College of Uncommon Knowledge, and look at another organization, Gargantuan Gears, Inc., which uses large sheets of metal in gear production.

At Gargantuan Gears, the metal sheets are fed into a flame-cutter machine, which cuts out circles. The circles of metal are sent to a grinding machine, which cuts notches into the circles to produce teeth on the gear. Next, a machine cuts the center hole into the gear. After each of these steps, the scrap is recycled. The entire process is initiated by an order stating number of gears to be made, and specifying diameter, tooth size, and center-hole size. The metal sheets themselves are delivered in large batches by a steel company, and are stored in one of Gargantuan Gears' warehouses to be used as needed. The delivery from the steel company is accompanied by a bill of lading (delivery document), which is checked for consistency against the actual metal sheets delivered. If the delivery is accepted, the bill of lading is filed away for later use.

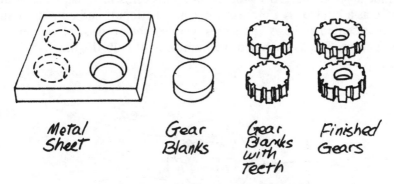

Figure 7.11. Stages in gear making.

Unless you're familiar with factory production techniques, you may not find the preceding text terribly clear. Figure 7.11 may help somewhat, by letting you visualize the raw material and the intermediate products, but the order and the bill of lading aren't part of the picture, although they're clearly important. The process schema shown in Figure 7.12 clarifies the situation by combining the documents with the material goods to produce a single diagram.

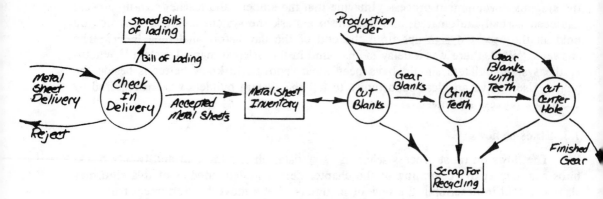

Figure 7.12. Process schema for gear making.

Flow symbols are used to represent movement of both data and material. Store symbols are used to represent time delays of data as well as inventories of material. Exactly what use can we make of a model of this kind? Clearly, our reason for studying this operation might arise from our wish to investigate the possibility of automating some portion of it. Although the handling of materials per se can't be automated,* the handling of raw materials and the handling of information contained in production orders, bills of lading, and other data are intimately connected. It's possible to build a model that shows only the handling of the data, but the model wouldn't provide as clear a picture as one that includes the material.

This expanded concept of the process schema is particularly important in industrial and scientific applications. Any process that transforms material, data, or energy can be represented as a bubble on a process schema. The inputs and outputs of such a process can be represented as flows and stores whether they consist of data or not. To illustrate this concept, I've diagrammed the humble light bulb (Figure 7.13).

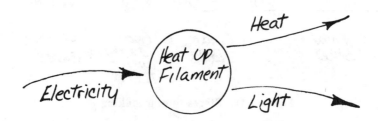

Figure 7.13. The light bulb.

---

*Robots could be built to handle the material, but in no case do we directly use computer technology to handle material.

7.4 Correcting mechanical errors

In practice, the development of automated systems is a kind of engineering, and is sometimes called software engineering or systems engineering. If a mechanical engineer handed me a paper-and-pencil model of some new gadget, my first question might be, How do I know this thing will work? Models of systems should be subject to the same kind of careful scrutiny as is common in other engineering fields. Models are communication tools: A person can use them to communicate ideas internally (for example, to lay out a problem so it can be thought about more clearly), or externally (to communicate something to other people). The communication process is flawed if the model has errors in it, and the product built from such a model will have corresponding flaws.

A mechanical engineer who is challenged about how well a model works might state that there are certain principles of physics to which every mechanical device is subject and that his model is consistent with these principles. Similarly, there are certain principles that apply to process schemas as well. Of course, if you're building a model of some existing organizational pattern, the most fundamental justification is that the pattern works in real life, and that the model matches the pattern. Nevertheless, it's useful to have some mechanical way to check the model. For example, a model describing a pattern that doesn't currently exist needs to be measured against some standard. Even if the pattern currently exists, it might contain undiscovered flaws that a mechanical check of the model will bring to light.

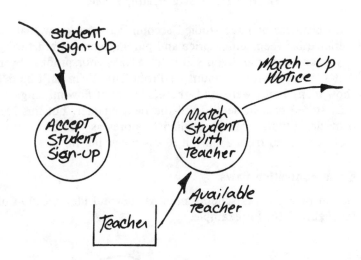

Figure 7.14. An erroneous process schema.

Examine Figure 7.14 to see whether you can detect any problems. In a way, it's a silly request; obviously, someone forgot to draw in the Accepted Student Sign-up dataflow. But the purpose of my request is to have you look at the two processes one at a time, because they have quite different problems. In the Accept Student Sign-up process, Student Sign-up disappears into some cosmic black hole and nothing emerges. In the Match Student With Teacher process, the Match-up Notice appears by magic. The only possible place it could have come from is the Teacher store; if it did come from there, that store is badly misnamed. The processes in Figure 7.14 demonstrate the following two general mechanical principles for process schemas:

- A flow that comes out of a process must have been input in some form.

- A flow that goes into a process should come out in some form.

Notice that the word "must" is used in the first rule and the word "should" in the second. It's possible to feed to a bubble a flow that it won't use; this isn't hopelessly wrong, just messy and unnecessarily complicated. Creating output flows from nothing, on the other hand, simply won't work.

Problems of this kind aren't always as easy to see as they are in Figure 7.14. Look at Figure 7.15, for instance, to see whether you can determine what's wrong.

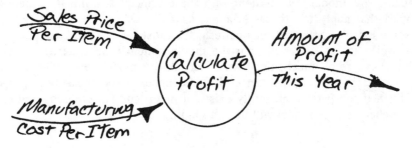

Figure 7.15. A data creating bubble.

If you are in business or have studied accounting, you know that, simply stated, profit is the difference between selling price and purchase or manufacturing cost. Thus, if an item costs you one dollar and you sell it for $1.25, your profit is twenty-five cents — *per item!* That's the problem: Amount Of Profit This Year can't be determined unless you know how many items were sold; there's an input flow missing.

I won't treat stored data in detail until the next chapter, but this idea of "no excess inputs, no magic outputs" can be applied to stores as well as to processes. Obviously, data can't be retrieved from a store if it was never put in.

7.5 Correcting communication flaws

The evaluation of a process schema must go beyond identification of mechanical errors. Consider Figure 7.16, for example.

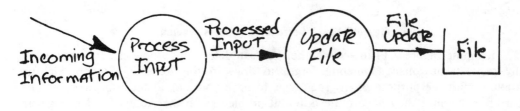

Figure 7.16. An uncommunicative model.

Does it contain any mechanical errors? Hard to tell, isn't it? In fact, there are no mechanical errors. Nevertheless, there's still one rather significant problem: *The model communicates virtually nothing about the system it represents.* It's impossible to tell whether Figure 7.16 represents an inventory control system, an accounts payable system, a library catalog system, or something else entirely. So, in addition to being checked for mechanical errors, process schemas must be subjected to some further tests to determine whether the model is an effective communication tool.

An extremely important test, suggested by Figure 7.16, concerns the *names* used on the process schema. The test is really very simple: A good process schema, if used as part of an essential model, must have names drawn from the natural vocabulary of the subject matter of the system. What do inventory control people talk about when they talk business? They talk about receipts, issues, balances on hand, inventory items, and so on. These, then, are the names that should be used to label the processes, flows, and stores on an essential model of an inventory control system. In contrast, insurance people talk about policies, claims, risks, and settlements, and these terms should appear on a process schema for an insurance system's essential model.

Some care must be exercised when determining a natural vocabulary, however. In many organizations, people use a shorthand jargon based on form numbers, storage locations, and so on ("Hey, Sam! Hand me the pile of X-5s from Section 2"). Labels such as these have two disadvantages: First, they don't mean much to anyone but the people who work with the details; and second, they're implementation dependent (changing the form numbers won't change the nature of the system in any way). The test would evaluate whether a diagram is clear to someone who works on similar systems in another organization. What's sought is a *generic* vocabulary for inventory control, accounts payable, or life insurance.

This test, of course, doesn't apply to an implementation model the same way it does to an essential model. What's an appropriate vocabulary for discussing an implementation? Clearly, if the system is to be automated, it must refer to computers, input-output devices, and so on. Names like Remote Data Entry Processor, Report Printer, and the like are preferable to specific brand names or model numbers, for the same reasons you avoid form numbers and the other jargon of manual systems. A generic vocabulary for implementation, which is specific but not unnecessarily technical, is not hard to create.

There's another very useful test that can be applied to a process schema, one that involves examining *connections* (flows and stores). The amount of traffic between processes on a process schema has substantial impact on its usefulness as a communication tool. The reason is very simple: The more connections a process has to other processes, the harder the process is to understand by itself. Think of writing a job description for someone whose job involves communicating with only a few people, versus writing a job description for someone who must communicate with many people about many different things. Similarly, packaging a system into processes with few connections will produce a diagram that is easier to understand than one with many connections between processes. When comparing two versions of a diagram for complexity of connections, consider the following:

- Flow connections between processes add more to the complexity than store connections. A flow from one process to another triggers the second process and produces a tight (causal) connection. A time-delayed connection is qualitatively different, in that the flow goes from the first process into storage and sits there until the second process (triggered by something else) gets around to using it.

- Flows that contain two or more individual pieces of data add more to the complexity than do flows that contain a single piece of data. (Visualize them as quantitatively different, as "thick flows" and "thin flows.") A single dataflow containing name, phone number, account number, and balance is just as complex as two flows, one containing name and phone number, and the other, account number and balance.

The most useful measurement is the number of flow connections *per process,* weighted for flow complexity. (The total number of flows on a diagram will of course be greater if the diagram is divided into many small processes, but that's not the point.) However, interface complexity is a useful measurement for evaluating essential models only. When modeling an implementation, the packaging imposed by the implementation technology doesn't allow sufficient flexibility to permit creating and comparing alternatives.

Let's test the interface complexity of two versions of The Un-College matching operation, shown in Figure 7.17 below, and in Figure 7.18 on the next page.

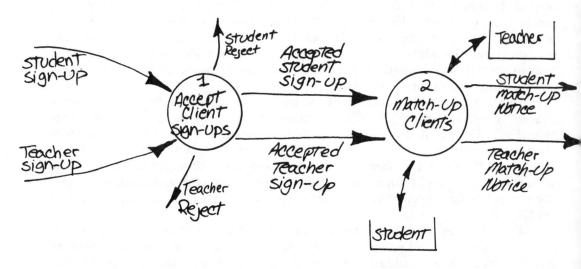

Figure 7.17. Comparing connections (version 1).

The easiest way to test is to count flow and store connections for each process:

	Version 1		Version 2	
	flow	store	flow	store
Bubble 1	6	0	4	2
Bubble 2	4	2	4	2

There's a decrease in the number of flow connections from version 1 to version 2. Look at the difference another way: If you hired two people to do a job, they'd be less dependent on each other under a version 2 work arrangement than under version 1. Notice also that the names of the version 2 processes relate specifically to the purpose of the system: matching students and teachers. Within The Un-College example, the differences between students and teachers are certainly more significant than the similarities. By reinforcing this distinction, version 2 makes the naming more specific. Simpler connections and specific names tend to go together in an essential model.

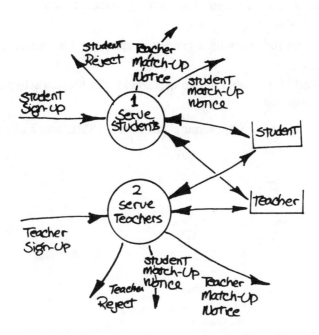

Figure 7.18. Comparing connections (version 2).

7.6 Organization of stored data

If you examine process schemas carefully, you will find that the methods for naming and packaging stored data have many similarities to the methods for naming and packaging processes. For example, the two stores in The Un-College matching operation are called Student and Teacher rather than Male Client and Female Client or Person Who Signed Up In The Morning and Person Who Signed Up In The Afternoon. The choice of stored data naming and packaging is closely related to the question of why the processes should be packaged as in version 2 rather than as in version 1 in the previous example. Although Student and Teacher seem clearly superior to the other labels, the best organization for a more complex system may not always be so clear. In addition, the job of dividing stored data into categories can get quite complex if there's a lot of data.

Notice that when I discussed organizing processes for clarity of communication, I de-emphasized connections that passed through stores (actually, they could have been ignored). Stored data, too, can be organized by ignoring the processes. How we organize stored data is the subject of the next chapter.

7.7 Summary

In this chapter, we have taken a detailed look at the process schema, including

- the meaning of the symbols used to draw a process schema,

- the use of process schemas in building essential models and implementation models,

- the criteria for checking a process schema for mechanical correctness, and

- the criteria for evaluating the usefulness of a process schema as a communication tool.

In the next chapter, we'll examine the other ASML schematic model, the data schema.

Chapter 7: Reference

1. T. DeMarco, *Structured Analysis and System Specification* (New York: Yourdon Press, 1978), pp. 40-62.

    The data flow diagram, as described by DeMarco, is the basis for the process schema.

8

Data Schemas

The basics of the data model were presented in Chapter 6, but as we turn our attention from processes to data, I want you to be sure you understand the difference between data schemas and process schemas. In process schemas and data schemas, the subject being described doesn't change; only our point of view is different. As an analogy, think about a photographer first snapping a ground-level view of a forest, then climbing aboard an aircraft to take a photograph from above. The subject matter is the same, but the different point of view affects selection of detail and thus changes what's communicated to the viewer. The advantage of multiple viewpoints is that we gain insight from seeing things from different perspectives.

The viewpoints taken by the process and data schemas aren't arbitrary. They are rooted in a distinction between *knowing* and *doing* that is fundamental to the human experience. Although knowing and doing are inseparable in practice, one can choose to focus on one or the other when thinking about a person; process and data schemas allow the same choice in modeling systems.

8.1 Basics of the model

The data schema describes a situation in which the things you know fall into different *categories* and where there are *connections* between these categories [1]. To illustrate this definition, let's return to the blackbird pie example. Something I didn't tell you when building the process schema was that the king's kitchen staff is renowned for catering to the whims of individual guests. It is said, for instance, that no guest has ever been served the same dish twice in a row. It is also rumored that if a guest indicates even the slightest displeasure with a dish, he or she will never be served that dish again. Conversely, anyone expressing particular enjoyment of some delicacy will be sure to be served that dish in the future, although not at the next visit. Finally, the royal waiters and waitresses are said to monitor the table talk carefully, and chance comments about culinary preferences will often lead to a guest being served his or her favorite dish on the next visit.

If we discount the possibility that the royal kitchen's staff members have magic powers of some sort, we can only conclude that meal planning is not based on chance, but on what the king's staff *knows*. We can further conclude that the staff members must store data (either in their memories or by recording facts on some external medium) and then use this stored data for meal planning. Finally, it seems clear that the staff's knowledge includes which guests were served which dishes during visits to the royal table.

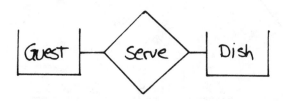

Figure 8.1. A simple data schema.

Look now at Figure 8.1. The three-sided shapes represent the data categories, and the diamond the connection. Notice that, as in the simplest example of a process schema (refer back to Figure 7.1), I've only shown certain details on the graphic model. The facts that are stored about guests (name, culinary preferences, and perhaps even age and weight to determine food portions) do not show up. Neither do the facts that are stored about the dishes served. These details will be placed elsewhere in the overall system models. Suppose, however, that it's necessary to remember the date on which a guest was served a particular dish, and the guest's reaction to the dish. In which data category do these facts get placed? Although both of these facts apply partially to guests and partially to dishes, neither category provides a perfect fit. A better solution to the problem is to add an additional category, which might be called Visit, Food Experience, or Tasting, and which is shown in Figure 8.2.

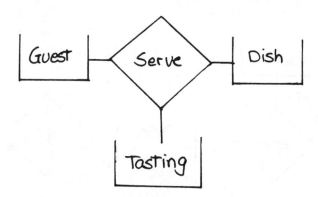

Figure 8.2. An expanded data schema.

In the previous chapter, I described a process schema as being a diagram of an imperative sentence. Remember your English grammar instruction? (You'd probably rather not, but . . .) Mine included a lot of practice diagramming sentences. For example, take the sentence, The guest tasted the dish after it was served. This can be diagrammed as shown in Figure 8.3, which shows the grammatical pattern of the sentence: subject, predicate, modifiers, and so on. Now look back at Figure 8.2. This is also a diagram of the same sentence, but instead of a grammatical pattern, it describes a pattern drawn from the day-to-day business of the royal kitchen. This pattern provides a framework for storing the facts relating to the operation of the kitchen.

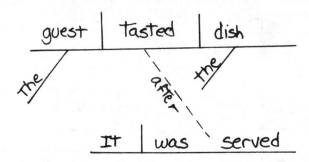

Figure 8.3. Diagramming a sentence.

In order to be useful, a data schema has to be capable of describing more complex patterns than the ones illustrated so far. Since dishes are concocted from ingredients and ingredients in turn are purchased from vendors, the model can be extended to describe the larger pattern (see Figure 8.4). In a process schema, successive transformations of a piece of data define paths through the model. In a data schema, there are also paths that represent complicated interconnections among facts. Suppose it were necessary to find all the guests who had eaten tomatoes at the royal table. Using the connection called Prepare allows identification of all dishes containing tomatoes. Using the connection Serve allows finding the guests who have eaten these dishes. In order to track the royal tomato eaters, all one needs to do is trace a path in the model from Ingredient through Dish to Guest.

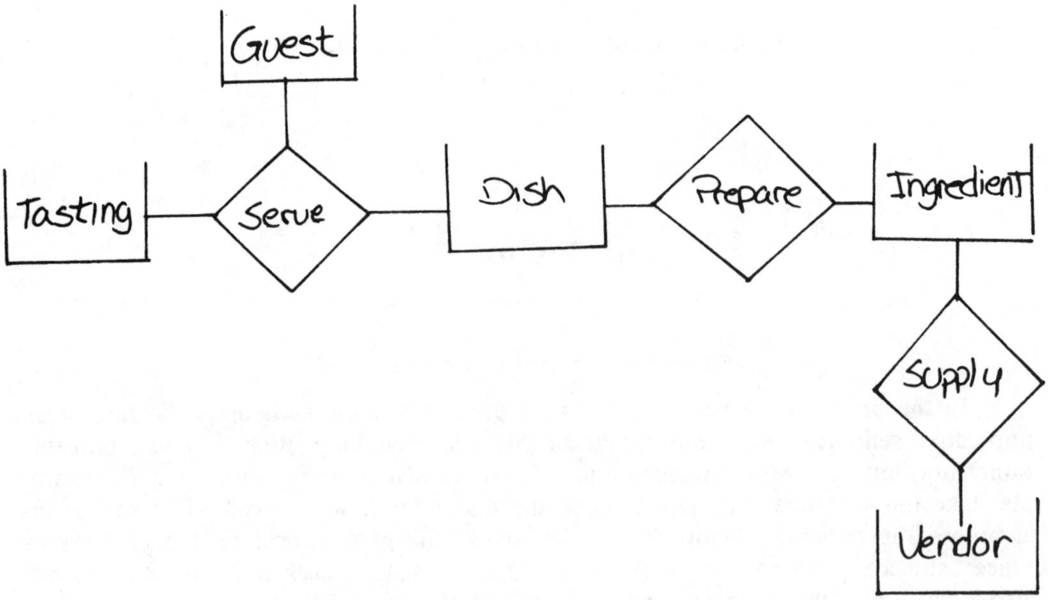

Figure 8.4. More expansion of the model.

Let's look closely at Figure 8.4 and ask some questions:

Q: Is it possible to have vendors who are not associated with existing ingredients?

A: Yes. Facts can be stored about a new vendor who hasn't yet supplied any ingredients.

Q: Can there be ingredients that are associated neither with existing dishes nor with existing vendors?

A: Yes. A new ingredient being considered for use may not be used in any existing dish or supplied by any existing vendor.

Q: Can there be dishes that aren't associated with existing ingredients or with existing facts about guests or tastings?

A: Yes, for the same reason that applies to ingredients.

Q: Can there be guests not associated with existing dishes or tastings?

A: Yes. There may be guests who have been invited to an upcoming dinner and haven't been guests previously.

Q: Can there be tastings not associated with an existing guest or dish?

A: No! The idea of a tasting doesn't make sense if there is no existing guest to do the tasting and no dish to be tasted.

It seems that *tasting* is different from the other data categories; its existence depends on the existence of the categories to which it's linked.

There's another peculiar thing going on here. Notice that the connection called Serve is not of any great intrinsic interest to the kitchen staff. If the king and queen decided to give a buffet dinner at which the guests served themselves, there still would be a connection of interest between guests and dishes; namely, that a particular guest actually tasted a particular dish. This suggests that the connection between guests and dishes should be called Taste not Serve, which further suggests that the data category called Tasting and the connection called Taste are really the same.

We can modify the model to incorporate this data. The superimposition of the three-sided figure and the diamond in Figure 8.5, shown on the following page, means that the tasting category is subordinate to the other categories to which it's connected, and that the term Tasting applies both to the category and to the connection. Another way to think of this is that the tasting category is a place to store facts about the connection between a guest and a dish.

As a last example, let's look at a rather different model of the royal kitchen's data pattern. Figure 8.6 contains categories that emphasize where the data is stored rather than what it's about. (Compare this with the graphic process schemas shown in Figures 7.5 and 7.6.) Like process schemas, data schemas can be adapted to describe either the essentials of a system or its implementation.

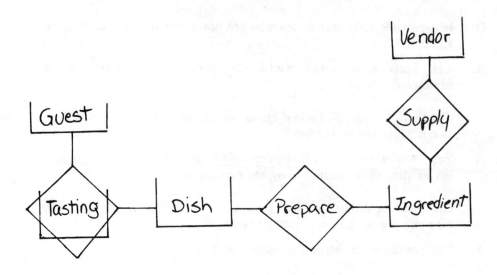

Figure 8.5. Refinement of the model.

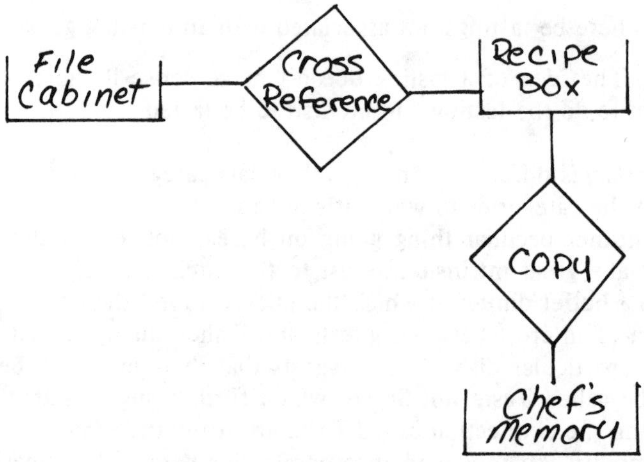

Figure 8.6. Stored data locations.

Following is a formal description of stores and relationships, which constitute the pieces of the data schema:

- The three-sided figures with labels in them are called *stores*. This is the same symbol used on the process schema, and represents the same concept from a somewhat different point of view. In the data schema, a store is a representation of something that is important to a system, that serves as a data storage category, and that describes a collection of individual things that can be distinguished from one another. (The inability to distinguish means that after storing a fact, it can't be retrieved unambiguously. This can happen with people's names: Imagine filing facts about two dinner guests named John J. Jones, one of whom loves fish and one of whom hates it. When John J. Jones reappears as a guest six months later, how can the two sets of facts be distinguished? Problems like this cause employers to assign numbers to their employees.)

- The diamonds with labels in them are called *relationships*. A relationship is a specific type of association between two or more stores. It's there because the real-world things represented by the stores are connected in a way that's important to the system. Just as a store represents a collection of individual things, a relationship represents the set of connections between two or more such collections. Think of the relationship symbol as being a link in a chain connecting the stores.

- When the store and relationship symbols are superimposed, the label represents both a connection and a data storage category.

The data schema represents the data stored within a system by picturing it as a network of stores connected by relationships.

8.2 Data schema details

Let's return once more to The Un-College example to explore the data schema in more depth. Remember that for data schemas, the question of interest is, What's important? rather than, What happens?

At The Un-College, students are matched with teachers on the basis of the teacher's proficiency and the student's interest in a subject. After being matched, the student may join a class given by the teacher. A variety of classrooms are available, with characteristics suited to the demands of different subjects, such as large and small sizes and availability of audio-visual equipment.

The description states what is important to this portion of The Un-College system; however, a graphic presentation would be easier to understand. The process of translating the text into the graphic model involves diagramming certain parts of the narrative. The basic rule is to turn the important nouns into stores and the important verbs into relationships. Figure 8.7 illustrates the data schema for the first part of the first sentence.

Figure 8.7. Basic data schema.

Notice that we've applied lumping to this model just as we applied it to the process schema in Chapter 7. Although a student's name, address, phone number, and so on, need to be stored, the single label Student is used to represent the whole collection. The level of detail presented on such a model is thus quite important, and careful decisions are required. For example, the first sentence of the narrative description contains the word "subject." Is this a store in its own right, or simply a piece of data about a student or a teacher? To answer this question, we'll need to do some digging. In an earlier discussion of The Un-College, I pointed out that certain subjects have health requirements (a course entitled "Training for a Marathon," for example). Into what store do facts about health requirements fit? Neither Student nor Teacher seems a good fit. Subject, on the other hand, is just perfect, so I've added it to the model to derive Figure 8.8. In addition, I have represented "proficiency" and "interest" as relationships even though they're nouns in the description: I did this because in the sentence, The teacher is proficient in the subject, "is proficient in" acts like a verb.

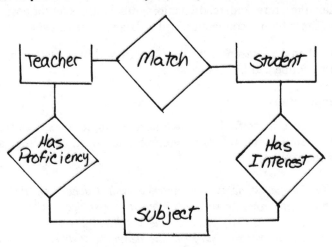

Figure 8.8. Expanded data schema.

The expanded model raises another question. If a student is interested in a subject, and a teacher is proficient in the same subject, doesn't that pair of connections constitute a match? If so, is a separate relationship called Match necessary? The answer depends on what a match means to The Un-College system. If it simply means that a teacher and a student share a common subject, the extra relationship isn't needed. Suppose, however, that in order for a match to exist, The Un-College system requires that

- the teacher is willing to take on additional students, and

- the student has been informed of this by phone or mail.

In this case, Match describes a specific connection that is different from a mere identity of subject. Our example shows the use of a data schema to investigate the policies of an organization. This will be discussed further in Section 8.3.

First, however, let's continue the thought process described above, so as to extend the data schema to cover the entire narrative. This produces Figure 8.9. Notice that "class" has been made both a store and a relationship. It's a data category, since it is described by facts such as number of sessions and meeting time. Furthermore, it can't exist without students, a teacher, and a subject, and it serves as the connection between these other stores. As an exercise, you might try thinking of some facts that are relevant to The Un-College's work to see how well they fit into the framework depicted by this model.

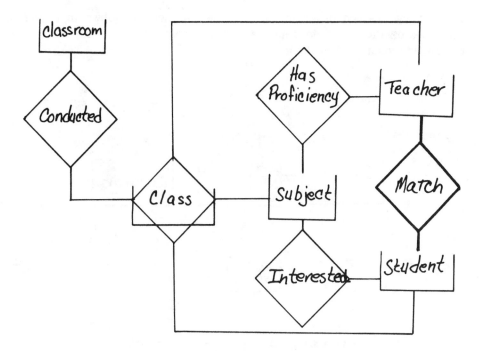

Figure 8.9. Completed data schema.

8.3 Problems and benefits of data modeling

My experience as a teacher has shown me that people grasp the idea of process schemas more easily than they grasp the idea of data schemas. I think this happens because the data schema is more abstract in nature than is the process schema. The answer to the question of what happens is closer to day-to-day experience than is the answer to the question of what is important. A specific source of difficulty is that the chunks of data people deal with on a daily basis are at a different level of abstraction than are the stores and relationships of a data schema.

To get a better idea of the scope of this problem, imagine that you're trying to set up a filing system for your personal papers. You've purchased an accordion organizer, and have decided that "auto" and "insurance" are two useful subdivisions. After stuffing your life and health insurance policies in the "insurance" pocket, and your automobile title certificate in "auto," you come across your automobile insurance policy. Does it go under "auto" or under "insurance"?

The problem arises because data categories were intended to be used for organizing data, not for organizing documents. A document such as an automobile insurance policy is typically a package, which contains facts drawn from various data categories. If you take a close look at any automobile insurance policy, you will see that it contains facts about

- insured drivers (name, address, age)
- insured vehicles (year, make, model, serial number)
- insurer (company name, agency name)
- insurance (policy number, liability limits)

These categories can be organized into the data schema shown in Figure 8.10. Since the facts on the policy document are drawn from all the stores, the document can't be assigned to any one of them.

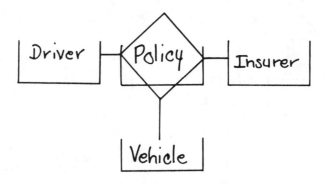

Figure 8.10. Automobile insurance model.

Data packages (forms, documents, files, and so on) play an important role in nearly all organizational patterns. The creation or modification of automated systems is often motivated by problems with the existing packaging; stored data may be confusing, error-prone, or inaccessible. The creation of new packaging cannot effectively be done by trial-and-error re-shuffling of the existing packaging. The data schema, because of its abstract nature, allows an examination of the patterns behind the packagings, and this is a very real benefit.

If you can't grasp the idea of a data schema by thinking of it as a set of document filing categories, how *can* you make it more accessible? One strategy is to think of the data schema as a question answering machine. To get a question answered, you start at a store and trace through one or more relationships until you've collected the needed facts. When looked at as a machine, the model shown in Figure 8.9 can answer the following questions:

- Which students have been matched with a particular teacher?
- Which teachers have been matched with a particular student?
- In which subjects is a particular teacher proficient?
- In which subjects is a particular student interested?

- Which teachers are proficient in a particular subject?

- Which students are interested in a particular subject?

- Which classes does a particular teacher teach?

- Which classes does a particular student attend?

- Which classes are given in a particular subject?

- Which teacher is teaching a particular class?

- Which students are attending a particular class?

- What is the subject of a particular class?

- In which classrooms is a particular class given?

- Which classes are given in a particular classroom?

There are many other questions that either are combinations of the questions listed above (for example, In which classroom is a particular student currently attending class?) or are subsets of these questions (Which male students between the ages of 25 and 30 have been matched with a particular teacher?).

As a matter of fact, there are automated systems, called database or inquiry systems, which are fundamentally question answering machines. Whether or not you're involved in building this type of system, it's useful to adopt the question answering point of view when modeling data.

Actually, once you've become comfortable with the idea of data modeling, you can turn its abstract nature to your advantage. Earlier in this chapter, there's an example involving the definition of what The Un-College system means by a match between a teacher and a student. Focusing on definitions is a way to use the data schema for policy research, so as to capture the rules of an organization by defining them as linkages between items of importance. Of course, the process schema can also capture policy: Presumably, the definition of what a match means could be extracted from the rules for the matchmaking activity. However, there are circumstances in which modeling organizational activities is difficult. For example, it is difficult if

- existing activities aren't carried out in a standardized way,

- existing activities are not working effectively, or

- new activities need to be defined.

In these cases, the abstract nature of the data schema provides an advantage. Although answering the question of what's happening isn't always helpful, the question of what's important invariably is helpful. Once a model of the stores and relationships has been created, the desired activities can be derived by identifying what activities are necessary to capture the data, and what activities are necessary for decision making and creation of outputs.

8.4 Correcting mechanical errors

Process schemas can be thought of as output producing machines; a mechanical error in such a model involves an inability to produce the desired output from the available input. Since the data schema is a question answering machine, a mechanical error in this type of model shows up as the inability to answer a desired question.

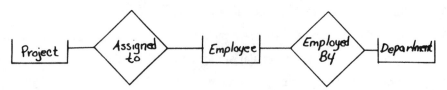

Figure 8.11. Project tracking model.

Consider the simple model of a project tracking system, such as that shown in Figure 8.11. On the surface, it looks as though the question, Which department is responsible for a particular project? can be answered by tracing through the Assigned To and Employed By relationships. The department responsible is the one that employs the employees who are assigned to the project. Suppose, however, that a project becomes the responsibility of a department prior to the assignment of any employees. In this case, there's no way to attach the instance of Project to the instance of Department, and thus no way to answer the question until employees are assigned. The only way to correct the model is to add a Responsible For relationship as shown in Figure 8.12. The policy represented by the Responsible For relationship must be incorporated into the model for it to answer questions.

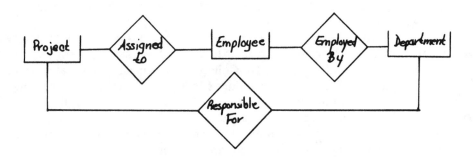

Figure 8.12. Corrected project tracking model.

There is another type of question answering problem that is caused not by an error in the model but by the nature of the subject matter. Suppose a company makes bread by mixing barrels of flour (along with other ingredients) to make batches of dough, which in turn are baked into loaves of bread. The individual barrels of flour, batches of dough, and loaves of bread are all given identification numbers. The model in Figure 8.13, although correct, will not answer the question, Which barrel of flour was used to make a particular loaf of bread? if more than one barrel of flour is mixed into a batch of dough. The problem is with the bread making process, not with the model. Individual barrels of flour lose their identity when mixed into dough. The best the model can do is trace a loaf back to the group of barrels that went into the dough.

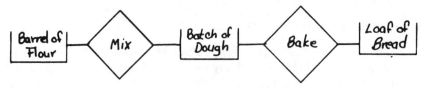

Figure 8.13. Bread baking model.

8.5 Correcting communication flaws

Although the mechanical issues discussed in the previous section are important, a data schema can be mechanically correct and still not function well as a communication tool. This happens because the data schema is either too general or too detailed. The main purpose of the graphic model is to lay out the interconnections among the main topics within the subject area of the system. A model whose data categories are too general will be vague, and will mask important topics by lumping categories and connections together. A model with overly detailed categories will cause important topics to be spread out among many lower-level categories and connections and, thus, to be lost in a mass of detail.

Guidelines for first recognizing problems in stores and relationships and then correcting them to the appropriate level of detail or generality are presented in the remainder of this section.

Let us first look at the problem of *overly general stores.* Imagine that you're building a banking system and that you have identified a store called Customer. Among the facts that need to be stored are "monthly loan payment" and "amount of last withdrawal." Monthly loan payments, of course, don't apply to all customers, only to those who have outstanding loans. Similarly, only customers holding deposit accounts would be making withdrawals. This indicates that the store Customer is too general. Let's consider replacing it with the two stores Loan-holder and Depositor. But this simply trades one problem for another, since there are data like "name," "address," "social security number," which really do apply to all customers. The fact is that there are two different levels of generality relevant to this system. The answer is to keep *both* the Customer store and the Loan-holder and Depositor stores, as shown in Figure 8.14. A person who does business with this bank plays a dual role in this model. He or she is represented as a customer, and also as either a loan-holder or a depositor, or possibly both.

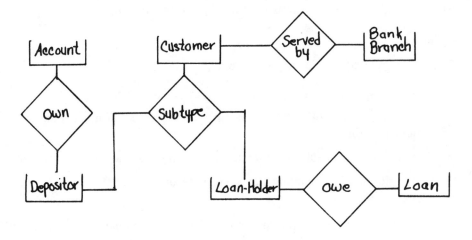

Figure 8.14. Banking model.

Answering a question about a specific customer using this model may require extracting data from one, two, or all three stores. The connection between the more general and the less general stores is shown by the Subtype relationship. Figure 8.14 shows that retention of the two levels of generality serves more than data storage purposes; there are relationships (such as being served by a particular branch of the bank) that affect all customers the same way, and also relationships that are specific to the depositor or loan-holder roles. Of course, if there were no data and no relationships that applied to all customers, the more general store would simply be dropped and replaced by the more specific ones.

In the case of *overly general relationships,* the trick is to identify the conditions necessary for the connection to exist. If you find two or more distinct sets of conditions, you may have two or more individual relationships. (There's absolutely nothing wrong with the same group of stores being linked by two or more relationships.) A data schema within a court system might contain the stores Lawyer and Case connected by the relationship Assign. In examining the details of an actual assignment, it will become clear that lawyers play two very different roles in a case, namely, prosecution and defense. The pair of relationships Defend and Prosecute, which connect lawyers and cases, represent the subject matter much more clearly. Notice also that the names are much more a part of the vocabulary of the legal profession than the vaguely named Assign.

The symptoms of *overly specific stores* are that two stores are described by the same facts and have the same relationships. Suppose a division of a large corporation is modeling its purchasing operation. Goods are purchased both from outside vendors and from other divisions of the parent company; initially, Inside Vendor and Outside Vendor are set up as separate stores. It turns out, however, that both types of vendor are treated identically in terms of storage of data, placement of orders, requests for quotations, and so on. From the point of view of the purchasing system, there is only one Vendor store, since both inside vendors and outside vendors play the same role. This situation might change, of course, if the purchasing model were to be incorporated into a model with a different scope.

The problem of *overly specific relationships* typically occurs because of aliases; two different terms are applied to a connection and end up in the model as two different relationships. This problem, like the problem of overly general relationships, can be detected by examining the conditions for forming the relationship.

8.6 Summary

The topics covered in this chapter were

- the meaning of the symbols used to draw a data schema,

- the employment of data schemas in building essential models and implementation models,

- the criteria for checking a data schema for mechanical correctness, and

- the criteria for evaluating the usefulness of a data schema as a communication tool.

In the next chapter, we'll explore methods for describing data in greater detail.

Chapter 8: Reference

1. M. Flavin, *Fundamental Concepts of Information Modeling* (New York: Yourdon Press, 1981), pp. 7-8, 62-71.

    The entity-relationship diagram, as described by Flavin, is the basis of the data schema. His term "object type" is equivalent to my term "store." Flavin also discusses how to refine the model by identifying the appropriate level of detail.

9

Data Descriptions

9.1 Levels of description

Look back at one of the process schema examples in Chapter 7: What does the model tell you about the data within the system? In addition to providing a graphic description of what's connected to what, the model contains

- the names of the chunks of data that are used by processes,
- the names of the chunks of data that are produced by processes, and
- the names of the chunks of data that are stored.

Now look back at one of the data schema examples in Chapter 8 to find out what it tells you. In addition to the graphic layout, you will find

- the names of the data categories and
- the names of the connections between the categories.

As useful as both of these types of schematic model are for providing a high-level picture, they give very little detailed information about the data within a system. As I introduced you in Chapters 7 and 8 to schematic models, I remedied this deficiency by filling in details about flows, stores, and relationships as necessary. However, a complete system model needs a well-organized method for describing the data within the system.

Before we begin to look at methods for precisely describing data, let us first think about describing something a little less abstract. Suppose it's necessary to characterize a first-aid kit. The simplest possible description is simply its *name*. The name serves as a tag or place marker, and is useful, for instance, in relating it to other items: "The safety equipment that should be present in any automobile consists of an emergency light, flares, and a first-aid kit." A more complete description might indicate what the first-aid kit is to be used for, by providing a *definition:* "The first-aid kit provides immediate assistance for minor injuries such as burns or cuts." Finally, an even more detailed description might give the actual *composition* of the kit: "The first-aid kit contains sterile gauze, adhesive tape, scissors, and burn ointment." Notice that the definition is more fundamental and less modifiable than the list of contents. It would not be unusual to modify the contents, say by substituting adhesive bandages for gauze, tape, and scissors. It would be highly unusual if we were to redefine the purpose of the kit.

Following the approach used to describe the first-aid kit, let's define a chunk of data to the name, definition, and composition levels. Let's take Student Sign-up from The Un-College system as our example. Name, obviously, is Student Sign-up, and a definition of Student Sign-up describes its purpose: "The purpose of Student Sign-up is to provide data required to maintain communication with a student, to determine his or her subjects of interest, and to evaluate his or her fitness to receive instruction." The composition of Student Sign-up would list the elemental pieces of data that are collected to form the chunk. The composition might include the student's name, address, home or business phone number, subject description(s), and perhaps health status. The individual data elements describe or measure the general characteristics included in the definition; address and phone number describe ways of maintaining communication; information about health status measures a student's ability to receive certain kinds of instruction. As in the first-aid kit example, changing the composition is less fundamental than varying the definition. For example, a decision could be made to store *both* home and business phone numbers to better maintain communication, or to add date of last medical exam to measure fitness.

9.2 Using definitions to refine the model

Definitions of flows, stores, and relationships play a unique and critical role in describing a system. However, their importance is easy to overlook because definitions seem irrelevant to the actual business of transforming and storing data. It's easy to see the practical usefulness of a process schema, because it serves as a blueprint for setting up a system and shows the pathways that must be established for transporting data so that processing can occur. In the same way, a data schema serves as a blueprint for cross-referencing stored data so that it can be retrieved to answer questions.

Descriptions of the composition of flows and stores serve a practical purpose at a more detailed level: They are blueprints for the internal organization of transactions, documents, and files. Pieces of an implemented system can be matched with pieces of a model: For example, a computer program carries out a process, and the printout that it produces can be described as a flow that is used by a clerk to carry out the next process; an item of data on the printout is a data element within the flow. But where in a working system can something corresponding to a definition be found? The answer is that it cannot be found, but it is nonetheless relevant to the business of transforming and storing data.

The role of the definition then is not to serve as a blueprint for the ultimate *system,* but to *ensure the quality of the model.* A system will only be as good as the model from which it was built. The stored data in a system, for example, will be well organized and easy to retrieve *only* if the people who create the storage scheme have a clear idea of the significant stores and relationships. The stores and relationships appear on the data schema simply as labels without any supporting details, and the labels convey an implicit definition to the person viewing the model. It is crucial to make certain that the definition becomes clear and precise, that it is not the result of fuzzy thinking. Let me illustrate this point by asking you to imagine that two people working on a data schema agree on a name for a store. How can you be sure that their definitions match?

If the definitions do not match, and if these two people are using the same name for two different stores, the quality of the model will be affected. Clearly, the working out of definitions plays an important role in refining the process and data schemas.

Definitions also serve to *ensure the completeness of the set of data elements* that flow through, and are stored in, the system. How do you know whether the collection of facts that describe a store is adequate, unless you know what's important about the store?

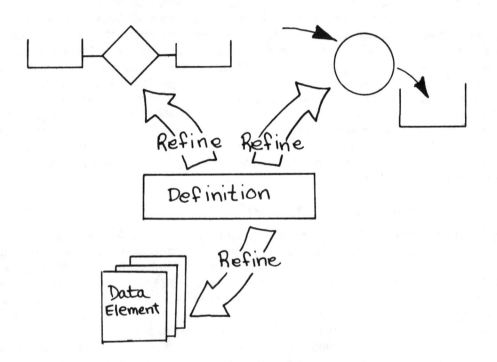

Figure 9.1. Role of the definition.

In terms of level of detail, the definition occupies an intermediate position in the model, coming between the name and composition levels. The definition level requires more detail than is needed for the labels for flows or stores found on the schematic model, but less detail than for the set of individual data elements that describe these chunks of data. Definitions can thus improve a model by clarifying data labels on the schematic model. They can also improve the model by ensuring that the data elements reflect the important features of the definition.

Let's apply the idea of refining models by means of definitions. Take a look at the Teacher store in Figure 9.2. A preliminary definition of Teacher might be, A person who is proficient in teaching a subject. Although this definition sounds reasonable, there are some problems. For one thing, The Un-College will not match teachers and students for just any subject; it must approve of the subject. Also, a teacher may teach more than one subject. The modified definition becomes, A person who is proficient in teaching at least one approved subject.

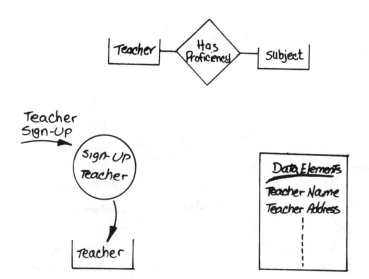

Figure 9.2. Pieces of The Un-College model.

If The Un-College wants to ensure that its teachers are proficient, it must do more than create noble-sounding definitions. It must also be able to measure a teacher's proficiency. In practical terms, this means acquiring data about the academic backgrounds and career accomplishments of the teachers. But this raises some further issues. The fact that a person has a degree in nuclear physics does not have any bearing on that person's ability to teach magic tricks. Facts about training and experience are relevant only in relationship to a teacher's proficiency in a particular subject. More precisely, training and experience are the components that describe the relationship Has Proficiency in Figure 9.2. The most appropriate place to put these pieces of data is in the combined store and relationship called Qualification, which replaces Has Proficiency in Figure 9.3.

It's also necessary to determine where verification of a teacher's qualifications is to be sought. Clearly, verification must come from someone other than the prospective teacher. This means that the process schema must be modified. When a teacher signs up, form letters will be sent to his or her schools, former employers, and so on, requesting verification of qualifications. This will require names of schools and former employers to be included in the Teacher Sign-up dataflow. A new process must also be added to accept and store the verifications.

Notice that our work on the definition of Teacher has led us to add some new stored data elements, to change the data schema, to add a new output flow to an existing process, and to add a new process. The definition has served its purpose in improving the quality of the model; the improved model, in turn, will make the implemented system more satisfactory.

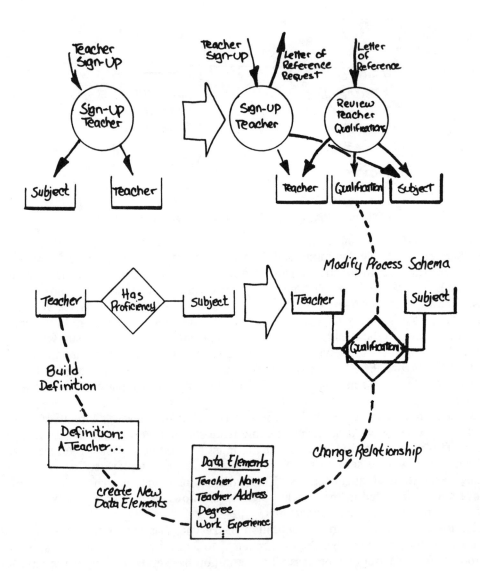

Figure 9.3. Refinement by definition.

9.3 Organizing data descriptions

Figure 9.4 shows the types of data descriptions necessary to completely describe the data within a system. The picture isn't as complicated as it might seem at first glance; it simply applies the ideas we used for the first-aid kit to pieces of the process and data schemas.

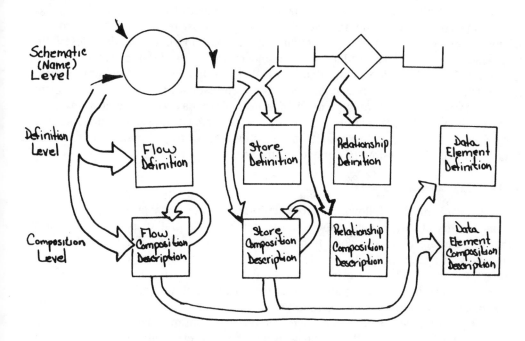

Figure 9.4. Data description types.

Notice that the name, definition, and composition levels in Figure 9.4 correspond to the levels of description in the first-aid kit example. The name level corresponds with the schema level, since the names of flows, stores, and so forth, appear as labels on the schematic models. Before we leave Figure 9.4, I want you to notice a few details:

- The stores on the process schema and on the data schema are equivalent. Although the process schema emphasizes the use of the stored information, and the data schema emphasizes the connections between storage categories, both models describe something that ultimately will be implemented as a file of some kind.

- The boxes labeled Flow Composition Description and Store Composition Description have arrows that circle back on themselves to the same box. In the case of a flow, this indicates that sometimes a flow is composed not of data elements but of smaller flows, called subflows, which in turn are described as being composed of data elements. Defining large flows in terms of smaller flows is useful for describing very complex chunks of data; the idea of flows within flows may be repeated for as many levels as necessary. In the case of the store, the circling arrow indicates that a store may be described as being composed of component stores.

- Descriptions of flow composition and of store composition may contain many data element names in common, since data that is stored within the system often finds its way into the system via flows.

- Although data elements are low-level pieces of flows and stores, they too have definitions and composition descriptions.

If you're trying to describe the data within a system of any size, you're going to have a large collection of bits and pieces of text that must be organized in some way. The most convenient form of organization is a *dictionary* in which the data descriptions are arranged in alphabetical order by the name of the thing defined. Thus, if you're looking for the composition of the dataflow called Teacher Sign-up, you simply look at the T entries. You may choose to have a single dictionary with all the definitions, composition descriptions, and so on mixed together, or to have separate dictionaries for flow definitions, store definitions, and so on. In either case, the most convenient way to maintain a dictionary is to enter it on an automated word-processing or text-editing system, but it is also possible to put each entry on a separate index card.

9.4 Defining flows and stores

Several examples of flow and store definitions have been given in the previous sections of this chapter, but I now want to remind you that it is important for the definer to be aware of what a definition will be used for. If the definer is specific about the meaning of a chunk of data, the definition can be used to refine a model both at the schema level and at the data element level. At the schema level, a precise definition may expose fuzzy or conflicting ideas about the nature of flows and stores. If you find, for example, that defining a store involves an either-or construct, there may well be two stores, which have been lumped together under a common name. At the data element level, the definition will tell you whether the data elements describe or measure what is important. For example, if the definition of a customer states that the customers of a business must be worthy of credit, and there is no piece of data that measures this credit worthiness among the data elements for the store Customer, something is obviously amiss.

If you have difficulty defining a flow or store, you can approach creating the definition in the following way: For a store, ask yourself, What couldn't the system do if the real-world thing represented by the store wasn't part of it? If The Un-College didn't have teachers, it couldn't arrange for subjects to be taught to students. Therefore, the definition, Someone who teaches subjects to students, is at least a start. For a flow, ask yourself, What couldn't the system do if it didn't have this chunk of information? Much of the information about the store called Teacher in The Un-College system comes from the flow called Teacher Sign-up. Without the sign-up, the system wouldn't know who the teachers were, what subjects they wanted to teach, who to check with to see if the teachers were qualified, how to contact teachers about potential students, and so on. The definition then starts out, The information necessary to identify and maintain contact with the teacher, determine what subject he or she is interested in teaching, and obtain data about qualifications.

9.5 Describing flow and store composition

If you look back at the description of a Student Sign-up in Section 9.1, you will find that it consists of the student's name, address, home or business phone number, subject description(s), and optionally health status. All that's needed to make this a good description of flow composition is to reorganize it a bit, like this:

```
STUDENT SIGN-UP consists of
        NAME
and     ADDRESS
and either
            HOME PHONE
    or      BUSINESS PHONE
and one or more
            SUBJECT DESCRIPTIONs
and optionally
            HEALTH STATUS
```

I've modified the original narrative description of the data elements as follows:

- The names of the pieces of the sign-up have been set in capital letters to make them stand out from the words that show how those pieces fit together.

- A standard set of phrases has been used to describe the composition; for example, "consists of," "one or more," and so on.

- The list of data elements has been indented to emphasize its organization.

All these changes have a common purpose: to assure that everyone who reads the description will interpret it the same way.

Let's run through the interpretation of Student Sign-up to make sure the rules are clear. The phrase "consists of" means that what follows is a prescription for a sign-up. The data element names connected simply by "and" are *required*. A collection of data elements that doesn't include a name just doesn't qualify as a Student Sign-up. The either-or means that a valid sign-up can have either a home phone or a business phone, but if it has neither it's not legal and *if it has both it's not legal*. If it's desirable to allow both, this must be stated specifically:

```
either
        HOME PHONE
    or  BUSINESS PHONE
    or  both
```

The same goes for specifying that neither is required. The phrase "one or more" means just what it says: a valid sign-up may have one subject description, two subject descriptions, or even 7,854 subject descriptions. "One or more" can be replaced by "zero or more," "twelve or fewer," "between three and nine," and so on, as circumstances require. Finally, "optionally" means that it's still a legal sign-up even if there's no health status included.

To summarize, the method allows an unambiguous description of the connections among the pieces of a flow. The method distinguishes among

- required pieces (connected by "and")

- a choice of one from a set of pieces (set preceded by "either" and pieces connected by "or")

- repetition of pieces (piece preceded by "one or more" or a similar expression)

- optional pieces (piece preceded by "optionally")

The indentation helps to visually connect pieces that go with one another. Notice in the example at the beginning of this section that Subject Description is indented to the right under "and one or more" and that the following line is moved back to the left. This indicates that "and one or more" applies only to Subject Description and not to any of the following lines. Here's another indentation example:

```
optionally
            HEALTH STATUS
    and     MARITAL STATUS
    and     AGE
```

This use of indentation allows treatment of the three data elements as a single piece, and means that either all three must be present or all three must be absent. If they were independent options, the description would read

```
        optionally
            HEALTH STATUS
    and     optionally
            MARITAL STATUS
    and     optionally
            AGE
```

At this point, you may be wondering why I present all this in such detail. Imagine that some of The Un-College operation has been computerized, and that clerks enter student sign-ups into the system by typing data into a data entry terminal. Messages on the terminal's display screen prompt the clerk to enter various pieces of data, show what he or she has entered, and indicate errors. *The system insists that Health Status be entered as part of every student sign-up.* The fact that Health Status is completely useless data about a student signing up for Eighteenth-Century Lithuanian History means nothing to the system. It keeps blinking out error messages unless the hapless clerk enters "N/A" for health status, time and time again, for the 99 percent of the students to whom health status doesn't apply. A minor annoyance, perhaps, but it's an accumulation of such minor annoyances that makes workers in many organizations feel the computer is a detriment rather than a help.

Why did this happen? Clearly, it happened because the fact that Health Status is optional never got incorporated into the computer system's pattern. It's probably not the poor programmer's fault; chances are, the programmer was never told. Something the users knew just never got passed on to the system builders. The purpose of describing flow and store composition so carefully is to prevent things like this from happening.

Remember that flows can be defined in terms of smaller flows. The original definition of Student Sign-up can be rephrased as follows:

```
STUDENT SIGN-UP consists of
        STUDENT ID INFO
and one or more
        SUBJECT DESCRIPTIONs
and optionally
        HEALTH STATUS

STUDENT ID INFO consists of
        NAME
and     ADDRESS
and either
        HOME PHONE
    or  BUSINESS PHONE
```

The two descriptions above are equivalent to the single description given earlier. The idea of describing larger flows in terms of smaller ones is particularly useful for flows containing many data elements, or for those that would require messy indentation if written in one piece. A collection of data elements that are repeated as a group, for example, may be given a single name and broken down in a separate description. If a charge card invoice contains an entry with date, place, and amount for each purchase, its description might read

```
INVOICE consists of
        NAME
and     ADDRESS
and     CARD NUMBER
and one or more
        PURCHASEs

PURCHASE consists of
        DATE
and     AMOUNT
and     PLACE
```

This description could also be written in one piece:

```
INVOICE consists of
        NAME
and     ADDRESS
and     CARD NUMBER
and one or more instances of
            DATE
    and     AMOUNT
    and     PLACE
```

Notice that "one or more" has been changed to "one or more instances of" so the description reads less awkwardly.

This manner of description may also be useful when relating the *composition* of a flow to the *definition* of a flow. If the definition includes several characteristics of the flow, a name may be assigned to the group of data elements measuring or describing each characteristic.

Defining the data composition of a store is quite similar to defining the data composition of a flow. A store represents data about a collection of similar things, each of which must be distinguished from the others by some data element or elements. In the case of stores that represent people, this usually means identifying them by an arbitrary number to allow for duplication of names. The Un-College Teacher store has the following description:

> TEACHER consists of zero or more instances; each one
> is identified by TEACHER NUMBER and
> consists of
>   TEACHER NAME
> and   TEACHER ADDRESS
> and   . . .

All the rules for indentation, standard phrases, and so on, apply. A group of data elements may be given a single name and broken down in a separate description, just as for flows.

9.6 Defining relationships

Relationship definitions play a role in the model that is similar to that of store definitions; clarifying the meaning of a relationship may prompt a revision of the data schema. Despite these similarities, relationship definitions have a different flavor than flow or store definitions. Two questions to remember when defining relationships are,

- What are the rules for forming a legitimate relationship? and,
- If the relationship information were destroyed, what would be required to reconstruct it?*

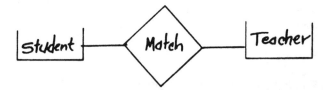

Figure 9.5. Fragment of data schema from The Un-College.

Using these questions to guide us, let's try to define the relationship shown in Figure 9.5. Just what is it that constitutes a legal match between a student and a teacher? First of all, the teacher must be proficient to teach the subject the student wants to learn. But that immediately brings up a potential refinement. A Match relationship doesn't just exist between a student and a teacher, it exists between a student, a teacher, *and* a subject. After all, a student may be interested in learning more than one subject, and a teacher may be proficient at teaching more than one subject. The data schema in Figure 9.5 simply isn't specific enough, and will need redrawing, as shown in Fig-

---

*This point was first made to me by my former YOURDON colleague Gary Schuldt.

ure 9.6. The definition so far is, An association between a teacher, a student, and a subject based on the student being interested in learning the subject, and the teacher being qualified to teach it.

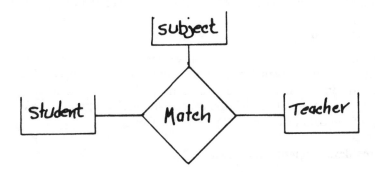

Figure 9.6. Data schema refined by relationship definition.

There are more conditions that must be added to this definition to make it useful. For example, suppose 4,697 students are interested in taking a course in log rolling. The poor teacher would be overwhelmed! Therefore, it's probably necessary for a teacher to indicate a temporary unwillingness to accept more matches in a particular subject. (This information about willingness or unwillingness, of course, must be stored somewhere, which requires a further refinement based on the definition process.) A final condition might be that the student and the teacher must be informed of the match, since it doesn't do any good to match them if they don't know about it. The finished definition is, An association between a teacher, a student, and a subject based on the student being interested in learning the subject, the teacher being qualified to teach it, the teacher being willing to accept additional students in the subject, and the teacher and student being given identifying information about each other.

Suppose a demon came along in the night and destroyed all the information in The Un-College's files about which students had been matched with which teachers. Neither the commonality of subjects between students and teachers, nor a teacher's current willingness to accept students will allow reconstruction of the linkages. The criterion for reconstruction of the relationship would be a record of the teacher's willingness to accept students on the date the match was made; but this information was not recorded within the system. This is where the definition proves its worth; it states that the student and teacher were given information about each other. Therefore, students and teachers can be contacted and the relationships can be reconstructed from information they provide.

9.7 Describing relationship composition

In addition to a definition, the description of a relationship includes some information about the relative numbers of stores connected by the relationship. Let's look back at Figure 8.9 at Class (in its relationship role). Each instance of a class connects a single teacher with one or more students. However, a particular teacher doesn't necessarily have to be involved in any class relationships, nor does a student. (A class, of course, requires the existence of a teacher and one or more students; that's the nature of something that is both a store and a relationship.)

This numeric information is important because you can use it to check the stored information for correctness. Suppose The Un-College found in its files a reference to a class composed of two teachers and two students. Either the description of class is inadequate and should be revised to allow multiple teachers of a class, or someone made a recording mistake. In either case, the discrepancy between the stored data and the description of relationship composition allows identification of a problem.

9.8 Defining data elements

If the name of a data element isn't self-explanatory, a definition should be provided. The same basic rules given for flow and store definitions apply. For example, The Un-College's Student store might have a Sign-up Date data element. Since sign-ups can come in by mail, the definition would need to specify whether the date referred to the recording of the data or its receipt by The Un-College.

9.9 Describing data element composition

There are several things about data elements that may be important to describe. The first is that if a data element is a number, it's *range* might be important. A bank, for example, might require a minimum checking account balance or impose an upper limit on a loan amount. Please don't confuse limits of this kind with the ones imposed by poor implementation planning, for those limits are due to the computer system's inability to store numbers over a certain size! Ranges should reflect organizational policy, not technological accidents.

The second point to be noted is that numeric data elements may also require a description of *units* and *precision*. For example, an international bank may store its currency amounts in U.S. dollars to the nearest penny; a room measurement might be in meters to the nearest centimeter.

Third, data elements that represent types or categories may need a description of *permitted values*. An airline might have a "ticket type" data element, which can have only the values "first class," "coach," "economy," or "military." In many organizations, abbreviations or number codes are used on forms or in computer files to represent values. The airline might use "F" for first class, "Y" for coach, and so on. The data element description should spell out the values, so that a reader unfamiliar with the code can understand the description. The shorthand version could be included as well, if desired.

Finally, data elements consisting of descriptive information like names and addresses have caused implementation problems in many systems because of the limitations of automated technology. Arbitrary restrictions like "names must be less than thirty characters long" reflect technological limitations rather than policy. However, it *might* be useful to record the expected range of these descriptive elements as an aid to planning the technology, for example, to note the longest name that has been encountered to date.

Some examples of element composition descriptions follow:

```
LOAN BALANCE
     range:  $0.00 - $99,999.99
     units:  U.S. dollars
     precision:  nearest penny
```

CUSTOMER TYPE
    permitted values:
    LOAN
    SAVINGS
    CHECKING
    TRUST MANAGEMENT

9.10 Aliases

In a large project, it is probable that two different names will be applied to the same chunk of data by two different groups of people. This is a problem only if it's not caught! If the two names slip into the model as though they describe different things, problems can arise as the system is being built. If an alias is identified, both names should be entered in the dictionary. The details should be listed under one name, and the entry for the other name should be simply a cross reference. As an example:

INVOICE consists of
       NAME
and   ACCOUNT NUMBER
and   AMOUNT DUE

STATEMENT same as INVOICE

9.11 Summary

This chapter dealt with filling out the system model with detailed descriptions of the data within the system. The elements to be described are flows, stores, relationships, and data elements. These elements must be defined, and their composition must be described. In the next chapter, we'll look at completing the system by filling in *process* details.

Chapter 9: References

1.   T. DeMarco, *Structured Analysis and System Specification* (New York: Yourdon Press, 1978), pp. 129-47.

     The data composition notation used in this chapter is an informal version of the one proposed by DeMarco; he uses the term "data dictionary."

2.   M. Flavin, *Fundamental Concepts of Information Modeling* (New York: Yourdon Press, 1981), pp. 55-61, 76-83.

     Flavin discusses defining stores and relationships and assigning data elements (he uses the term "attributes") to stores.

10

Process Descriptions

In the preceding chapter, I asked you to look back at Chapter 7 at a process schema to see what the model told you about the *data* in the system. Now I'd like you to repeat the exercise, this time to see what the process schema tells you about the *processes,* the basic transformation work of the system. You'll find that the only information the diagram gives you consists of the names of the processes.

Now look back at Chapter 8 at a data schema to see what it tells you about the processes that are part of the system. This may seem like a strange request; after all, the whole idea of the data schema is to create a picture of the system that is divorced from what happens. However, if you look closely you'll find that some (although not all) of the relationships on the data schema represent *aftereffects of the operation of processes.* For an example, think back to the relationship between students and teachers called Match in The Un-College data schema. For a Match relationship to exist, the student and teacher not only needed to share an interest in a subject, they also had to be given information about each other. In other words, the Match relationship is an aftereffect of a process carried out by The Un-College system.

Although both the process and data schema models give some information about processes, neither provides full details. How we identify and record those details is the subject of this chapter.*

10.1 Restricted context

Although it's clear that details about processes must be incorporated into the model, it's critical to take a close look at exactly which details need recording.

If a person has to describe a complex system without the benefit of a well-organized modeling technique, he or she usually asks, Where do I start? How do I know what needs describing, or when the description is complete enough, or how to arrange the pieces of the description? With a model of the type described in this book,

---

*Our discussion will focus exclusively on data transformation processes. It's often useful to include material transformations in a process schema, and the ideas in this chapter can easily be adapted to describing them. However, the subject won't be addressed directly.

there is a separate process description for each process; this reduces the actual work of process description to a series of small, well-defined description jobs that can be attacked one at a time. The schematic portions of the model and the data descriptions provide a context for the individual descriptions; that is, they show the placement of the separate processes within the system and the relationships of those processes to other parts of the system.

The only elements to be included in a process description are activities that

- put data elements into stores,

- get data elements out of stores,

- form or find connections between data·in one store and data in another, and

- manipulate data elements to create and issue output flows.

It may seem as though there are important things about the process left unsaid. However, the work that's been done previously in creating the rest of the model, as illustrated by Figure 10.1, has already provided these details:

- The labeled flows entering the bubbles on the process schemas show *what chunks of data are processed.*

- The pieces of the model connected to the tails of the labeled input flows show *where the data that's processed comes from.*

- The composition descriptions of the labeled input flows show *which individual data elements are processed.*

- The composition descriptions of the stores connected to unlabeled input flows show *the set of stored data elements available for processing.*

- The relationships on the data schema and their composition descriptions show *what stored data connections can be made or used by the processes.*

- The labeled flows leaving the process schema bubbles show *what chunks of data are produced by the process.*

- The pieces of the model connected to the heads of the output flows show *where the data that's processed goes.*

- The composition descriptions of the labeled output flows show *which individual data elements are produced by the process.*

- The composition descriptions of the stores attached to unlabeled output flows show *the set of stored data elements that can be changed by the process.*

- The descriptions of the input and output data elements show *the ranges, units, and precision of the data that is used or created.*

I don't want you to leave this section feeling too rosy about the technique for describing processes, so let me point out a disadvantage. *It's nearly impossible to make sense out of an isolated process description.* The same restricted context that makes the description so easy to write must be *re-created* in order to read it with understanding.

That means that the process schema containing the process bubble in question, the data descriptions for that process schema, the data schema containing the relationships between the stores referenced by the bubble, and the data descriptions for that data schema must all be assembled. This takes some getting used to if you're accustomed to getting your information from conversations or from informal, rambling written descriptions. However, I think you'll find that the effort involved will pay off.

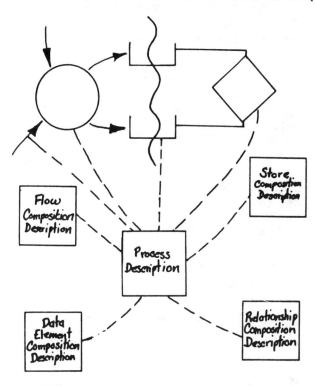

Figure 10.1. Process description context.

10.2 Size restrictions on process descriptions

If you think carefully about the last section, you'll find that the whole idea makes sense *only if the process you're describing is reasonably small.* Imagine a one-bubble process schema for a very complex system. In writing its process description, you'd have to describe dozens of input and output flows and stores; the task wouldn't be much easier than describing a system in the traditional narrative fashion. The advantage of this type of process description is realized only if the process schemas consist of processes, each of which is small enough to be dealt with by a description less than a page long. Multi-page descriptions are inherently harder to deal with since flipping back and forth between pages interferes with concentration.

Unfortunately, deciding whether a bubble is small enough to be described in a page is a matter of trial and error. If a description seems to be getting too long, the process schema must be revised by breaking the original bubble down into two or more smaller ones. The strategy for breaking a bubble is to identify an intermediate flow; in other words, some chunk of data must be identified that is a combination or transformation of the inputs but which still needs some work done on it to become an output.

If such a chunk can be identified, the bubble splits naturally into two pieces: the piece that creates the intermediate, and the piece that turns the intermediate into an output.

The process in Figure 10.2 depicts a system chunk that is undoubtedly already small enough, but breaking it into pieces will be good practice. Both Profit Per Item and Total Profit are pieces of data that arise from combining inputs but that aren't yet the final output. Using these as intermediates produces the three simpler processes shown on Figure 10.3. Because they are smaller pieces of the system than the original process in Figure 10.2, the description of each of these processes will be roughly one-third the length of the original process description.

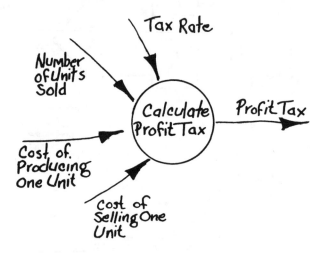

Figure 10.2. Process to be further partitioned.

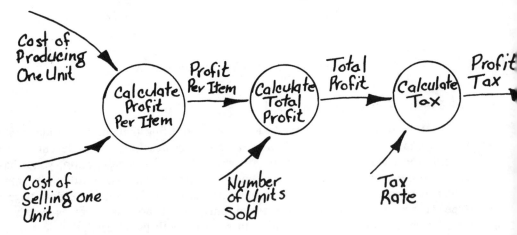

Figure 10.3. Process after partitioning.

10.3 Describing processes graphically

Whenever possible, a process description should be in graphic form. When used appropriately, graphics convey more information in less space and are easier to understand than narrative text.

Let's see how to build a process description by building one for the piece of process schema in Figure 10.4, which describes part of the processing of a new membership application carried out by a museum. Building a description for this process requires the assembling of all the relevant pieces of the model; since there's no stored data involved, the data schema isn't relevant, but data descriptions for the input and output flows are needed.

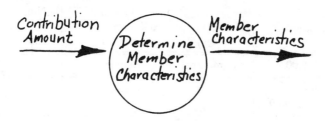

Figure 10.4. Museum membership processing.

CONTRIBUTION AMOUNT
      range: any positive amount
      units: U. S. dollars
      precision: nearest penny

MEMBER CHARACTERISTICS consists of
      MEMBERSHIP CATEGORY
and   TYPE OF ACKNOWLEDGMENT LETTER
and   NUMBER OF FREE MUSEUM PUBLICATIONS

MEMBERSHIP CATEGORY
      Permitted values are
            NONMEMBER
            NORMAL
            SUPPORTING
            SUSTAINING
            PATRON

TYPE OF ACKNOWLEDGMENT LETTER
      Permitted values are
            STANDARD
            FLOWERY
            FAWNING

NUMBER OF FREE MUSEUM PUBLICATIONS
      Range is $0-3$

Note that Contribution Amount is simply a number and has no smaller pieces. The process description for Determine Membership Category must describe the rules for determining the details of the Member Characteristics output flow based on the Contribution Amount input flow. Although the rules could be spelled out in narrative text, a *table* is clearer and more succinct (see Table 10.1). Notice what the process description *does not say*. It doesn't say, Go get a Contribution Amount, or Follow these rules when a Contribution Amount turns up; the bubble already describes this. Neither does it say, Produce an outgoing Member Characteristics flow. Again, the bubble describes this; only if the flow were produced intermittently would it be necessary to describe the conditions for producing it. In short, the process description provides just exactly the information needed for the bubble to do its work, in the clearest form possible.

Table 10.1
Process Description

Contribution Amount	Membership Category	Type of Acknowledgment Letter	Number of Free Museum Publications
Less than $25.00	Nonmember	Standard	0
$25.00 or more but less than $100.00	Normal	Standard	1
$100.00 or more but less than $250.00	Supporting	Flowery	1
$250.00 or more but less than $500.00	Sustaining	Flowery	2
$500.00 or more	Patron	Fawning	3

Another very useful graphic layout for process description is the *decision tree* [1]. A common type of decision tree is the one used in athletic elimination tournaments. Figure 10.5 can be thought of as a tree tipped over on its left side. The leftmost branches represent the starting set of teams; as the branches coalesce toward the right, each meeting point represents a decision that eliminates a team.

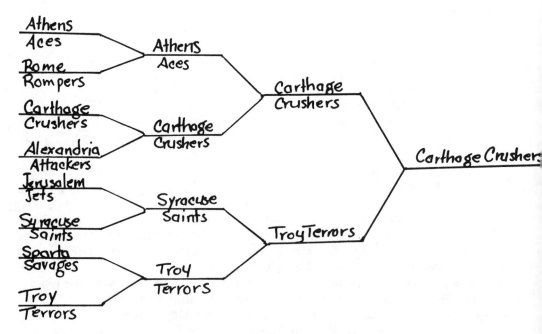

Figure 10.5. An elimination tournament.

Figure 10.6 shows another process, part of a tax calculation that determines the number of allowable exemptions.

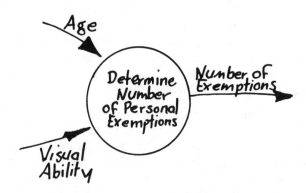

Figure 10.6. Exemption calculation process.

As in the membership application example, the full context must be assembled to build the description; in this case, descriptions of the input data elements are needed. They are presented as follows:

AGE
          permitted values:
                  UNDER 65
                  65 OR OLDER

VISUAL ABILITY
          permitted values:
                  SIGHTED
                  BLIND

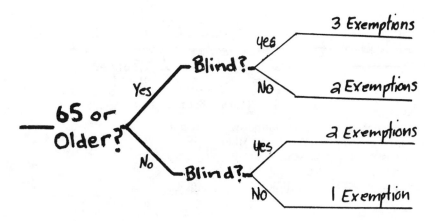

Figure 10.7. Decision tree for exemption calculation.

To use a decision tree to describe process logic, it must be turned on its right side, as in Figure 10.7. The decision making process starts from the root rather than from the outer branches; each branch point represents a decision whose outcome leads to a particular branch, until finally one of the rightmost branches is reached.

10.4 Textual process descriptions

As useful as graphic descriptions are, they are simply inadequate to describe some kinds of processes. While it might be tempting in these cases to fall back on narrative text, this is not the optimal solution because narrative text as used by many writers is unclear, ambiguous, and sometimes downright misleading. What's needed is a discipline, a set of rules that can be imposed on the writing of narrative descriptions to ensure their clarity and precision. Such a discipline exists, and is often called structured English [1].*

My three rules for structured English follow:

1.   Refer only to the collection of names that can be found in the data context for the bubble. This collection includes the names of the flows, the stores and their associated relationships, and the names of the components of the flows, stores, and elements as shown in the data descriptions. Since the context for the process description has been laboriously assembled, ignoring it means that you've wasted all the work by describing something the process couldn't do in that context.

2.   Phrase the logic of the process in terms of simple instructions. Assume that you have an intelligent and competent assistant willing to carry out the process for you, but that this assistant knows nothing about the subject matter of the system.

3.   Organize the simple instructions only in the following ways: as a list preceded by either "carry out in the order shown" or "carry out in any order"; as a series of alternatives preceded by a rule for making the choice; or as one or more instructions to be repeated, preceded by the rule for repetition.

Seeing concrete examples will make these three rules more meaningful. Figure 10.8 depicts the production of a list from a data store. The context is

Figure 10.8. Teacher list process.

```
TEACHER consists of zero or more instances; each one
        is identified by  TEACHER NUMBER
        consists of       TEACHER NAME
        and               TEACHER ADDRESS
        and               TEACHER PHONE NUMBER
        :
        :
TEACHER LIST consists of zero or more instances of
        TEACHER NAME
and     TEACHER PHONE NUMBER
arranged by TEACHER NAME
```

---

*Actually, it might well be called structured language, since any language can be organized this way.

The structured English process description is simply

>   for each TEACHER
>   add the TEACHER NAME and the TEACHER PHONE NUMBER
>   to the TEACHER LIST

Notice that the three rules have been followed; the text refers only to names found in the context, and the simple instruction beginning with "add" is preceded by the rule for repeating it. It isn't necessary to describe the ordering of the list by teacher name since the data description does this. On the other hand, it *is* necessary to say that there's an entry on the list for each teacher. It's precisely to describe transformation rules such as this that we build process descriptions. A list of this kind could be created from a great many sources; the job is to describe the details of its creation.

Notice that the Teacher store contains repetitions of the same chunk of data, one for each teacher. Notice also that the instructions for building the output dataflow contain the instruction to repeat the adding of data to the flow for each teacher. The connection between the repetition in the data description and the repetition in the process description isn't accidental. If you look closely at the context of a process description, you will always find some clues in the organization of the data, which will help you to organize the description [2].

Figure 10.9 also describes the extraction of some data from the teacher store to produce an output flow. This time, however, the required output concerns only a single teacher.

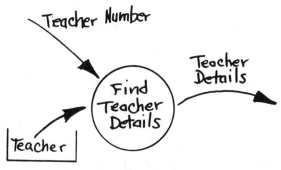

Figure 10.9. Teacher details process.

The Teacher store was described in the last example, and the data element called Teacher Number doesn't need any description; the only description that is missing is the one for Teacher Details. We can describe it as

>   TEACHER DETAILS consists of
>   either
>   TEACHER NAME
>   and   TEACHER PHONE NUMBER
>   or
>   "NO DATA FOR THIS TEACHER NUMBER"

(The output flow may not contain anything specific about a teacher.) The process description for Figure 10.9 is

> if there is data stored for the TEACHER NUMBER
> then
> > construct TEACHER DETAILS from TEACHER NAME
> > > and TEACHER PHONE NUMBER
> otherwise
> > set TEACHER DETAILS to "NO DATA FOR THIS TEACHER NUMBER"

As in the last example, the structured English rules have been followed. The instructions beginning with "construct" and with "set" are alternatives; they are preceded by a rule for selecting one of the alternatives. By the way, there is nothing special about words such as "add," "construct," and "set," which have been used in these examples. Any word or phrase that clearly describes the putting together of a chunk of information from its constituent pieces will do.

The example from Figure 10.8 was driven by the input data; the process description took its form from the list of individual teachers. The example given in Figure 10.9, on the other hand, was driven by the *output data*. Since the output could consist of one of two alternatives, the description of the process was also organized in this way. Again, the structure of the data in the context provided a valuable clue for organizing the description.

As a final example, let's look at a more complex process.

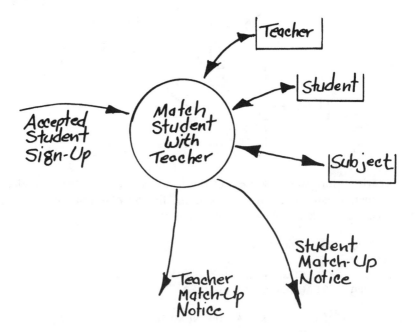

Figure 10.10. Process schema for matching students with teachers.

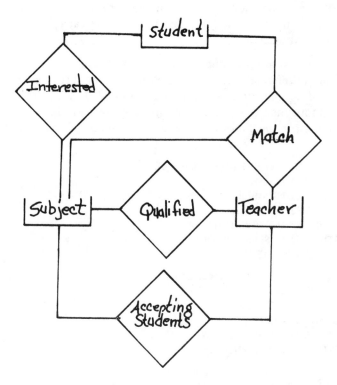

Figure 10.11. Data schema for matching students with teachers.

Figures 10.10 and 10.11 present schematic models, which depict the process of matching of new student sign-ups against the existing teacher data within The Un-College system. Since the process involves several flows and several stores, its context is more substantial than was the context of the ones previously described. First, here are some definitions:

ACCEPTED STUDENT SIGN-UP: data necessary to match a student who is interested and able to learn an approved subject with a teacher

TEACHER MATCH-UP NOTICE: data necessary to allow a teacher to contact a student

STUDENT MATCH-UP NOTICE: data necessary to allow a student to contact a teacher

TEACHER: a person qualified to teach at least one approved subject

STUDENT: a person interested in learning at least one approved subject

SUBJECT: an area of knowledge approved by The Un-College, which may be restricted to qualifying students only

MATCH: an association between one teacher, one student, and one subject based on the student being interested in learning the subject, the teacher being willing to teach it, the teacher accepting students in the subject, and the teacher and student being given identifying information about each other

INTERESTED: an association between one student and one subject based on the student wishing to learn the subject and being capable of receiving instruction in the subject

The only relationship definitions given were the ones for Match and Interested; the *existence* of the other relationships is important to this process, but their *details* are not important. The composition description of Interested is also important: A student may be linked to more than one subject by Interested relationships. Following are composition descriptions for the flows and stores (only some of the data elements for the stores are listed):

ACCEPTED STUDENT SIGN-UP consists of
      STUDENT NAME
and   STUDENT NUMBER
and   STUDENT ADDRESS
and   STUDENT HOME PHONE
and   STUDENT BUSINESS PHONE
and   SUBJECT NAME

TEACHER MATCH-UP NOTICE consists of
      TEACHER NAME
and   TEACHER ADDRESS
and   SUBJECT NAME
and   STUDENT NAME
and   STUDENT HOME PHONE

STUDENT MATCH-UP NOTICE consists of
      STUDENT NAME
and   STUDENT ADDRESS
and   SUBJECT NAME
and   TEACHER NAME
and   TEACHER HOME PHONE

STUDENT consists of zero or more instances; each one
is identified by STUDENT NUMBER and consists of
      STUDENT NAME
and   STUDENT ADDRESS
and   STUDENT HOME PHONE
and   STUDENT BUSINESS PHONE

    :
    :

SUBJECT consists of zero or more instances; each one
is identified by SUBJECT NAME and consists of

    :
    :

TEACHER consists of zero or more instances; each one is identified
by TEACHER NUMBER and consists of
      TEACHER NAME
and   TEACHER ADDRESS
and   TEACHER HOME PHONE
and   TEACHER BUSINESS PHONE
and   TEACHER SIGN-UP DATE

    :
    :

A final useful piece of information is that the Accepted Student Sign-up flow is produced by an Accept Student Sign-up process (which of course has its own process description). In brief, Accept Student Sign-up makes sure that the student's desired subject is stored in the Subject store, and that the student fulfills any special requirements (for example, health) for the subject. This process, however, does not store any data about the student. There's no profound reason for this; it's just a convenient division of labor.

It's now possible to create the process description for Match Student With Teacher (Figure 10.10):

```
record the data about the new STUDENT
        from the ACCEPTED STUDENT SIGN-UP
record that the new STUDENT is INTERESTED in the subject identified
        by the SUBJECT NAME
if there is at least one TEACHER who is both QUALIFIED and
        ACCEPTING STUDENTS in the SUBJECT
then
                pick the TEACHER identified above who has the earliest
                        TEACHER SIGN-UP DATE
                create a STUDENT MATCH-UP NOTICE
                        and a TEACHER MATCH-UP NOTICE
                        from the TEACHER, STUDENT, and SUBJECT data
                record the MATCH among the STUDENT, the TEACHER,
                        and the SUBJECT
```

In addition to manipulating data elements to create output flows, this process description does three additional jobs: It traces existing relationships ("a Teacher who is both Qualified and Accepting Students"), creates new instances of stores ("record the data about the new Student"), and creates new instances of relationships between stores ("record that the new Student is Interested"). This last is significant because it adds one more connection to the bundle of connections represented by the relationship on the data schema. Whenever a process is connected by flows to two or more stores, it is implicitly connected to the data schema and can use or create the relationships shown between those stores.

As in the earlier examples, the setup of this description is influenced by data structure, although in a more subtle way. After the process does its job, there may or may not be a new instance of a Match relationship and the associated Match-up Notice output flows. The choices are reflected in the set of instructions following the "then" ("pick the Teacher . . . ," "create a Teacher Match-up Notice . . . ," "record the Match . . .") and preceded by the decision making rule. In this case, the alternative is to take no action.

If you compare the definitions of Interested, Match, and the flows and stores with the process description, you will find a considerable overlap. The process description, in fact, *enforces the definitions.* Just as the data elements ensure that the characteristics of importance to the system can be described and measured, the process description ensures that the data is created, collected, stored, and organized so that it can be used.

Even though the rules of structured English reduce the freedom of the description writer, a variety of styles can be accommodated within the basic rules. For example, the instructions and groups of instructions may be numbered to give the description a rigorous outline format:

1. record the data about the new STUDENT . . .

2. record that the new student is . . .

3. if there is at least . . . then

    3.1 pick the TEACHER . . .
    and so on . . .

Conversely, the description may be made less formal by dropping the capitalization of data terms and running the sentences together:

In all cases, the information about the accepted student sign-up must be stored so that we have a record of the new student, and the student information must be cross-referenced to the subject for which the student has signed up, to record his or her interest. Whether anything else is done depends on whether there are currently any teachers. . . .

The criterion for selecting a style is simply the preference of the people who will have to write and review the descriptions.

10.5 Adding new data descriptions

Sometimes, the easiest way to create a process description is to first invent some new dataflows or data elements. Figure 10.12 represents an income tax calculation; the input flow compositions are

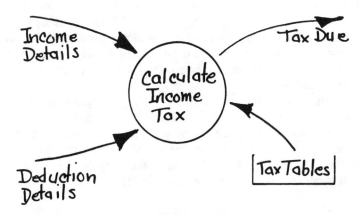

Figure 10.12. Calculating income tax.

INCOME DETAILS consists of
      WAGES
and   DIVIDENDS EARNED
and   INTEREST EARNED

```
        DEDUCTION DETAILS consists of
                CONTRIBUTIONS
        and     INTEREST PAYMENTS
        and     TAXES
        and     MEDICAL EXPENSES

        TAX TABLES consists of one or more instances of
                TAXABLE INCOME RANGE
        and     TAX AMOUNT
```

The process description for this bubble is

```
        add the WAGES, DIVIDENDS EARNED, and INTEREST EARNED
                to obtain the TOTAL INCOME
        add the INTEREST PAYMENTS, TAXES, CONTRIBUTIONS,
                and MEDICAL EXPENSES to obtain the TOTAL DEDUCTIONS
        if the TOTAL INCOME is smaller than the TOTAL DEDUCTIONS
        then
                the TAX DUE is zero
        otherwise
            subtract the TOTAL DEDUCTIONS from the TOTAL INCOME
                to obtain the TAXABLE INCOME
            set the TAX DUE to the TAX AMOUNT corresponding to the
                TAXABLE INCOME RANGE that includes
                the TAXABLE INCOME
```

Notice that Total Income, Total Deductions, and Taxable Income appear neither in the input flows nor in the output flows; they are internal data elements used exclusively within the bubble, to allow the calculation to be described conveniently. Such new data descriptions should be added to those for the other previously defined data elements. In addition to data elements, new flows may be defined that consist of groups of elements that are manipulated as a unit by the description.

Notice that there is a substantial difference between saying that a data element is *calculated from* several other data elements, and saying that a dataflow is *composed of* several data elements. An example of the former is Taxable Income; Income Details is an example of the latter. The formula for deriving one data element from others belongs in a process description, not in a data specification.

10.6 Checking for completeness

A process description is complete when it contains rules for all the kinds of work that might have to be done to transform inputs into outputs. This means that the process description must be checked closely to assure that it is complete. There are some obvious special cases that should be considered. For example,

- What if stored data necessary for the creation of an output can't be found?

- What if there is already an existing instance of a store or relationship when the process is supposed to create one?

- What if the data elements in an arithmetic calculation can't produce a sensible result (for example, the denominator in a division turns out to be zero)?

In these cases and in similar ones, an important distinction must be made. If the special case could only arise because of a technological failure within the system (a computer failure, for example), then the process description does not need to address the problem. On the other hand, it should address a special case that could arise even if the technology worked perfectly. Normally, there are alternatives for handling such cases, and choosing the correct one may well require an understanding of the subject matter of the system. Look back at the process description accompanying Figure 10.10. Suppose a student had already signed up for one subject, and was in the process of signing up for a second one. Data about that student would exist in the Student store, and the instruction to create a new instance of Student would not apply. What is to be done? It is certainly not satisfactory to ignore the problem; the programmer will then end up making the decision. An uninformed decision might result in an arbitrary rule restricting a student to one subject. This would clearly be opposed to the basic purpose of The Un-College system. In this case, the process description should allow for bypassing the creation of a new instance of Student. Notice, by the way, that this modification enforces the description of the relationship Interested, which specifies that a student can be linked to more than one subject.

10.7 Organizing process descriptions

The organization of process descriptions is quite straightforward. Put each one on a separate sheet of paper or in a separate section of the library on a text-processing system. Organize the descriptions alphabetically (the name of the process description is the same as the name of the bubble) so that you can cross-reference a process schema to the appropriate description. Thus, the process description for Match Student With Teacher would be found in the M entries.

10.8 Summary

In this chapter, we have examined the creation of detailed descriptions of processes. Such descriptions require the context of the process and data schemas and of the data descriptions. The descriptions may be graphic, or they may be created by the use of a disciplined narrative technique. The next chapter treats the ASML model as a whole.

Chapter 10: References

1. T. DeMarco, *Structured Analysis and System Specification* (New York: Yourdon Press, 1978), pp. 179-213, 222-25.

    DeMarco introduces the idea of using decision trees and structured English to describe processes.

2. M.A. Jackson, *Principles of Program Design* (London: Academic Press, 1975).

    A highly technical treatment of a strategy for using the structure of the data to derive the organization of the processing.

11

Leveling and Balancing

Now that all the bits and pieces of the model have been introduced and discussed, it's time to take a comprehensive look at the model as a whole. One major issue to be discussed is how to organize the model for presentation and review, and a second deals with methods for mechanically checking the overall consistency of the model. Leveling provides the organization; balancing provides the mechanism for checking consistency.

First, let us look at the issue of organization. If you are the model builder, you may know a model well enough to find a detail you want without any special organization. However, if you want someone else to review the model, or if you want to be able to come back six months later to find a detail, organization becomes very important. This issue was discussed in general terms in Chapter 2, in which I presented the idea that model builders must surmount the inherent noisiness of communication channels. We now need to look at specific details, because if the complex message about the behavior of a system — that is, the essential model — is to be successfully communicated, it must be organized so that it can be checked for errors and omissions. This means that the pieces of the model must be small enough not to overload a reader, and must be arranged so that you can focus on one area of the subject matter at a time.

Once the model has been properly organized, we need a mechanical means to check it. Checks have been introduced within individual portions of the model; in Chapter 7, we discussed ways to ensure that a process schema bubble doesn't create output flows by magic. Now we must consider how to apply this type of consistency checking to the model as a whole. Mechanical consistency checking must precede any review of the model's faithfulness to the system's subject matter. One cannot decide whether some behavior of a system is desirable if it is described two different ways in two different pieces of a model. Let's begin by looking at methods for leveling and balancing process schemas.

11.1 Leveling process schemas

Figures 11.1 and 11.2 show two different representations of The Un-College matching operation. Figure 11.1 is heavily lumped: All the stored data is condensed into a single store, all the transformation work is condensed into a single process, and so on.

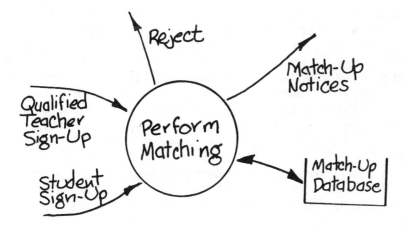

Figure 11.1. Lumped version of The Un-College matching operation.

Which representation is better, the lumped version of Figure 11.1, or the more detailed one, as shown in Figure 11.2? Both have pros and cons. The one-bubble version has the great advantage of simplicity. It would be very useful, for example, for presenting to a manager who wanted to understand the basic nature of the operation, but who would find the level of detail of the four-bubble version confusing and unhelpful.

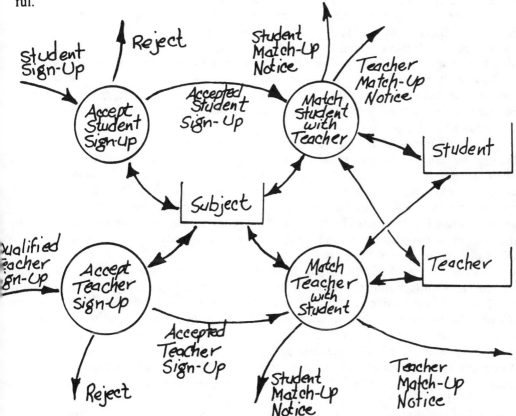

Figure 11.2. Detailed version of The Un-College matching operation.

Another advantage is that a much larger portion of a system can be shown on a single-page process schema. Suppose that a proposed system change encompassed the matching operation plus another four or five Un-College operations of roughly comparable size. A single process schema at the level of detail of Figure 11.1 would not be overwhelmingly complex, since it would contain a half-dozen bubbles or fewer. The level of detail of Figure 11.2, on the other hand, would result in a single-page process schema with roughly twenty bubbles to describe a system of this size. Such a schema would be hard to build and even harder to comprehend. The simplicity of Figure 11.1 has a negative side, of course: The masking of details, which makes high-level review possible, would cause great frustration to someone who needed to know about the lower-level details.

Since both versions have significant advantages, the intelligent course of action is to keep them both in the model. Figures 11.1 and 11.2, in fact, should be considered as two *levels* of a single model. The basic principles of the leveling process are quite straightforward:

- A collection of units (stores, flows, or processes) may be represented as a single unit (flow, store, or process) at a higher level.

- A single unit may be represented as a collection of units at a lower level.

Collecting a group of flows, stores, or processes into a single higher-level entity is a rather mechanical task; the only caution is that the collection should not be arbitrary. For example, a group of processes that cannot be given a name that will be meaningful in terms of the system's subject matter is a poor candidate for leveling upward into a single process. Breaking down a flow, store, or especially a process into a lower-level collection is somewhat harder. One strategy for breaking down processes was described in Chapter 10, and involved the identification of an intermediate flow, around which to partition the higher-level bubble. A much more powerful and general method for partitioning a system will be described in Chapter 14, but the ideas presented above are all that we need at this point.

Let's examine the building of a leveled system model step by step. What would the highest-level representation of a system look like? It would, of course, have only a single bubble, a "superprocess" into which was condensed all of the transformation work of the system. In a way, such a schema doesn't really describe the system at all. The processing and data storage details are all hidden inside the single bubble. This schema, however, does describe the system's *communications* with the outside world, by showing the flows that enter and leave the system boundary. For this reason, it is called the *context level* of the model.

In the next level of description, the context bubble is broken into a group of bubbles few enough in number to fit comfortably on a single page. This lower level of the model describes the same subject matter as does the context level, but here the system is shown in more detail. For obvious reasons, this lower level is called the *system level*. There are two useful ways to think about the relationship between the context level and the system level. One is that the context bubble is the parent bubble, and that the bubbles at the system level are its children (compare Figures 11.1 and 11.2). Another is to think of the evolving model as a hierarchy or upside-down tree. Figure 11.3 depicts this hierarchical arrangement, with the context bubble attached to the upside-down tree's roots and the system-level bubbles attached to the first level of branches.

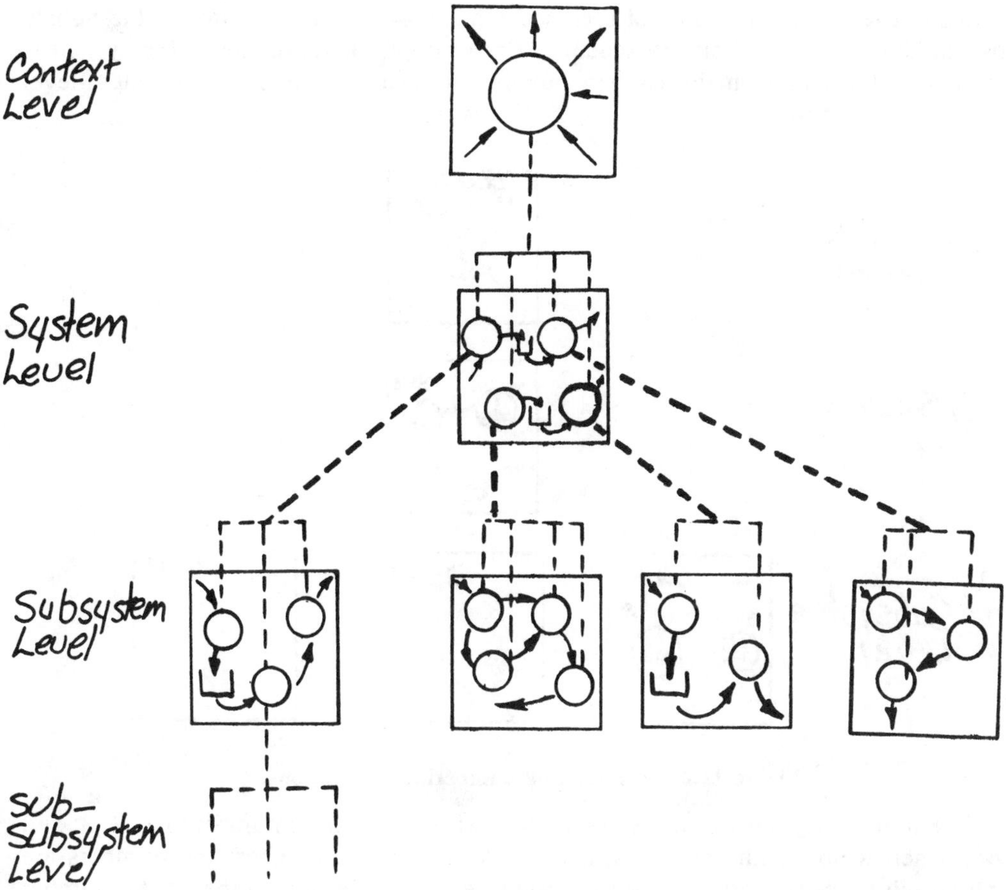

Figure 11.3. Leveled system model as tree.

Let's continue the leveling by breaking each of the bubbles at the system level into a lower-level group. This time, there are too many bubbles to fit on a single sheet of paper, so the bubbles that are the children of each individual parent will be collected on a separate sheet. You could also think of the whole system-level schema as the parent, and each lower-level schema as a child. This new level is called the *subsystem level* since each schema represents one process from the system-level schema. The tree continues to branch out: Each bubble on a subsystem schema is attached to a subbranch of the branch on which its parent bubble grows.

The leveling can be continued by breaking each bubble on each subsystem schema into a group of lower-level bubbles, called the *sub-subsystem schema*. Each schema at the sub-subsystem level corresponds to a bubble at the subsystem level. This process may be continued for as many levels as necessary to adequately represent the system.

As convenient as this method is, it needs some additional organization to prevent confusion. Specifically, there must be some way to tell which piece of system is being described when one schema is examined in isolation. Schemas are identified by assigning them names and numbers, as shown in Figure 11.4. All bubbles and all schemas have names, but if there is only one bubble or only one schema, no number is assigned. The context bubble bears the name of the system that is being modeled. From the system level down, the name of each schema is the same as the name of the bubble whose children are shown on the schema. For example, if the name of the system is XYZ, that is the name on the context bubble and also the name of the system-level schema.

Figure 11.4. Naming and numbering conventions.

The numbering starts at the system level, with the bubbles numbered 1, 2, 3, and so on. There's no significance to which bubble gets which number; the numbers are simply to tell bubbles apart. Below the system level, each schema inherits the number of its parent bubble as well as the parent bubble's name. If Bubble 1 at the system level is called ABC, its child schema at the subsystem level is called ABC and also given the number 1. The bubbles of Schema 1 are numbered by adding a decimal point and a second number to the parent bubble number: 1.1, 1.2, 1.3, and so on.

Suppose you picked up a schema headed RST — 2.3.1. This would tell you three things. First, it would indicate that the level being described is the sub-sub-subsystem level (there are as many ''subs'' as there are digits). Second, you would know that the bubbles on this schema, which are numbered 2.3.1.1, 2.3.1.2, and so on, are pieces of a higher-level process whose name is RST, whose number is 2.3.1, and that occurs on schema 2.3 at the sub-subsystem level. Finally, you would know that Bubble 2.3.1 represents a piece of the processing done by Bubble 2.3 at the subsystem level, which represents part of the processing done by Bubble 2 at the system level, which is part of the overall work of the system described at the context level. Thus, the notation allows tracing the work done by any fragment of the system back to its origin in the overall organization.

There are several important questions about the leveling process that we have yet to address. These are presented below:

Q: When does leveling stop?

A: Leveling stops when the lowest-level bubbles are small enough for their process descriptions to be written in a page or less. (This means that the leveling process won't progress evenly; if two bubbles of a five-bubble schema are small enough for single-page descriptions and the other three aren't, there will be only three child schemas.)

Q: How big should each schema be?

A: Research on human perception indicates that a drawing with more than a half-dozen or so elements will overload the right brain's ability to process pictures, and thus will be substantially harder to grasp than one with fewer bubbles. When examining a process schema, consider that an element is either a bubble with a few flows, or a store. Bubbles with many flows should probably count as more than one element. Don't feel obliged to force the child schema to have five or six bubbles; a two-, three-, or four-bubble breakdown is sometimes the natural one.

Q: How does leveling affect the organization of data and process descriptions?

A: The leveling process usually results in the same flows and stores appearing on a number of schemas. Therefore, it's not practical to have a separate set of definitions or composition descriptions for each schema. There should be a single set of data descriptions for the whole set of schemas. Process descriptions are a different case. Since the child schema for a bubble *is* its process description, only the lowest-level bubbles need separate process descriptions.

Q: What rules govern the leveling of data stores?

A: A data store should appear in the model at the highest level at which it's shared between two or more processes. Above that level, it should be hidden inside the parent bubble, since it's only used for local storage and doesn't serve as a connection. (If data is delayed on its way into a system, it's perfectly reasonable to show a store at the context level: It represents data shared with a process in some other system.)

Now that the process schema has been leveled, balancing methods can be applied to check it for consistency.

11.2 Balancing between levels of a process model

In a leveled set of process schemas, the group of bubbles on the system-level schema should represent exactly the same processing as the single bubble on the context schema; only the level of detail is different. The same idea applies to the other levels; a child schema represents the same piece of system as its parent bubble. The balancing process is a way of mechanically verifying this consistency.

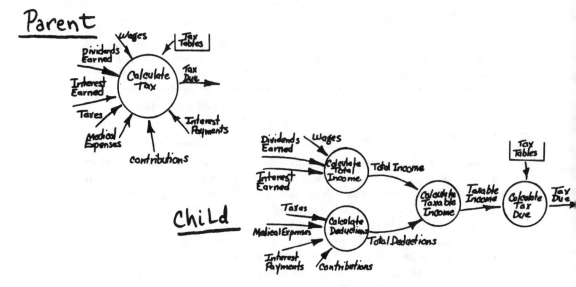

Figure 11.5. Direct balancing between levels.

Figure 11.5 shows a parent process and its child schema. To verify that the two are consistent, draw a rough outline around the bubbles on the child schema so that any flows that aren't connected at both ends to bubbles remain outside. The child schema is in balance with the parent bubble if all the flows on the parent bubble appear outside the boundary on the child schema, all the flows outside the boundary on the child schema appear on the parent bubble, and all the data stores attached to the parent bubble appear on the child schema. Note that it is possible to have stores in the child schema that don't appear attached to the parent bubble; they could be hidden inside.

The procedure described above, while tedious, is quite easy. In fact, it's too easy! Figure 11.6 represents a more typical leveling situation, one in which the flows have been lumped at the higher level. The boundary should be drawn around the child schema as in the previous example.

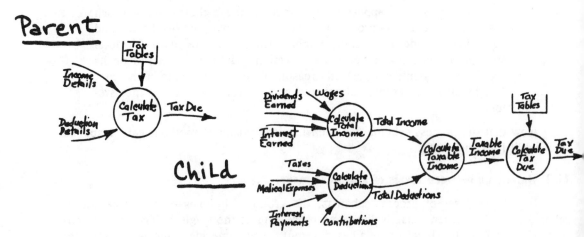

Figure 11.6. Balancing via data descriptions.

In order to assure that a balance exists, it's necessary to assemble the context of the higher-level bubble, which in this case consists of the composition descriptions of the flows, as follows:

INCOME DETAILS consists of
    WAGES
and   DIVIDENDS EARNED
and   INTEREST EARNED

DEDUCTION DETAILS consists of
    TAXES
and   CONTRIBUTIONS
and   MEDICAL EXPENSES
and   INTEREST PAYMENTS

In this case, a balance exists if all the flows on the parent bubble, or the components of these flows, appear outside the boundary on the child schema; all the flows outside the boundary on the child schema appear on the parent bubble or are components of flows that appear on the parent bubble; and all the data stores attached to the parent bubble, or their components, appear on the child schema.

The idea of balancing process schema levels is simply an extension of the mechanical check for "no extra inputs, no magic outputs" described in Chapter 7. If extra flows or missing flows appear at either the parent level or the child level, the simpler check prescribed in Chapter 7 must have been violated by the parent bubble or by one of the child bubbles.

11.3 Balancing processes against process descriptions

In the preceding sections, we determined that a lower-level process schema provides a process description for the parent bubble; that is, it supplies a detailed description of the process in graphic form. Look back at the structured English description for Figure 10.12 to compare it with the child schema shown in Figure 11.6. Clearly, these are alternate representations of the same piece of processing. In this case, the structured English description is a better choice than the diagram, since the low-level bubbles on Figure 11.6 still need short process descriptions themselves (strictly speaking, Calculate Total Income doesn't say *how* to obtain Total Income from the input flows; it's just a very familiar calculation). The diagram plus the process descriptions would add four pieces of paper to the model instead of one. Nevertheless, it's very instructive to compare the low-level process schema with the equivalent structured English description. If the low-level process schema can be balanced against the parent bubble, why can't the structured English description be balanced against it?

Remember that a process schema graphically depicts an imperative sentence. Using this idea, it's possible to create something that's halfway between a narrative process description and a process schema. Compare Figure 11.7 with the leftmost three, low-level bubbles on Figure 11.6. The data elements referred to within the sentences are exactly equivalent to the flows on the process schema. Some of them are inputs to or outputs from the process, and correspond to flows that are not connected at their tail or head ends. Some data references, however, are created in one sentence and used in another, and act just like the flows that connect bubbles inside the child schema.

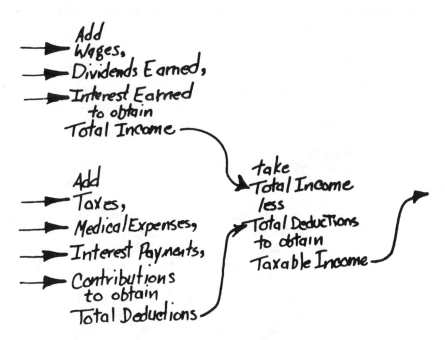

Figure 11.7. Structured English in semigraphic form.

Because of this close connection between a low-level process schema and a process description, it's possible to write balancing rules for process descriptions that are very similar to the process schema balancing rules: Begin the balancing process by eliminating from the process description any data term that is created and used completely within the description. Then, match any remaining data references against the flows or stores attached to the parent bubble, or to components of those flows or stores.

Notice that the fact that a process description balances with the bubble it describes does not guarantee its correctness. If the process description for Figure 10.12 were changed to read

> add the WAGES, the DIVIDENDS EARNED, and the INTEREST EARNED
> to obtain the TOTAL DEDUCTIONS
> add the TAXES, the MEDICAL EXPENSES, the INTEREST PAYMENTS,
> and the CONTRIBUTIONS to obtain the TOTAL INCOME

it would still balance perfectly. Balancing is a test for mechanical consistency, not for faithfulness to the subject matter of the system.

11.4 Leveling data schemas

A data schema can be made into levels by defining high-level stores that represent groups of low-level stores. At a high level, the data schema shows a small number of these parent stores and their relationships.

Leveling is necessary because practical difficulties arise in organizing a large data schema for presentation. If the schema contains dozens of stores and relationships, it's hard to draw on a single page and even harder to read. The solution is to break the data schema into smaller pieces and put each on a separate page. Look back at Figure

8.9: To break this model into pieces, we must determine a basis for partitioning that has some relevance to the subject matter. One possibility is to separate the providing of instructional resources from the providing of services to students and teachers. This partitioning results in the two data schemas shown in Figures 11.8 and 11.9. Notice that stores are duplicated on the two models, but that relationships are not.

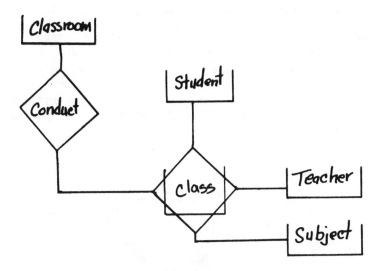

Figure 11.8. Un-College instructional resources data model.

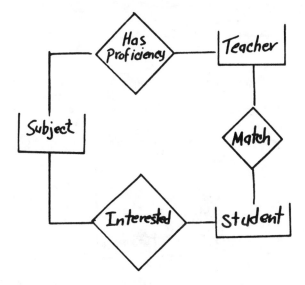

Figure 11.9. Un-College client services data schema.

The parent level for these two child schemas would have an Instructional Resources store (Class and Classroom) and a Client Services store (Student, Teacher, and Subject) connected by an unnamed relationship. This partitioning has the disadvantage that one must look on more than one data schema to find all the relationships that a store may enter into. Nevertheless, it is preferable to attempting to deal with a single complex data schema. In order to partition based on subject matter, one can make each piece of the data schema correspond to the stored data usage of a process schema bubble. For a small-to-medium system, each piece of data schema could correspond to a system-level bubble; for a larger system, each piece might correspond to a subsystem-level or lower-level bubble.

11.5 Balancing process schemas against data schemas

Since process schemas and data schemas share a symbol in common, it's possible to visualize a composite schema formed by joining the two diagrams at their common points. Figure 11.10 illustrates a composite schema that is drawn on a surface with a right-angle bend in it. If you viewed this surface from directly in front, rather than from the angle depicted in Figure 11.10, the portion of the surface containing the process schema would appear edge-on, and you would see the data schema shown in Figure 11.11.

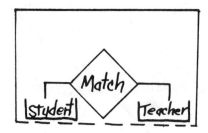

Figure 11.10. Composite schema.

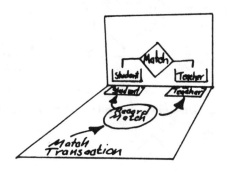

Figure 11.11. Composite schema viewed from the front.

Similarly, if you viewed this surface from the top, the data schema would be reduced to an edge and the process schema would look like that shown in Figure 11.12.

We have already discovered that process schemas and data schemas represent two different perspectives. However, matching the two in this detailed way suggests that we may be able to use this approach to check them for consistency. If you think of a data schema as a set of storage containers for data elements, it's reasonable to ask how the elements got there and what they're used for. If a data element is needed to describe a store but doesn't have a way to be captured, or if it *is* captured but doesn't seem to be needed, we have a situation very much like discovering an extra input to or a magic output from a bubble.

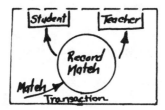

Figure 11.12. Composite schema viewed from the top.

Actually, not only the capture and use of data elements is at issue, but also the creation and use of instances of stores and relationships. An isolated data element can't be simply tossed into a data schema. The rules for balancing a data schema against a process schema are simply common-sense extensions of these ideas:

- There must be some bubble capable of creating instances of each store shown on the data schema.

- There must be some bubble capable of creating instances of each relationship shown on the data schema.

- There must be some bubble that uses each data element that is a component of a store on the data schema.

- There must be some bubble that uses each relationship shown on the data schema (that is, a bubble that needs to find instances of some store linked to instances of some other store by that relationship).

- Bubbles must not use or create instances of stores that do not appear on the data schema.

- Bubbles must not use or create instances of relationships that do not appear on the data schema.

- Bubbles must not store or retrieve data elements that are not components of data schema stores.

11.6 Summary

There is no practical way of modeling a complex system without procedures for organizing the model and procedures for verifying model correctness. This chapter introduced both the organizing principle (leveling) and the verification criteria (balancing), and concludes our treatment of modeling tools.

In the next five chapters, we will look at the model building process.

Chapter 11: Reference

1. T. DeMarco, *Structured Analysis and System Specification* (New York: Yourdon Press, 1978), pp. 71-88.

    DeMarco introduces the idea of leveling and balancing the graphic process model.

Part III
The Model Building Process

In Part II, we saw all the pieces of the ASML model and how they fit together to create an integrated picture of a system. The five chapters of Part III provide a systematic procedure for assembling those pieces into the various models required during systems development. The organization of these chapters, as shown below, follows the ASML model building sequence illustrated in Table 6.2.

Essential Model	Environmental Model	Chapter 12 Defining System Context
		Chapter 13 Describing Purpose and External Events
	Behavior Model	Chapter 14 Deriving the Schematic Behavior Model
		Chapter 15 Completing the Essential Model
Implementation Model	Processor Configuration Model	Chapter 16 Beginning the Implementation Model

Chapters 12 and 13 describe the building of the environmental model, with Chapter 12 focusing on the schematic level and Chapter 13 on the detail level. The creation of the schematic behavior model from the environmental model is discussed in Chapter 14, and its completion is taken up in Chapter 15. Chapter 16 describes the beginnings of the implementation model. Although we do not use The Un-College example in Part III, the ideas are applied to it in the book's Appendix.

12

Defining System Context

The process of building a model of a system begins with the "outside" of the system. A system, after all, can be thought of as a stimulus/response mechanism. Let me illustrate this by asking you to consider the example of a soft-drink machine. If given the stimulus of two quarters and a dime, the machine will respond by dispensing a can of soda. If given the stimulus of three quarters, it will dispense the can of soda, a dime, and a nickel. It makes sense to discuss the function of the soda machine only in the context of an environment containing someone willing to feed it money and someone willing to refill its soft-drink supply. A system within an organization is typically much more complex than a soft-drink machine, but it is nevertheless helpful to think of it as a mechanism that responds to its environment and to build an *environmental model* as the start of the development process.

The environmental model is part of the essential model of the system, and the essential model focuses on those things the system needs to have *regardless* of how it is implemented. This focus on essentials allows us to describe the system with as small a model as possible, since any implementation model must contain all the essentials of the system plus implementation details. It also allows us to use a vocabulary drawn from the system's subject matter. By using the small model and the natural vocabulary, we make the model understandable and reviewable, and maximize our chances of getting everything right.

Remember that ASML separates the schematic level from the detail level and separates process models from stored data models. Because the environmental model depicts the system from the outside, and since any stored data needed by the system will be described by the inside model, the environmental model doesn't include a schematic data model.

Before we begin our discussion of the context schema, let me outline our immediate chapter goals: The rest of this chapter describes the building of a schematic process model of the system's environment. Chapter 13 describes the detail level of the environmental model. Together, the two chapters serve as a prelude to modeling the detailed behavior of the system.

12.1 The context schema

The context schema, introduced in the previous chapter, in form is just another process schema, with circles representing processes, arrows representing flows, and three-sided figures representing stores. In actuality, however, it exhibits the following differences:

- The system being described by the model is represented by a single process; the bubble for this process is drawn larger than the others and is placed in the center of the schema.

- Other people, departments, automated systems, outside organizations, and the like, which communicate with this system by sending or receiving flows, are depicted as smaller bubbles around the outside of the central one representing the system. These bubbles are referred to as *terminators,* since they are "dead ends" for the flows shown on the context schema.

- All the flows sent or received by the system being modeled must be shown on the context schema although several individual flows may be lumped into a group and represented by a single higher-level flow.

- Only the flows sent to or received from the central system bubble are shown entering and leaving the terminators.

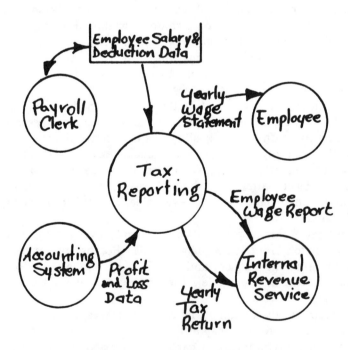

Figure 12.1. Context schema for tax reporting.

Consider the context schema for the tax reporting system shown in Figure 12.1. Placing the tax reporting system in the center of the schema shows that it's the subject of the model. The bubbles marked Payroll Clerk, Accounting System, Employee, and

Internal Revenue Service describe the *environment of the system being modeled.* In other words, the tax reporting system exists in order to serve the needs of these people, organizations, and systems. However, these terminators will not appear in the inside, or behavior, model of the tax department; they are not of interest in and of themselves, and are included only because the system *responds* to them.

Because of the subsidiary role of the terminators on the context schema, their input and output flows are not completely shown. Clearly, the employees must send data to the Internal Revenue Service, and the payroll clerk must provide data to the computerized accounting system. However, these communications are not of direct concern to the tax reporting system and are omitted from the schema. Therefore, the test of "no extra inputs, no magic outputs" can only be applied to the central bubble on the context schema because it is the only bubble whose communications are being fully modeled.

Although the terminators on the context schema aren't part of the system, they do provide useful services, as described below:

- Terminators show the sources and destinations of the flows entering and leaving the system. The flow called Profit And Loss Data will be the input to some process within the tax reporting system. Someone studying the schema in which the process appears may want to know where the input comes from. Showing the sources of input flows on process schemas would make them more complicated and thus harder to verify. Including the context schema as part of the essential model provides a way to identify sources and destinations without cluttering the lower-level process schemas.

- Terminators serve as an index to the needs to which the system responds. Before modeling the behavior of the system in detail, we must examine these needs. The people, organizations, and systems with which the system communicates are starting points for identifying needs.

The set of flows into and out of the system bubble on the context schema also serves an important purpose. The inputs and outputs of the lower-level process schemas must *balance* with those on the context schema. If data that don't appear on the context schema show up at a lower level, or if data shown at the context level aren't used or produced by the detailed model of the system, the model as a whole isn't coherent and may be in error.

Notice the store called Employee Salary And Deduction Data in Figure 12.1. It indicates that the payroll clerk and the tax reporting system have a shared responsibility for the stored data. If the data were owned by the payroll clerk or by the tax reporting system, the store would be hidden inside one or the other bubble, and only a flow would show on the context schema. Stored data owned by the system can be modified or reorganized without penalty. Stored data shared with a terminator, however, may be modified only with the knowledge and consent of the parties involved.

12.2 Naming pieces of the context schema

The name on the context bubble in Figure 12.1 is Tax Reporting, not Tax Department. This is deliberate: Although systems development efforts are often loosely referred to as "computerizing department X" or something similar, such terms are misleading. It would be very unusual to decide that *everything* done by a department be considered the subject of a systems development study. The name on the context bubble was chosen to avoid indicating that everything in the tax department will appear in the model, or that everything modeled is done by the tax department. In fact, the flows to and from the system bubble *define the limitations* of the scope of this particular system.

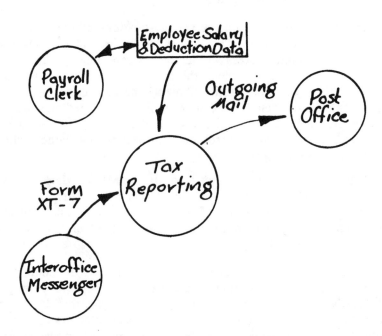

Figure 12.2. A context schema with inappropriate vocabulary.

Speaking of names, look at Figure 12.2 for an alternate description of the tax reporting system. What's wrong? Clearly, this diagram doesn't communicate what the system is all about as well as the one in Figure 12.1 does. One way of looking at the problem is in terms of vocabulary. Payroll Clerk, Employee Salary And Deduction Data, and Internal Revenue Service correspond to the natural vocabulary of a tax reporting system. On the other hand, Outgoing Mail, Interoffice Messenger, and Post Office are not specifically related to tax reporting. The model has slipped from describing the essentials of the system into describing an implementation. If the profit and loss data came by electronic mail rather than by interoffice messenger, the system would still be the same, having the same purpose and responding to the same needs in the outside world. Let me suggest some guidelines that can prevent you from putting the wrong sorts of details on the context schema:

- When identifying terminator bubbles, show the ultimate sources and destinations of the flows, not the intermediate handlers of the flows. Terminators should represent people and systems whose needs are being served by the basic purpose of the system.

- When naming flows, describe the data contained in the flow, not the medium of transmission. Form names and physical packagings do not convey useful information about the essentials of the system.

By the way, I'm not suggesting that there's anything wrong with modeling implementation details. However, modeling these details before nailing down the essentials of the system means jumping to a solution before you understand the problem.

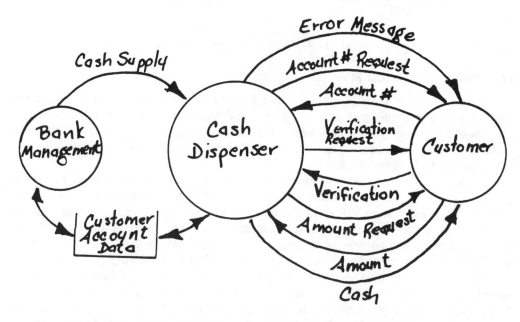

Figure 12.3. Cash dispenser with implementation details.

Figure 12.3 describes a more subtle problem involving implementation details. Here the most obvious problems (such as calling the input flow Plastic Card With Magnetic Strip instead of Account Number) have been avoided. Nevertheless, by modeling the customer's entry of data as three separate flows interspersed with prompts, the diagrammer demonstrates that he or she has taken implementation details into consideration, for only the limitations of mechanical technology would require such an approach. Figure 12.4 contains less distracting detail, and shows what any system of this nature would require. It could describe the job performed by a human bank teller as well as by a cash machine.

What the context schema should show is the net transfer of data from the environment to the system. Flows that prompt for a response tend to be implementation dependent, and add details to the model that don't aid the users' understanding of the system's essentials.

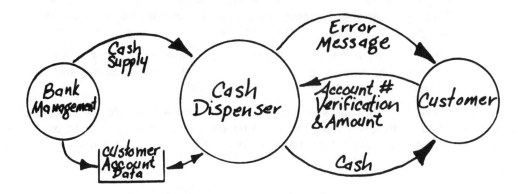

Figure 12.4. Cash dispenser essentials.

12.3 Mechanical context problems

Some decisions about system context lie outside the realm of the modeling process; these are decisions such as what system to develop, or how large or small the context should be for a particular project. We discuss these issues in Part V. However, there are some mechanical issues about system context that relate to the application of the modeling techniques themselves.

Suppose an organization wants to develop a new automated system to provide support for its purchasing department, which currently has an unsatisfactory automated system. The new system will re-implement the maintenance of computerized files on purchased products and suppliers, and will also automate some of the clerical work currently done by the purchasing department. The only guideline passed to the systems developers is that the creation of new computerized files be avoided if possible.

The work done by one of the purchasing clerks is shown in Figure 12.5. It involves the choosing of a single supplier from whom to buy a requisitioned part. (Typically, there are multiple suppliers for each part.) Although the Product and Supplier data come from computerized files, Delivery History consists of record folders kept in a file cabinet. This seems to present a dilemma: If the purchasing clerk's activities are incorporated into the new system, as depicted in the context schema of Figure 12.6, the Delivery History file will have to be automated. However, leaving out the clerical function will reduce the usefulness of the new system.

This dilemma is purely artificial. It is caused by another "essentials versus implementation" issue, namely the failure to distinguish between a *process* and a *processor*. Although the job of selecting a supplier is performed by a single processor (the purchasing clerk), it can be separated into two or more processes. Figure 12.7 is developed from Figure 12.5 by the identification of the intermediate flow called Candidate Supplier List. Although completing the job of selecting a single supplier requires a manual file, finding the group of suppliers that supplies a product can be done entirely with computerized data. Therefore, the latter process can be included in the system and the former one can be excluded.

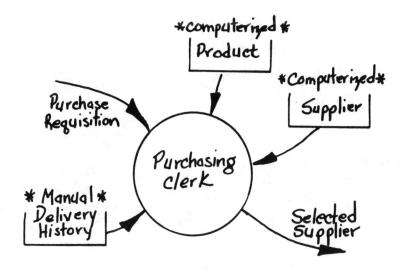

Figure 12.5. Purchasing clerk's activity.

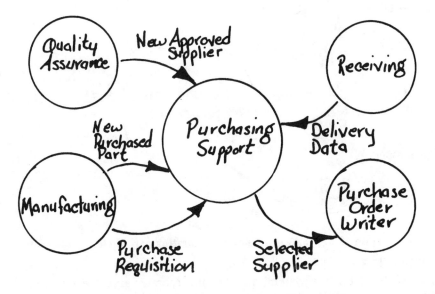

Figure 12.6. Context schema incorporating clerk.

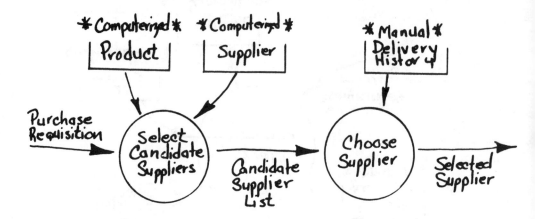

Figure 12.7. Partitioning of purchasing clerk's activity.

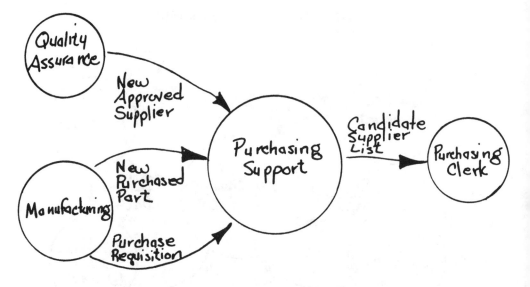

Figure 12.8. Context schema incorporating part of clerk's activities.

Figure 12.8 may look strange at first glance: It shows the purchasing clerk as the receiver of data from the system, and also incorporates an activity currently performed by the purchasing clerk. Remember that the boundary between a system and its environment is an *abstraction;* it does not represent a real physical boundary, and there's no reason a processor (either a person or a computer) can't be partly inside and partly outside.

Another modeling issue involving context determination concerns manual activities requiring human judgment. Including a process within the boundaries of a system does not commit the developers to automating it. There are good reasons for incorporating into a context schema processes that are, and will remain, manual. Often, the developers can't do a good job of determining what an automated system needs to do unless they thoroughly understand the manual processes that will provide its inputs and accept its outputs.

Nevertheless, it's important to be able to recognize whether a process *can* be automated. Fundamentally, automation requires the transfer of some pattern of activity into the computer. In order to do this successfully, one must be able to identify the input flows required by the activity, the output flows produced by the activity, and an exact set of rules for transforming the input into the output. If any one of these conditions is missing, the activity cannot be automated. In fact, to describe an activity as requiring human judgment is tantamount to admitting it can't be modeled in this way.

Consider the context schema shown in Figure 12.9. The system accepts data from the testing of manufactured products, determines whether the products meet quality standards, and issues appropriate outputs. Certain test results show that the product is obviously, hopelessly bad, and others show that it's incontestably good. However, there's a range of results that are near the borderline between good and bad. Interpreting these results and reaching a decision involves inputs that are not specifiable in advance and rules that can't be formalized. Therefore, the system in Figure 12.9 diverts these borderline results to a quality assurance expert, who may use human judgment to override the computer's decision.

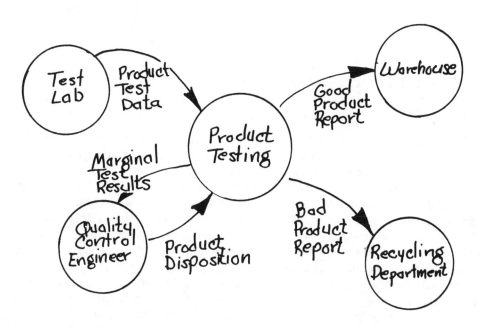

Figure 12.9. Context schema excluding human judgment.

By drawing the context as in Figure 12.9, we emphasize the nonautomatability of part of the evaluation process, and provide valuable information about the nature of the system. On the other hand, Figure 12.10, which incorporates the entire evaluation process into the system, is simpler, and focuses attention on normal flow through the system. Since both diagrams are quite simple, the relative complexity isn't a big issue. However, there are systems that contain a large number of activities of this kind, in which outputs produced by a set of routine rules are presented to an expert for evaluation. As demonstrated in Figure 12.11, a context diagram showing all the results that are sent out for review is unnecessarily complicated and distracts from the fundamental nature of the system. In cases such as this, it's more reasonable to simplify the context diagram, and to identify the processes that require human judgment on the inside model of the system.

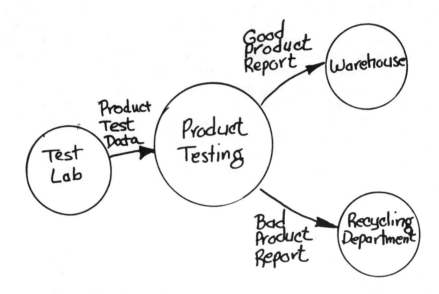

Figure 12.10. Context schema incorporating human judgment.

12.4 New versus existing systems

One final issue must be addressed before we conclude our discussion of context schemas: That issue is a system's "newness." At one extreme are systems that are genuinely new, that serve environmental needs that currently aren't being served at all, that accept and provide entirely new kinds of data, and so on. At the other extreme are systems designed to incorporate a set of routine manual activities lock, stock, and barrel into an automated system, or to transfer some processing en masse from an old automated system to a new one. Most systems development efforts fall somewhere in between: The content of the system is not entirely new, but will be added to or changed as a result of the development process.

The usability of the techniques described in this chapter does not depend on the degree of newness of the system. The symbol representing a terminator serves as well to describe a system or person who *will* provide or accept data as it does to describe a system or person who already does. However, the nature of the work will be different for a system with a large degree of newness than for a system without. The identification of people and systems whose needs aren't currently being served, and who aren't currently accepting or receiving communications, requires considerably more creativity than simply gathering information about an existing environment.

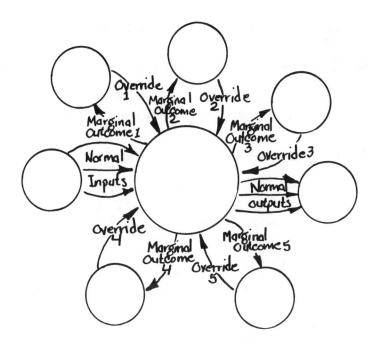

Figure 12.11. Context schema with surrounding override processes.

Because of this difference, developers can expect the context schema for a very new system to be far more tentative. It may be necessary to build a preliminary schema, go through the next steps in the modeling process, and then return and revise the preliminary schema extensively before performing another round of modeling.

12.5 Summary

The ASML systems development process begins with the examination and modeling of a system's environment. This chapter has focused on the schematic level of the resulting model, and on criteria for ensuring the model's correctness and communicational clarity.

In the next chapter, we'll complete our study of the environmental model by examining its detail level.

Chapter 12: References

1. T. DeMarco, *Structured Analysis and System Specification* (New York: Yourdon Press, 1978), p. 90.

    DeMarco introduces the concept of building a graphic model of system context.

2. K.T. Orr, *Structured Requirements Definition* (Topeka: Ken Orr & Associates, Inc., 1981).

    The context diagram notation used in this book is that of Orr's entity diagram.

13

Describing Purpose
and External Events

The context schema is the schematic level of the environmental model. In other words, it describes how the system and its environment form an overall pattern, but it doesn't provide any details. Figure 13.1 shows how the context schema is supported by more detailed descriptions of both the system bubble and the terminator bubbles. The context schema, system definition, and external event descriptions together provide a complete model of the system's environment.

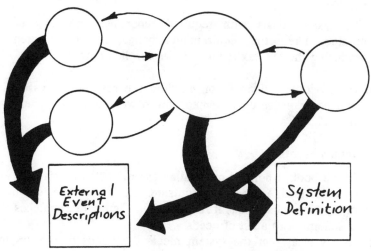

Figure 13.1. Organization of the environmental model.

The detailed level of the environmental model plays a role much like those of flow and store definitions as discussed in Chapter 9. Neither the system definition nor the external event descriptions can be directly used to build the system. Their purpose is to improve the model; they provide a standard by which to judge its adequacy and from which it can be refined. Like flow and store definitions, the system definition and external event descriptions occupy an intermediate level in the model; they provide more detail than the context schema and less detail than the inside model of the system's functioning. From this position, they can show where refinement is needed.

The system definition, for example, focuses attention on the system's purpose. It can make the model builders realize that the system needs to receive or produce some data not currently shown in the context schema in order to accomplish this purpose. Refinement in the downward direction might take the form of modifying the details of some process inside the system so that it responds more adequately to an external event.

13.1 Defining the system

The central bubble on the context schema gives the system's name; if carefully chosen, the name can provide a reasonable amount of information about the system's purpose. However, a name that described the system's purpose in detail wouldn't fit in the bubble; that's the reason for having a separate definition. Consider the tax reporting system shown in Figure 12.1. It might be defined as, The processes and stored data necessary to provide the required yearly federal tax reporting. This definition provides several pieces of information that the name on the context schema doesn't:

- The system deals with federal, rather than state or local, tax reporting. (This could have been inferred from the absence of terminators for other tax agencies; nevertheless, it's nice to know that the omission wasn't accidental.)

- The system deals only with yearly reporting requirements; there may be tax reporting required more or less often that this system doesn't handle.

- The system deals with required reporting, and may need to be modified if reporting requirements change; its purpose extends beyond producing the two tax reports shown on the context schema.

In addition to providing guidance for building the rest of the essential model, this definition would be very useful to someone who wanted a high-level overview of the system's operation.

13.2 Needs versus events

Earlier in the book, I pointed out that an essential characteristic of any system was that it responded to needs in the world outside. Let's continue looking at the tax reporting system, and ask what needs it responds to. Figure 13.2 matches the terminators on the context schema with a list of needs.

Although it's clear that the system meets the needs of the employees and the IRS, it's somewhat less clear that the accounting system "needs" to submit profit and loss data. In fact, it's common in many organizations to phrase things in terms of a tax reporting system *needing to receive* profit and loss data, but this isn't really the case: The system wouldn't be there if it wasn't serving some need beyond itself.

It's possible to see the accounting system's need to submit data as part of an overall organizational need to obey the tax laws. However, that's quite abstract. A much more practical point of view involves focusing on *external events* rather than on needs. This approach emphasizes the system's function as a stimulus/response mechanism, and asks the question, What are the events in the system's environment to which it must make some response? External events are related to needs, and many needs can be thought of as events, but the change in perspective will make things simpler.

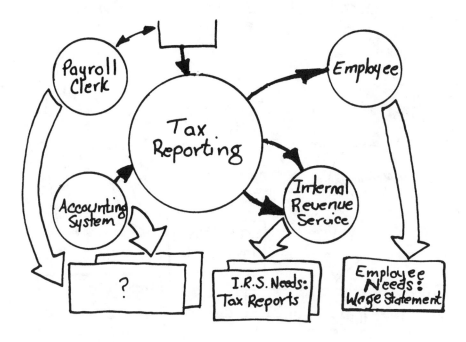

Figure 13.2. Needs satisfied by tax reporting.

Figure 13.3 provides a description of the tax reporting environment in terms of external events. The shift in perspective doesn't affect the Employee or Internal Revenue Service parts of the environment, but fits the Profit And Loss Data into the picture better. Notice that there's still not a one-to-one correspondence between the events and the terminators. There are two events related to the IRS, since the two outputs must occur at different times of year, but there are no events directly involving the payroll clerk. The lack of one-to-one correspondence is due to the delayed connection represented by the Employee Salary And Deduction Data store, which represents some storage scheme (a filing cabinet or a computerized file) accessible both to the clerk and to the tax system. There is no special external event needed here; the tax system simply reads the data from storage when required to do so by some other event. In fact, the payroll clerk and the tax system need not even be aware of each other's existence.

On the other hand, the Profit And Loss Data requires an event since it simply appears at some point. This data may reach the system before it is needed, so the system must make some provision for accepting and storing the data. In other words, the system must respond to the arrival of the Profit And Loss Data, and thus it's an event.

Figure 13.3. Events responded to by tax reporting.

13.3 Types of events

The discussion in the last section focused on *what events are,* and ignored the issue of *how the system knows the event has occurred.* To explore the *how,* I'll use the context schema of Figure 13.4, which represents part of the work done by a garden-variety book club system. Some flows that would be part of a real system, such as membership cancellations and book refusals, have been omitted in order to simplify the example.

Notice the effort that has been made in this schema to treat only essentials. Most book clubs provide members with a single form on which to indicate either the desire to receive a book or the desire not to receive one. Nevertheless, the alternatives are quite different and have quite different consequences. I've shown them as separate flows.

In a similar way, the shipped book and the invoice normally travel together, but because they have different consequences, they are thus shown as two separate flows.

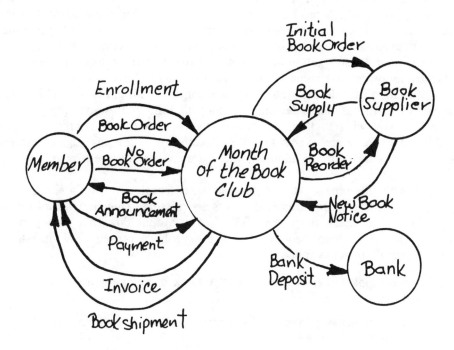

Figure 13.4. Month of the Book Club context schema.

Let's list some of the more obvious events to which this system responds:

Event 1: A potential member wishes to enroll.

Event 2: A member wishes to order a book.

Event 3: A supply of books arrives from a book supplier in response to a book order.

Event 4: A book supplier reports that a new book is available.

Event 5: A member submits a payment for a book in response to an invoice.

All the events in this list have something in common: A dataflow arrives to signal that the event has occurred. Although an event signaled by a dataflow is the most obvious type, it is not the only type. For example, if you watched the Month of the Book Club system carefully, you would observe that around a certain time of the month *it started up all by itself* and shipped books to various members. Since systems don't carry out activities in a random fashion, it was necessarily responding to *something*. But what was it responding to? There was certainly no input flow that triggered the response.

Those of you who are veteran book club members have no doubt solved the mystery. The rules of most book clubs state that if, by a certain date, you don't order a specific book or don't specify that you want no books, the club will assume that you want its main selection for that month. The lack of an input flow is not relevant. There *was* an event, which can be described in any of the following ways: It was time to send out default book shipments to members. Or, the grace period for members to refuse a book expired. Or, a member has ordered a book by default.

If the system doesn't get an input flow to signal that the event has occurred, how does it become aware that some response is necessary? You can think either of an alarm clock going off inside the system, or of a continuous input flow labeled Time being watched by a process that is deciding whether it's time to do something.

However you wish to think of the mechanism, there are clearly two different kinds of events: There are events that are triggered by a flow that signals the system that a response is needed. In addition, there are events triggered by the passage of time.

Armed with this broadened definition of an external event, let's revisit the context schema to see if any time-triggered events are missing. One straightforward way to find omissions is to check the output flows. Any output flow that isn't part of the response to an already identified event might have been caused by a time-triggered event. The existing matches follow

- Initial Book Order is caused by "A book supplier reports that a new book is available."

- Bank Deposit is caused by "A member submits a payment for a book in response to an invoice."*

- Book Shipment and Invoice are both caused by "A member wishes to order a book."

This leaves the output flows called Book Reorder and Book Announcement unaccounted for. It's tempting to think of the book reorder as a response to "A member wishes to order a book," since if there weren't any book orders from members the stock of books on hand would never decrease. Likewise, Book Announcement might be considered to be a response to Event 3 above: A supply of books arrives from a vendor in response to a book order. However, the purpose of the book club system no doubt involves making money as well as serving book lovers. A book should be reordered from a supplier only if the number of orders suggests that more books can be sold than are in stock. The book club also wants to avoid the expense and inefficiency of issuing book announcements haphazardly. It is more likely that the club reorders from suppliers periodically on the basis of a book's popularity, and also issues book announcements on a periodic basis in order to save money through mass mailings.

In both of the above cases there is a delay between an input flow and the issuing of some related output by the system. Contrast this with the response made to an individual member's book order. Although a club might intentionally stack individual orders and ship them periodically, let's assume that this club's policy is to ship immediately. Under this policy, it's possible that there will be a delay before shipment of an order. However, a delay of this kind would be an *implementation accident,* unrelated to

---

*The decision about what is a delay is often arbitrary. Although one could argue that there is a delay between Member Payments and Bank Deposits, the delay is typically short, and the system's money-making purpose would involve minimizing this delay.

the system's purposes or the needs it serves. In contrast, the delay in placing reorders with book suppliers is a deliberate one, a matter of organizational policy. Because of the usefulness of emphasizing policy determined delays, it's clearer to say that there are separate events, driven by time, that cause the system to issue book announcements and book reorders.

The event that causes the book announcement could be stated "Time to issue book announcement," but that's rather uninformative. The *reason* the system issues the announcement is that members want to know what books are available so that they can place orders. Since it's not economical to give members this information one at a time, the system makes the simplifying assumption that everyone wants to know at the same time of month. The full set of events for the book club follows:

Event 1: A potential member wishes to enroll.

Event 2: A member wishes to order a book.

Event 3: A supply of books arrives from a book supplier in response to a book order.

Event 4: A book supplier reports that a new book is available.

Event 5: A member submits a payment for a book in response to an invoice.

Event 6: A member has ordered a book by default.

Event 7: Members wish to know what new books are available.

Event 8: Members have ordered more copies of a book than was originally anticipated.

It's very easy when building a list of this kind to slip in events that aren't external. For example, "Book is shipped to member" is something that the *system* does, not something that happens in the environment; it is a response by the system. This whole procedure may seem quite arbitrary and artificial when you already know how the system will respond and are anxious to document it. It's worth the effort, however; the purpose of the procedure is to focus attention on one item at a time, so that nothing is accidentally omitted.

13.4 A strategy for building event lists

The full-set event list in the previous section was built by trial and error, with the assistance of some ideas about the system's purpose and of the flows on the context schema. This is practical when the system's inputs and outputs are well defined and are not likely to change substantially. However, if a new system is being built, or an existing one heavily modified, the context schema may be tentative and unreliable in the early stages of the modeling. An approach is needed that is independent of the system's existing input and output flows. In fact, an independent procedure may be the only way to assure that the system's connections with its environment are adequate to fulfill its purpose. As events are discovered, the context schema can be changed to reflect the system's communications relating to these events.

The only necessary raw materials for this method are a knowledge of the system's purpose and an identification of the terminators (the people, organizations, and systems) that are crucial to its purpose. The stripped-down context schema of Figure 13.5 will be the starting point for a reinvestigation of the book club's events. In addition to this schema, the definition of purpose for the system is needed: "The Month of the Book Club provides selected books to book lovers in exchange for sufficient money to make a profit."

Figure 13.5. Stripped-down book club context.

The object of the method is to identify events relating to each of the terminators to which the system *might* want to respond; that is, events that have some bearing on the purpose of the system. This list of potential events is then looked at more closely to determine whether a response will actually be made and how the system will determine that the event has occurred. The method is similar to brainstorming, in the sense that the tactics require not exactness but imagination; it's quite all right to come up with unlikely events, since the questionable ones will be filtered out later. The important thing is not to miss any events.

Suppose this method is tried for the Member terminator on the Month of the Book Club schema. To which events involving the member might the club respond? The obvious first choice is that a member wants a book. To discover more events, systems developers can begin speculating from this point; some of the more obvious questions are

- Are there variations on this event that are significant?

- Is the *opposite,* or *negative,* of the event of interest to the system?

- Are there events that must precede this event?

- Are there events that must follow this event?

Applying these questions to "Member wants a book," it becomes clear that there are at least two varieties of this event. The member may want a book that is currently offered by the club, or one that is not currently offered. The distinction is important, since the club would have to respond very differently in the two cases.

How about negatives or opposites of an event? The two possible varieties are that a member decides he or she doesn't want a book to be shipped, or that a book already received isn't wanted. Again, the system would have to respond differently to these two events. Are there events that must precede the member's wanting a book? Well, the member can't discover which books are to be had by mental telepathy. Presumably, the member must have wanted to know what books were available prior to deciding which one was desirable. Also, since the club makes its services available only to members, the member's wanting to join would precede or accompany the desire for a specific book. Finally, an examination of following events produces "Member wants to pay for a book," "Member wants to know how much he or she owes for books," "Member refuses to pay for a book already received," and "Member wishes to quit club."

This list is certainly not exhaustive, but it's a good illustration of the thinking process involved. Having created the list, the systems developers must look at each potential event and ask two questions:

- Will the system respond to this event?

- How will the system determine that this event has occurred?

A possible answer to the first question could be a simple yes. Other answers might be that some other system currently responds to the event and so no response is required, that the event isn't closely enough related to the purpose of the system and will be ignored, or that the event is unpredictable and an ad hoc response will be made to it. Suppose the potential event list contained, Member wishes to pay for a book prior to receiving it. The decision might be that the system needs machinery for accepting prepayments, or that they will be handled outside the system in an unplanned way.

The question of how the system determines that the event occurred may be harder to answer. An obvious possibility is that some dataflow from the terminator to the system will signal that the event has occurred. Another possibility is that the system will assume that the event has occurred periodically, based on some prior communication from the terminator. The book club may decide that when a person wants to join, he or she has explicitly or implicitly made the following requests:

- I want to be informed monthly which books are available.

- I want to receive a selected book once a month unless I tell you otherwise.

- I want to be told how much I owe each time you ship me a book.

A different possibility is that the system may conclude that an event has occurred by collecting information about other events. The book club may conclude that members want a book not yet offered on the basis of new book information from suppliers and a history of orders for books in the same category. Although the mechanism is very indirect, the connection is very strong. It simply wouldn't make sense for the club to announce a book without a good probability that the members will want the book. Therefore, the basic reasoning that triggers a book announcement is, "Members want the books offered in this announcement."

By building event lists, we can examine existing systems by investigating how their current inputs and outputs relate to their basic purposes. It will help you see if perhaps something the system does is irrelevant or even inimical to its purpose. The method provides a comprehensive way to enhance existing systems or build new ones while staying close to the essentials.

13.5 Event description format

Since the event list will be used to create a detailed model of the system, it's important that it contain all relevant information. Event descriptions should be as complete as possible. For example, if the event involves making a request or providing information, the nature of the request or of the information should be spelled out. Saying that a member orders an available book, or a member wishes to have an available book is more informative than saying that an order is placed. It's also useful to indicate what prompted the event to occur, if that is related to the system's purpose. For example, stating that a member orders a book after learning what books are available gives some useful additional information.

13.6 Summary

The system definition and the external event descriptions provide detailed information about the environment in which the system operates. Together with the context schema, the definition and event descriptions constitute a complete environmental model.

In the next chapter, we'll examine how this environmental model can be used as the basis for a model of the system's behavior.

Chapter 13: Reference

1. J. Palmer and S. McMenamin, *Essential Systems Analysis* (New York: Yourdon Press, 1984).

The basic concepts of event modeling are described in detail.

14

Deriving the Schematic Behavior Model

Systems do the work they do and store the data they store in order to accomplish within their environment the purposes for which they were created. The environmental model, constructed as described in the previous two chapters, describes both the system's purpose and its surroundings. It thus serves as an excellent starting point from which to build a model of the system's behavior. The behavioral model is best built from the top down, with a schematic level to show the overall layout first, and descriptions of the lower-level details following. This chapter addresses the building of the schematic level.

Although building a schematic model for a complex system takes time, thought, and careful planning, the basics of the schematic model couldn't be simpler. Let's review the fundamental ideas: The process schema and the data schema contain only four symbols: circles, arrows, three-sided figures, and diamonds. We have seen that by combining these symbols, we can describe all elements of any system. The circle, which represents a process, indicates some work that is done. The arrow, which represents a flow, describes something that gets worked on. The three-sided figure, which represents a store, indicates a repository for something that is worked on. The diamond, which represents a relationship, connects whatever is stored.

Processes, flows, stores, and relationships are important in everyday life, and have nothing specific to do with computers. Even when only data is being worked on and stored, the majority of human activities involve all these elements. We are constantly doing work on facts, remembering them, recalling them, extracting new facts from old, making and using connections between facts. Since facts are important in themselves and also are required for carrying out many activities, the store symbol is used by both the process and data schemas.

The distinction between the process and data schemas is not based on computer technology, although similar distinctions are made there. Instead, it is drawn from the fundamental human distinction between doing and knowing. Although most things done by humans involve both knowing and doing, some activities involve a greater degree of knowing than do others. In these activities, the making and using of connections between facts is of primary importance. Let me illustrate my point: Certain African tribes have a man called a *griot*, whose role it is to remember stories (both those passed on from earlier generations and those occurring in his lifetime) and to retell them. Describing what a griot does (listen and talk) is not particularly enlightening. It is what the griot *knows* that is of interest. Conversely, most people are more interested in what a professional athlete *does* than in what he or she knows.

The model building process is greatly facilitated if the distinction between doing and knowing — that is, between process and data — is kept in mind. Clearly, this distinction occurs in the patterns that are incorporated into computers just as it does in storytelling, sports, and all other areas of human experience.

14.1 Systems with dominant schemas

Among systems found in typical organizations, the closest analogue to the griot is the inquiry/response or database system. Like the griot, its job is to remember things and then recall them on demand. Consider a system that stores and retrieves information about articles published in technical journals. Such a system might be found in a college library, to assist students writing research papers. A student can request all the articles on taxation published in the *Harvard Business Review* between 1979 and 1981, all the articles on quarks published by authors affiliated with Stanford University, and so on. Notice that I haven't indicated that the system is computerized, although it certainly could be. A system operated by librarians using index card files would be modeled in the same way. What would a schematic model of such a system look like? One can easily draw a generic process schema for such a system, and Figure 14.1 depicts one such generic representation.

Figure 14.1. Generic process schema for database system.

Unfortunately, Figure 14.1 isn't really very helpful. The more detailed process schema of Figure 14.2 is better, but still isn't what we need. This model focuses on the processes that store and retrieve the data, but anyone knows without looking at a model that systems such as this *must* store and retrieve information. We need a schematic model that tells us more. The really interesting thing about this system is *the questions it will answer.*

Although some information can be extracted from the process schema shown in Figure 14.2, the information has not been presented in a form that is easy to see and to comprehend. In contrast, study the data schema of Figure 14.3. By starting at the stores and tracing through the relationships to other stores, you can easily learn about the questions the system will answer.

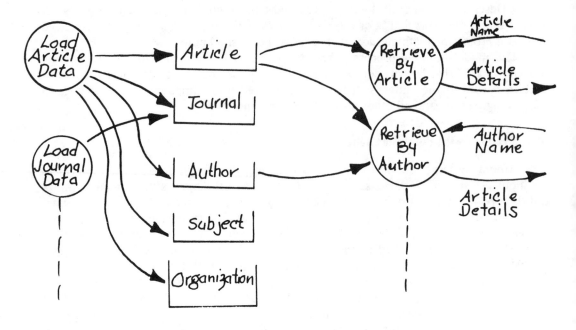

Figure 14.2. Process schema for literature search system.

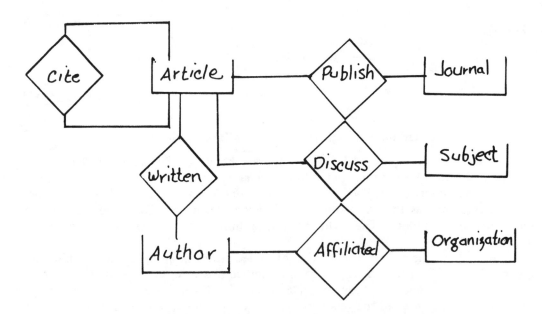

Figure 14.3. Data schema for literature search system.

For example, you can learn which articles were written by a particular author, which articles appeared in a particular journal, and which other articles were cited in a given article. You can even learn about an author's organizational affiliation. A succinct way to express the points just made is to say that the literature search system is *dominated* by its data schema.

There are also systems that are dominated by their process schemas. Consider the yearly income tax calculation modeled in Figure 14.4. The data for this calculation shows up all at once, wends its way through the system, and emerges at the other end, leaving no internal traces. (A system of this type *could* store data about its calculations; it just happens that this one doesn't.) The only store in this model is the one called Tax Tables; I'll let you figure out for yourself what the data schema for this system would look like, and why it's not worth drawing.

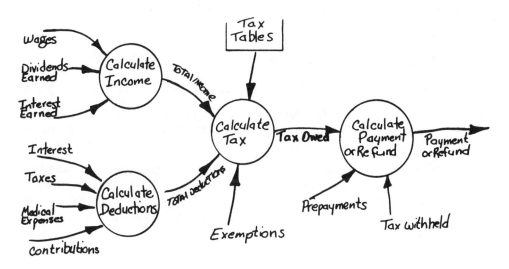

Figure 14.4. Yearly income tax process schema.

From the preceding discussion comes our strategy for building the behavioral model from the context schema and the event list. If the system falls at one extreme or the other (a trivial process schema or a trivial data schema), then only a single schema need be built. If both schemas are nontrivial but one or the other dominates, the dominant one should be built first: The dominant schema identifies the nature of the system, and will provide assistance in building the other schema. Of course, if both schemas are of approximately equal importance, either one can be built first or the two can be built together.

But how can the dominant schema be predicted in advance? It's actually not very difficult. Let's work backward from the literature search system of Figures 14.2 and 14.3 to discover what the event list must have contained. There would have been a group of events involving the arrival of data to be stored: For example, "Data about article is available," or "Data about journal is available." There would also have been a group of events involving questions asked of the system, such as "Student wants to know what articles were written by an author" or "Student wants to know what articles appeared in a journal." A possible variation on this would be a system that issued periodic reports on its stored data. In this case, the questions would be presumed to have been asked at some regular interval.

To discover which schema will dominate a system, look for events of the kinds described above. If they are in the majority, the data schema dominates the system. If they are in the minority or if the system only deals with a few types of input data (so that the interconnections can't be too complex), the process schema dominates.

14.2 Deriving the process schema

The procedure for building the process schema has four steps. I'll explain each of the steps, using the tax reporting system from Figure 12.1 to illustrate the process. The process schema may be presumed to dominate in this system, since there is only one input dataflow. The events for this system follow:

Event 1: The IRS needs to know how much profit the company made.

Event 2: The IRS needs to know what employees earned.

Event 3: The employees need to know what they earned.

Event 4: The accounting system has profit and loss data ready.

Now let's look at the four steps in the procedure for building our process schema:

Step 1: Draw a bubble for each event, naming the bubble according to what response the system will make when the event occurs. Use the definition of the system to determine exactly what the response should be.

The result of Step 1 for the tax system is shown in Figure 14.5; the number of the corresponding event is shown on each bubble. Don't forget that the behavioral model describes what happens *inside* the system, not what happens outside. By the way, the Store Profit And Loss Data bubble simply stores data because the system can't use it until it's time to issue the reports.

Figure 14.5. Step 1: Tax reporting process schema.

Step 2: Attach the input and output flows and stores from the context schema to the bubbles. To identify the appropriate connections, for each bubble ask the question, What data are needed by this response, and what data are produced?

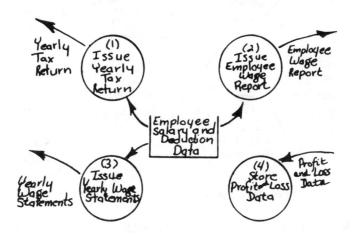

Figure 14.6. Step 2: Tax reporting process schema.

Figure 14.6 shows the result of the second step. In order to complete this step, you may need to have some knowledge about the details of the processes; for example, the stored data about employee salaries and deductions needs to be incorporated into all the outputs.

Step 3: Fill in any additional data stores that are needed. (A data store is needed when the response to one event needs data about another event.)

Figure 14.7 shows that the Issue Yearly Tax Return process needs data from the Store Profit And Loss Data process. Since events can occur at different times, all connections added in this step are necessarily delayed. The processes that need stored data inputs can be identified by applying the "no magic outputs" test: Does each bubble have sufficient input data to produce the output data shown? If the answer is no, the event from which the extra data is available must be identified, and a data store connection made. If the system is at all complicated, it may be difficult to identify stored data categories. If so, plug in a general-purpose data store, attach it to all the bubbles requiring extra data, and leave the cleanup till the next step.

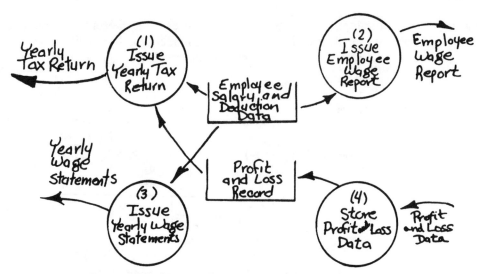

Figure 14.7. Step 3: Tax reporting process schema.

Step 4: Refine the process schema. This involves two parts: First, check the schema for mechanical errors. (The most likely errors are flows from the context schema that can't be assigned to processes, and processes that need data not available in the system's environment to produce their outputs. In both these cases, the event list or context schema is in error and must be corrected.) Second, check the schema for communication flaws. (If a process has a vague name, or seems to require excessively complicated stored data connections to produce its output, the event to which it responds may be ill defined. In such cases, the event needs to be replaced by two or more events that are more specific. If a data store has a vague or general-purpose name, it should be replaced by more specific stored data categories from the data schema.)

The tax reporting schema shown in Figure 14.7 is correct as it stands, and needs no refinement (except possibly if the output flows need some data other than Profit And Loss Record or Employee Salary And Deduction Data).

The example doesn't present much of a challenge. The names of the events strongly suggest the nature of the responses, and the system as a whole is so simple that it hardly requires such an elaborate procedure. Let's try a somewhat more complex system, the book club whose context schema was shown in Figure 13.4 and whose event list was given in Section 13.3. The event list contains some database entries: For example, the system collects data about new books available from suppliers (Event 4), and reports selected portions of it to the members (Event 7). Nevertheless, such events don't predominate, and building the process schema first is reasonable.

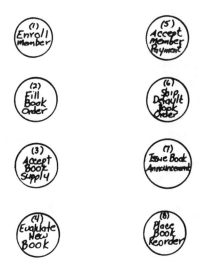

Figure 14.8. Step 1: Book club process schema.

The result of applying Step 1 to the book club environmental model is shown in Figure 14.8. Applying Step 2 results in Figure 14.9. Notice that the Enroll Member process produces a Book Shipment output; the club gives new members a free book as an enrollment benefit. Speaking of book shipments, notice that three different processes create a Book Shipment output. You might be tempted to merge all the processes that create book shipments into a single bubble, or to send data from the Enroll Member bubble to the Fill Book Order bubble instead of issuing a shipment from Enroll Member. *Resist these temptations!* Anything you know about computer programming will probably be a bad influence as you build this type of model. The kind of generalization done when writing computer instructions is not appropriate here. The fact that some responses duplicate the work done by other responses will not cause any problems. In fact, the duplication is usually only partial.

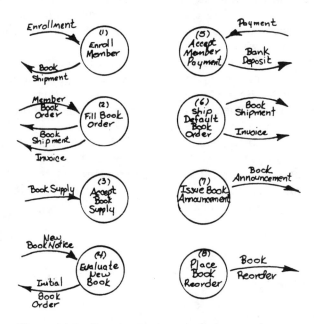

Figure 14.9. Step 2: Book club process schema.

Figure 14.10 shows the result of applying Step 3. Since books as well as data move through this system, a store for the books (called Shelves) is necessary. Filling in the other stores turns out to be fairly complicated. For example, Issue Book Announcement needs data from Enroll Member and also from Evaluate New Book. Rather than trying to work out these complications using the process schema, I have simply plugged in a database store and attached it to all the processes. A more detailed stored data breakdown will be obtained from the data schema.

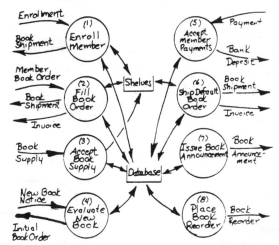

Figure 14.10. Step 3: Book club process schema.

Finally, the result of Step 4 is shown in Figure 14.11. An unaccounted-for flow on the context schema (No Book Order) has been found, leading to the correction of the event list to include "Member declines book shipment" and the addition of another process to the schema. Furthermore, the vaguely named Database store has been replaced by stores borrowed from the data schema, which we will build in the next section of this chapter. Filling in complex store connections on a process schema is much easier if a data schema is available. For each process, the question is not, What other events does this process need to know about or need to provide data for? but, What stores does this process need to get data from or give data to? The latter is generally an easier question to answer.

For example, the Enroll Member process clearly needs connections to the stored data about members. Since the system ships an available book to new members, a connection to the Available Book store is needed. However, there's no direct relationship between the member enrollment process and book suppliers, and thus no connection to the stored data about suppliers.

If you look ahead to the data schema in the next section of the chapter, you will see that the stores on Figure 14.11 don't correspond to the individual stores on the schema. They represent groups of stores; the grouping process is shown in Chapter 15. Even with this simplification, Figure 14.11 is a monster. Methods for simplifying data schemas are also covered in the next chapter.

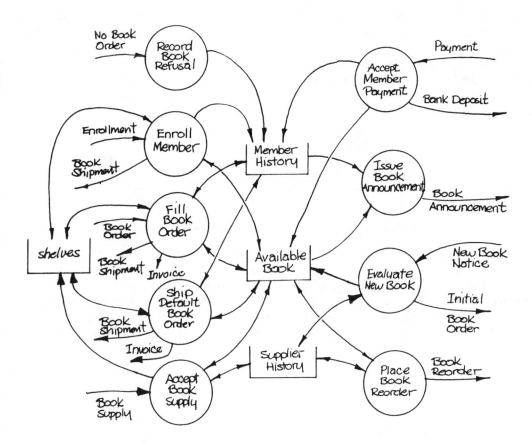

Figure 14.11. Step 4: Book club process schema.

14.3 Deriving the data schema

Let's assume that the data schema for a system is dominant, or that the process schema has already been built. The procedure for building the data schema has four steps. Since the data schema for the tax reporting is too simple to be interesting, let's use the book club example. Look again at Figure 13.4, and the event list given in Section 13.3.

Step 1: Build a data schema fragment for each event. Use the nouns in the event description as stores and the verbs as relationships. Keep in mind, however, that nouns describing groups of stores, instances of stores, data elements, values of data elements, and the like may be found in the descriptions, and that judgment must be exercised. Also keep in mind that grammatical constructions that are not formally verbs may play the role of verbs, and are valid candidates for relationships.

The first event on the book club list is, "A potential member wishes to enroll." This sentence is incomplete. What does the potential member wish to enroll in? The essence of this sentence is that a member enrolls in a book club, and the associated fragment of data schema is shown in Figure 14.12. Does it make sense that a book club system would have a stored data category called Book Club? If the system being studied keeps records for more than one book club, it would make perfect sense. The questions, Which book club does this member belong to? and, Who are the members of this book club? then become essential. However, the system being studied deals with only a single book club, and so the fragment of schema derived from this event is simply the Member store. (That's why the sentence was incomplete.)

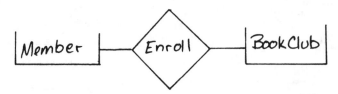

Figure 14.12. Step 1: Event 1, book club data schema.

The second event is straightforward. The sentence essentially is, "Member orders book," and yields the stores Member and Book linked by the relationship Order.

The third event, "A supply of books arrives from a book supplier in response to a book order," is a little trickier. This sentence could be just as well stated, "A book supplier supplies books in response to a book order." Is Supply a store or a relationship? For now, I'll use it as a relationship, but I'll return to the issue in the next step.

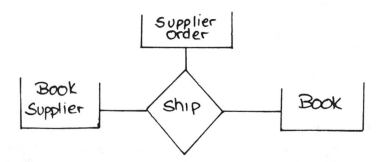

Figure 14.13. Step 1: Event 3, book club data schema.

Figure 14.13 translates Event 3 into a data schema fragment. I've replaced Supply by Ship, and changed the name Book Order to Supplier Order. The name change is necessary because the term Book Order is ambiguous, since it can refer to books ordered from the supplier by the club, or to books ordered from the club by the customer. Note that Event 6, "A member has ordered a book by default," will cause the system to store data as though the member has ordered the book; the schema needs no additions for this event. Note also that the event that is missing from the list, "Member declines book shipment," isn't about a connection between a member and a specific book. The member is refusing the shipment of any book. The information that a refusal has taken place is data about a member, and need not appear on the schema.

Step 2: Identify stores that can serve as relationships and relationships that can serve as stores. Look for terms that can be used in both noun and verb forms.

This situation has already been encountered in the third event; the word "supply" can be a verb or a noun. This is more than a grammatical peculiarity; the data schema concerns itself with both things (stores) and happenings (relationships). The event list contains the subject matter vocabulary relevant to the system's environment, and thus is a source for those things and happenings. Certain nouns, like "book," are irrevocably things. Words such as "supply" can be either things or happenings. Identifying these terms ensures that the model will be as complete as possible. Instead of the word "supply," I've incorporated its equivalent into the model: "ship" as the verb or "shipment" as its noun form. Other terms of this type are "to order" and "order," "to bill" and "invoice," and "to pay" and "payment."

Applying Step 2 to the second event, "Member wishes to order a book," results in the revised schema shown in Figure 14.14.

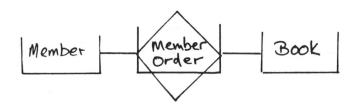

Figure 14.14. Step 2: Event 2, book club data schema.

Step 3: Assemble the fragments into a single data schema. Change names as necessary to prevent ambiguity; no two stores or relationships should have the same name.

Assembling the pieces results in Figure 14.15. Like Figure 14.11, this is a rather monstrous diagram, but the guidelines for simplifying it will be presented in the next chapter.

Step 4: Refine the data schema, using the guidelines discussed in Chapter 8. In particular, drop any store out of the model for which there's no stored data of interest to the system. Then, check for overly general stores. Try some sample data elements to see if they describe all instances of the store; if not, split the store as necessary.

14.4 Summary

If an environmental model is available, a schematic model of a system's behavior can be derived fairly easily. In this chapter, we have presented rules for carrying out the derivation.

The topic of the next chapter is completion of the essential model, and focuses on building the detailed level of the behavioral model.

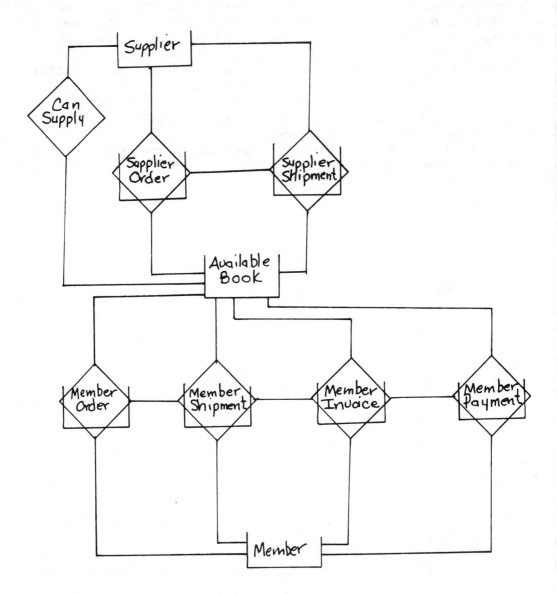

Figure 14.15. The complete book club data schema.

Chapter 14: Reference

1.   J. Palmer and S. McMenamin, *Essential Systems Analysis* (New York: Yourdon Press, 1984).

The authors address ways to translate an event list into a process model.

15

Completing the Essential Model

A preliminary model of the system's behavior can be created from the context schema, system definition, and external event descriptions as shown in the previous chapter. This model shows in schematic form the network of processes that do the work of the system, and the network of facts that form its memory. Let us now turn this preliminary schematic picture into a complete essential model of the system. We will do this first by reorganizing the preliminary schemas for maximum clarity and readability, and then by filling in the lower-level details of the system's behavior.

15.1 Leveling the preliminary model

In the previous chapter, the diagram in Figure 14.15 describing the book club's data schema was overly complicated. The number of elements clearly exceeds the half-dozen that can be absorbed by the right-brain communication channel. To reduce the complexity, we need to apply the techniques for leveling a data schema that were described in Chapter 11.

The leveling process involves finding a group of stores that are tightly connected to one another and loosely connected to the other stores. The group containing Supplier, Supplier Order, Supplier Shipment, and Available Book seems to qualify. The only connection of this group to the rest of the schema is through the Available Book store. Therefore, Supplier, Supplier Order, and Supplier Shipment will be represented as a single higher-level store. Available Book is excluded from the group since it serves as the connection to the rest of the schema. Using similar reasoning, Member, Member Order, Member Shipment, Member Invoice, and Member Payment will form a high-level group. The two groupings make sense in terms of the system's subject matter as well as in terms of their connections. One group involves dealings with suppliers, and one involves dealings with members. The names Supplier History and Member History will be given to the high-level stores.

Figure 15.1 shows the results of the grouping. The unnamed relationship between Member History and Available Book represents all the relationships *among* the lower-level stores in Member History as well as all the relationships between these stores and Available Book. Figures 15.2 and 15.3 depict the lower-level pieces of the data schema; they were formed by separating Figure 14.15 into two pieces around Available Book.

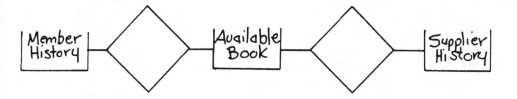

Figure 15.1. Book club data schema at the system level.

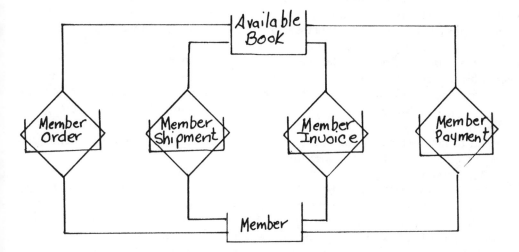

Figure 15.2. The Member/Book segment of the book club data schema.

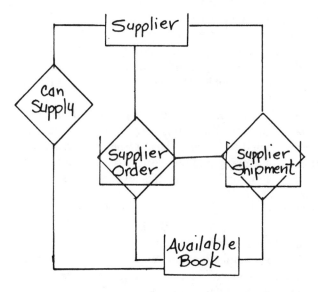

Figure 15.3. The Book/Supplier segment of the book club data schema.

Now that the composition of Supplier History and Member History has been explained, you might wish to re-examine Figure 14.11 to assure yourself that the process-to-store connections make sense. For example, Evaluate New Book is connected to both the Supplier History and the Available Book stores because it must form the Supplier Order relationship between these two stores.

Figure 14.11, which describes the processes carried out by the book club, is even more complicated than the data schema. Counting processes and stores, it contains thirteen elements. To remedy the situation, the procedure of leveling will be used to lump together processes, flows, and stores.

One of the guidelines for the essential model is that the connections between the processes should be as simple as possible. Therefore, the strategy for lumping will be to pull together processes that are tightly connected and to separate processes that are loosely connected. Since all the processes in Figure 14.11 are connected to each other through data stores, we try to combine processes in such a way that stores are eliminated from the diagram. For example, there are four processes (Enroll Member, Fill Book Order, Ship Default Book Order, and Accept Book Supply) that are connected to the store called Shelves. Lumping these four processes together would allow the Shelves store to be hidden, since it would no longer serve as a connection between processes. A different possibility would be to lump together into a single process all the processes connected to the Available Book store. We compare the resultant process schemas for complexity of connections and choose the simpler one.

There is another way of lumping processes that produces a simpler diagram than either of the two just mentioned. All the processes are connected either to the Member History store or to the Supplier History store, but none is connected to both. Lumping all the bubbles from the first group into a single high-level bubble, and doing the same for the bubbles in the second group, will allow hiding both the Member History and the Supplier History stores. Think of the leveling process in the following way: First, snip Figure 14.11 into two pieces, one containing Member History and all the bubbles connected to it, the other containing Supplier History and all its connected processes. Since Shelves and Available Book are used by bubbles in both groups, copies of these two stores must be carried on both pieces. Each piece of the original figure is a child diagram. On a separate sheet of paper, draw two bubbles, making each the parent of one child diagram. Copy all the external flows (those not having connections at both head and tail) from each child diagram onto its parent bubble. Copy the connections between the parent bubbles through the Shelves and Available Book stores as well.

All the bubbles sharing the Member store have something to do with providing books to members; that's not surprising, given the purpose of the system. Likewise, all the processes that are connected to Supplier History relate to procuring books from suppliers. The fact that each of these groupings performs a single function provides an obvious way to name them, and confirms that the leveling is reasonable in terms of the system's subject matter.

Figures 15.4, 15.5, and 15.6 show the results of leveling. Not only are processes lumped, but so are flows. The Enrollment, Book Order, No Book Order, and Payment flows have been joined into a single flow called Member Transaction. A similar grouping has been applied to communications to members and to supplier orders. Figure 15.5 is still rather complicated since it has nine elements. As an exercise, you might try regrouping it and pushing the details to a lower level.

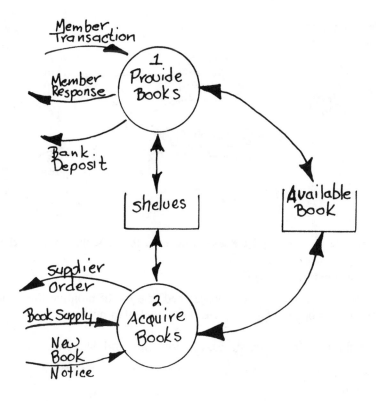

Figure 15.4. Book club process schema at the system level.

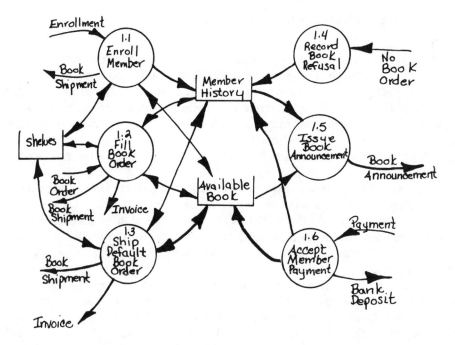

Figure 15.5. The Provide Books segment of the book club process schema.

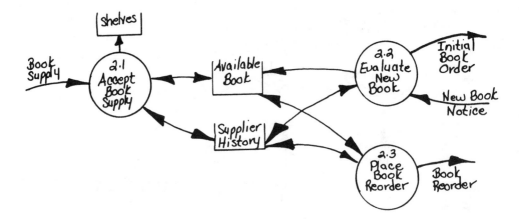

Figure 15.6. The Acquire Books segment of the book club process schema.

15.2 Filling in lower-level details

Once the schemas have been reorganized, the job of building the remainder of the essential model can begin. To complete the model, it is necessary to add

- definitions for flows, stores, relationships, and data elements;

- composition descriptions for flows, stores, relationships, and data elements;

- lower-level process schemas for any bubble whose process description can't be written in a page or less; and

- process descriptions for all low-level bubbles.

The actual work of creating these pieces of the model will be quite different for revising an existing system than it will be for building a brand-new system. For a new system, the lower level of the essential model literally must be *invented*. For example, it will be necessary to determine what's important about each stored data category, and to select data elements that will describe or measure these things of importance. It will also be necessary to select the rules for each process that transforms input flows into output flows, and to build lower-level process schemas when these rules become too long. Identifying an intermediate flow will often help you partition a schema into lower-level schemas.

Although most systems development efforts involve some changing of the system's behavior and thus some inventing of lower-level details, they typically incorporate existing behavior into the model. This incorporation involves gathering of information rather than inventing of details, and thus can be approached in a more systematic fashion. The process and data schemas can be of immense value in guiding this information gathering.

Now let's look at a typical information gathering task carried out *without* the guidance of high-level schemas. Consider an insurance company that sells various types of policies (health, property, or business failure, for example). One strategy for building a detailed model of this company's claim handling system would be to visit its departments one by one, creating a data schema for each department. Figure 15.7 shows a model developed for the Claim Verification Department. The question marks on the output dataflows emphasize that these are loose ends; in many organizations, departments perform only fractions of an overall task, and pass uncompleted work to other departments. Notice the disconnected nature of the processes on this schema. The processes are more closely related to processes carried out in other departments than they are to each other. The schema as a whole is thus not very illuminating.

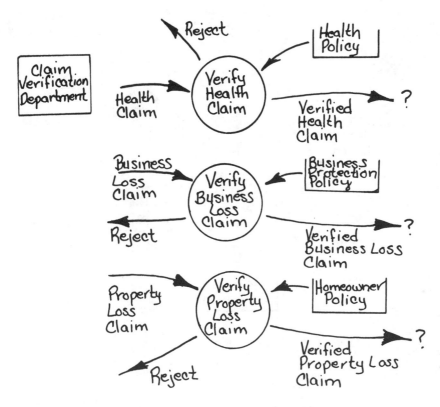

Figure 15.7. Geographical approach to gathering information.

Let's now assume that a high-level schema for the policy handling system is available. Figure 15.8 shows one of the processes from this schema. It's the response to the external event, "Policyholder submits health claim." This process tells us that the system contains lower-level processes that accept or reject health claims, use stored data about health policies and store data about payments and health statistics, and create health claim payments. Notice that this information was derived not from low-level details, but from an examination of the purpose of the system and its connections to its environment. Given its basic character, the system simply *has* to do these things. In particular, this information does depend on the way the pieces of the job are split among people and departments.

This high-level process can be used to organize a search for details that is quite different from the geographical approach of modeling office by office. You start the search by identifying the place where the health claim enters the system; this turns out to be the Claim Verification Department. Instead of modeling everything done by the department, the searcher need only find out *what happens to the health claim*. In this case, it's checked against the health policy file, and either rejected or passed on as a Verified Health Claim. Having determined this, the searcher can serenely ignore everything else in the department and *follow the Verified Health Claim.* As shown in Figure 15.9, this process leads the information gatherer through two other departments and finally to a halt. There are no loose ends here; all outputs and all uses of stored data shown on the high-level process have been accounted for. The three processes discovered in this fashion constitute the child diagram for the Satisfy Health Claim process.

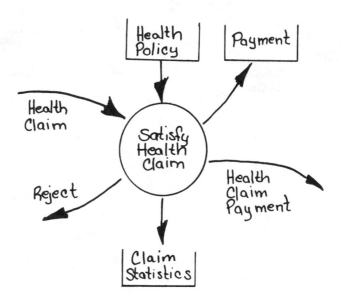

Figure 15.8. Event response from process schema.

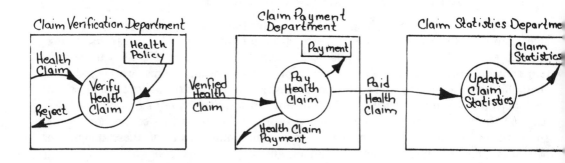

Figure 15.9. Flow approach to gathering information.

There is little danger of overlooking information when using this method. The activities in the three departments that were ignored in this part of the model will be picked up as the lower-level details of some other high-level process, *if they are relevant to the work of the system.* Otherwise, they need not be studied at all and will be bypassed.

This method of collecting information will undoubtedly require more moving around (by a single searcher) or more coordination (among several searchers focusing on different parts of the organization) than the geographical approach. However, the payoffs in avoiding unnecessary details and creating a well-organized model are immense.

In Figure 15.9, the boxes drawn around the bubbles show in which departments the work was done. The model would be perfectly understandable without the department references; after all, it's meant to describe the essentials of the system. However, knowledge of where activities are carried out is useful, since it can aid in verifying that the model has captured the details correctly. For example, a model with department references can be reviewed with the supervisors of those departments for accuracy. Rather than drawing boxes around bubbles as in Figure 15.9, you could insert a location reference under the process name.

Department references are only one method for tagging process schemas to show where the details are to be found in the real system. As illustrated in Figure 15.10, flows and stores may be tagged in a similar way. Models created with tags of this kind are somewhat messier than pure essential models; the tags might well be dropped from the model once their purpose is accomplished.

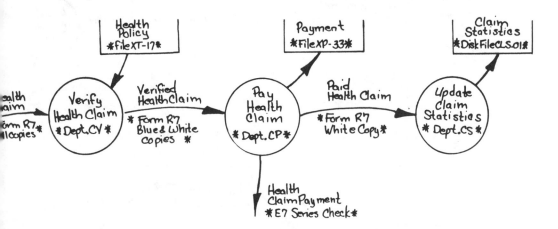

Figure 15.10. Tagging processes, stores, and flows.

Remember that in building an essential model by extracting details from an existing system, neat correspondence between the actual files, forms, and transactions and the flows and stores from the essential schematic model isn't very likely. As the model builder, you are likely to find two or more flows lumped together on a single form, a single flow split between two or more forms, data from several stores lumped into a single file, or data from a single store split between two or more files.

The data schema can be used to disentangle data storage details from the existing files for incorporation into the model. When confronted by a process that uses stored data from an existing file, you should determine which data elements from the file are used by the process, and then use the data schema to identify which stores these data elements describe. Next, draw a bubble for the process and attach the stores from the data schema, tagging them with the name of the actual file used. Finally, add the data elements to the composition descriptions for the stores. Models built in this way contain implementation details, but they are not organized around those implementation details. Descriptions of people, departments, form numbers, and so on are reduced to comments, so they don't interfere with the model's organization.

There are other kinds of implementation details encountered in actual systems, which are somewhat less obvious than departments and form numbers. One example of this is a system in which dataflows change form. These changed flows constitute implementation details and should be included in an essential model only as comments. Figure 15.11 shows some low-level details of the book club's Enroll Member process. Neither the Load Enrollments process nor the Diskette store relate to the essentials of the system. Changing the diskette to a deck of punch cards or loading Form X9 directly to the Member store wouldn't change the system's purpose or its response to external events. Therefore, the details should be reduced to comments as shown in Figure 15.12. (Temporary stores and changes of form like the ones illustrated tend to occur together. However, temporary stores alone and changes of form alone should be reduced to comments in the same way.)

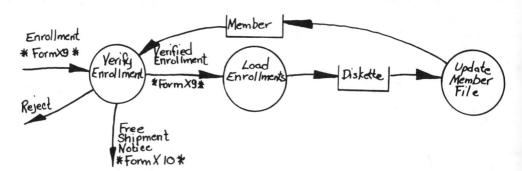

Figure 15.11. Modeling temporary storage and form changes.

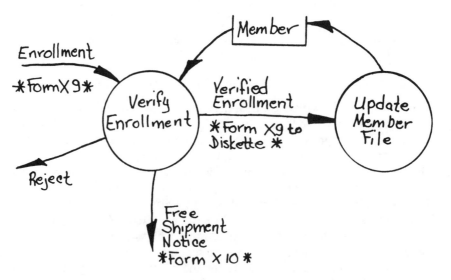

Figure 15.12. Tagging temporary storage and form changes.

Error checking within a system is implementation dependent and should be modeled only as a comment. Figure 15.13 represents another selection of details from the book club's Enroll Member process. The Free Shipment Notice, which is created in Department A, is checked for correctness as it enters Department B, and rejected if incorrect. The points at which such checking is appropriate in actual systems depend heavily on how the systems are implemented. The best way to model this situation is shown in Figure 15.14. Note that the checking of data that enters a system from the outside world is *not an implementation detail*. Since the system has no control over the creation of this data, any implementation would need to verify its correctness.

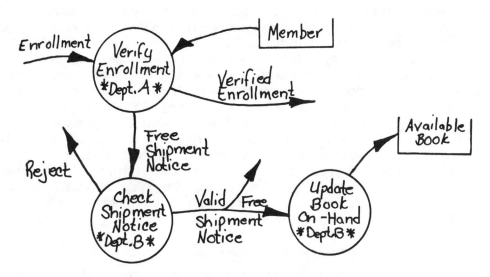

Figure 15.13. Modeling internal editing.

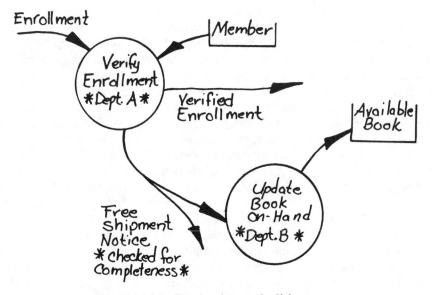

Figure 15.14. Tagging internal editing.

Most of the examples in this chapter have pertained to existing manual systems. Modeling the low-level details of an existing automated system is no different in principle, but the practical problems of information gathering are quite different.

It's only fair to begin by asking why a non-data-processing person should get involved in modeling an automated system. There certainly are situations in which such involvement *isn't* necessary. Moving a system from an old computer to a new one without changing its behavior in any way is a job needing only knowledge of automated technology. However, it's very common for an existing automated system to have flaws and to need modification of its essentials as well as its implementation. Unfortunately, it's also common to discover that *no one in an organization actually knows what an existing automated system does* because of poor or nonexistent documentation. In cases such as these, the non-data-processing people who provide the inputs and use the outputs will benefit from participating in the development effort.

The ideal way to approach such a situation is to ask someone from the data processing department to build an essential model of the automated portion of the system. However, as a last resort, a user project team might have to interview data processing people about the functioning of an automated system, taking care to bypass the technical details and to get a grip on the essentials of the processes and stored data.

At the other extreme from automated systems are activities that require human judgment. If the choice is made to include such activities in the model, one must recognize that complete process descriptions cannot be written for them. Either omit the process description or write a rough summary, noting that the process can't be completely modeled. In either case, add a comment to the corresponding bubble on the process schema.

15.3 Verifying the correctness of the model

After the essential model has been completed, use the balancing processes described in Chapter 11 to verify its mechanical correctness. A model that is reasonably large or that was created by two or more people is almost certain to have consistency errors that need to be discovered and corrected.

After the model has been shown to be mechanically consistent, its adequacy as a description of system behavior should be checked. One vehicle for this checking is the *playthrough*. The playthrough takes advantage of the fact that the essential model has game characteristics such as those described in Chapter 4. Several people are required to conduct a playthrough. Each person is assigned to play one or more of the low-level processes in the essential model. In addition, one person acts as the overall manager of the game, and one person is given the job of recording any problems that are identified.

The key role in the playthrough is not that of player, however, but that of creator of the scenario or script, which guides the playing. The job of the script's creator(s) is to demonstrate that the model is *wrong*. This is done by creating a script for which the model fails to predict what the system will do, or for which the model predicts that the system will misbehave. Although this sounds rather nasty, a resourceful scriptwriter can provide an invaluable service to a development project. An error discovered while a system is still in the form of an essential model is relatively cheap to correct. An error discovered after the system has been implemented can be disastrously expensive.

A script consists of a statement of initial conditions and a list of events. The statement of initial conditions may include a description of what data is stored within the system, for example, or the time the game starts. The listed events should be more specific than those given on an external event list, and should describe not only which dataflow occurs, but also the values of the data elements. In order to play through the script, the manager of the playthrough needs a copy of the script and a copy of the essential model; the other players need copies of the process descriptions for the processes they're playing. Dataflows and data stores are simulated by information written on paper. Suppose the following script was used to check the segment of the book club's essential model shown in Figure 15.12.

Initial   Member store contains the data
conditions: "Jerry Jones, 100 Elm St., Peoria, IL"

Event: Enrollment arrives from Jerry Jones, 100 Elm St., Peoria, IL

The manager of the playthrough first would consult the model to determine which process should receive the enrollment dataflow, write the data on a sheet of paper, and hand it to the appropriate player. The player would then carry out the instructions in his or her process description.

If the process receiving the enrollment was Verify Enrollment and the process description required checking the Member store for an already existing enrollment with the same name and address, the enrollment would be rejected. Otherwise, Jerry Jones would get a second free book and the model would have failed.

After being used to check and correct the model, the scripts should not be discarded. They should be attached to the model, along with a description of what the model predicts the system will do under the script. When the system is implemented, these scripts will serve as acceptance tests. In order to pass muster, the system must behave as the model predicts it will when the script is fed to it.

15.4 Summary

The essential model is complete when the preliminary schematic model has been reorganized by leveling and when the lower-level details of processes and data have been filled in. This chapter has provided guidelines for carrying out these tasks in an organized fashion.

In the final chapter of Part 3 we will treat the implementation model.

16

Beginning the Implementation Model

When completed, the essential model is a comprehensive description of the required behavior of a system. The intended users of this system may have organized and directed the model building, or they may have worked under the direction of data processing personnel. Whatever the form of the development effort, the intended users clearly have a major concern with the details of the essential model.

The essential model cannot be used as a blueprint for creating the hardware and software configuration that will actually do the work of the system. It must first be developed into an implementation model, through reorganization and expansion. The low-level technical details, which must be added to describe the implementation, are not of direct concern to the users. However, there are some features of the implementation that are very much of concern to users. For example, a decision to lease or purchase a new computer rather than incorporate the system into an existing one may substantially raise the cost of implementing the system. Or, the selection of a network of computers located at remote sites rather than a single centralized computer can drastically affect the accessibility of certain data to certain users. Or, the presence or absence of direct user access via terminals with keyboards and display screens, and the details of the possible interactions, can sometimes determine whether the system is workable in practice.

These high-level implementation decisions normally cannot be made by non-data processing experts without technical assistance, and should not be made by the data processing experts without user input. Therefore, the beginnings of the implementation model require a close collaboration between those who will use the system and those who will direct its building.

16.1 Implementation guidelines

The architect Louis Sullivan stated, "Form ever follows function."* This could be paraphrased as, "The solution should have the same organization as the problem," or if

---

*L. Sullivan, "The Tall Office Building Artistically Considered," *Lippincott's Magazine,* March 1896.

we tailor his words to correspond to our specific needs, "The implementation model should look as much as possible like the essential model."

One major reason for distorting the essential model as little as possible when developing the implementation is to keep the system maintainable. Almost all systems regularly require some revision after they become operational. If the implemented system is organized along the same lines as the essential model, an individual group of computer instructions can be traced back to a process description in the essential model. A user can thus formulate a request for system maintenance by referring to the essential model, such as "Please change the process description of Bubble 2.3.1 from xxx to yyy."

Not all difficulties with system maintenance, of course, are caused because instructions can't be traced. Sometimes limitations in the existing technology (for example, file or record size limitations) make changes difficult to accomplish. However, the traditional conflict between the user who wants to make a "small change" and the data processing professional who insists that the request requires a major revision is often preventable. Responsibility for the problems with maintenance lies with both users and data processing professionals, for the following two reasons: The users aren't sufficiently aware of organizational patterns to formulate maintenance requests coherently, and the existing automated implementations aren't faithful to organizational patterns and thus are unnecessarily awkward to modify. The building of an essential model, and the following of the model's organization in the implemented system, helps correct both these problems.

Another argument for organizing the implementation along the lines of the essential model is that it minimizes interface complexity. In general, the connections among the pieces of a complex mechanism are its weakest links. The relatively low prices of many modern technological gadgets are due to their modularity. Connections are designed to be simple, so that a malfunctioning component can be unplugged and replaced. Let's look at the modularity of the essential model to see how it makes implementation easier.

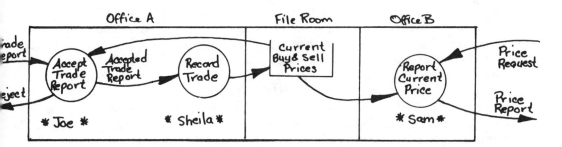

Figure 16.1. Trading information center.

Figure 16.1 describes a small organization that keeps track of stock market activity and maintains data about current trading prices. Since Sheila must update the central file each time Joe accepts a trading report, they must coordinate their activities closely; that's no big problem, since they work in the same office. There's no need for Joe and Sheila to coordinate their activities with Sam, whose work is triggered by price requests. In fact, Sam never even has to talk to Joe and Sheila. He simply needs to get out of the file the information they put in. If Sam is taking a nap because it's a slow day for price requests, Joe and Sheila will not even know, much less be affected.

Now consider the effect of moving Sheila from office A to office B. Figure 16.2 indicates that the connection between office A and office B now involves not only the file that Joe uses to verify trade reports, but also the passing of trade reports between Joe and Sheila. Coordination is now necessary *between* the two offices. If Sheila is out for coffee when Joe arrives with a trading report, problems will ensue.

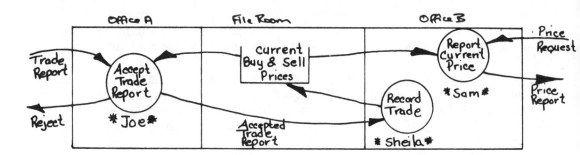

Figure 16.2. Modified trading information center.

In Figure 14.11, all the connections between event responses are through stores. This also is true of the situation in Figure 16.1; the absolute minimum of coordination between processes has been arranged. An implementation that followed the essential model would put all the pieces of an event response (for example, a single process from Figure 14.11) in a single computer, or better still, in the same computer program. Then the programs could communicate entirely through shared files; no coordination between them would be needed. On the other hand, an implementation that split pieces of the response to an event between two computers or two programs would be analogous to Figure 16.2. The operation of the programs or of the computers would have to be coordinated, and the possibility of an unwanted delay in the system's response to an external event would be increased.

Everything described so far in this section has been model-oriented; that is, we have looked at the problems of building a system strictly from the perspective of the essential model. There is another set of important criteria, which considers system building from the point of view of the capabilities of available technology, and suggests that the implementation should be guided not by "Form ever follows function" but by "Make the best use of the available resources." Unfortunately, model-oriented criteria and technology-oriented criteria often point in different directions. Let me give some examples: If the essential model contains transformations of material as well as of data, the processes that handle both data and material either must be assigned completely to a human (or possibly a robot), or must be split so that the material transformation parts are excluded from the automated portion of the system.

A second example is that the capacities of existing equipment may dictate splitting the pieces of an event response between two computers or two programs. Multipurpose computers often make the most efficient use of their resources by managing many small programs rather than a few large ones. This may dictate splitting the essential model into programs of a certain size rather than into programs that each carry out an event response.

In a third case, we see that if the people who communicate with the system are geographically dispersed, the costs and problems of transmitting large volumes of information may dictate a distribution of processing that violates the boundaries of the essential model. Suppose, for example, that a system needed to create an output in Chicago on the basis of an input in New York. It may be necessary in this case to split the pieces of the response between Chicago and New York computers so that the least amount of information has to be exchanged to complete the work.

The resolution of the conflict lies in an understanding of the overriding criterion for system building: Find the implementation that minimizes the overall lifetime costs of the system. The model-oriented implementation criteria increase the understandability of the implemented system, and therefore tend to minimize the testing and maintenance costs. The technology-oriented criteria tend to minimize the costs of implementation hardware and of normal operations, since they emphasize efficient use of resources. The total lifetime cost of a system includes both these factors. The graph in Figure 16.3 suggests that the best implementation strategy lies somewhere between a completely model-dominated strategy and a completely technology-dominated strategy. This intermediate point can be found only by careful examination of both the essential model and the technological environment.

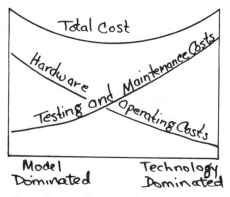

Figure 16.3. Factors of system cost.

16.2 Allocation of the essential model

The basic component of the essential model is the *event response,* a chunk of work that enables the system to deal with a stimulus from the outside world. The basic component of the implementation model is the *processor.* A processor is simply a person or machine capable of carrying out instructions and storing data. Computers of all sizes and shapes from pocket calculators on up fit this definition, but people of all sizes and shapes also fit this definition. Although most current-day systems development intends to automate systems, it's quite possible that the best implementation strategy will have some of the work carried out by people.

One of the first tasks of changing the essential model into a high-level implementation model is to repackage it by assigning the work of the system to processors. The choice of the processors and the decisions about which processes will be assigned to which processor are outside the scope of the modeling process. These activities involve cost and benefit analysis and evaluation of available technology rather than model building. Nevertheless, developing an implementation model will ease the choice of processors and the allocation of the processes, by permitting what's being done to be visualized and reviewed.

The amount of work required to repackage the model will vary greatly from project to project. At one extreme, everything inside the context diagram will be automated, and only a single computer used. In this case, no repackaging needs to be done;

the essential model and the repackaged implementation model are identical. At the other extreme, if several human processors and a network of computers will share the work of the system, the repackaging work will be extensive.

One easy way to think about repackaging is to imagine that the process schema of the essential model consists of tennis balls (the processes) connected by lengths of string (the flows and stores). Each processor that has been chosen to do some of the work of the system is represented by a bucket (Figure 16.4). The decision to assign a process to a processor is visualized as the tennis ball dropping into the appropriate bucket. Figure 16.5 shows the result of assigning processes 1 and 2 to processor A and assigning process 3 to processor B. The connection through store Y between processes 1 and 3 appears as a string looping out of one bucket and into the other one. In an actual implementation, a stored data connection between processors may be accomplished in one of two ways: Either the two processors must actually share access to a data storage device, or the data must be duplicated and a separate copy kept in each processor. In the latter case, the processors must be able to transfer data to each other in some way, and extra processes must be added to copy the stored data from one processor to the other, or to send updates to the data to both processors.

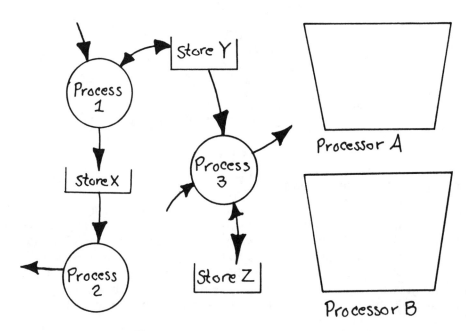

Figure 16.4. Imagining process repackaging.

The effect of repackaging on the data schema can also be thought of in terms of dropping things into buckets (Figure 16.6). Suppose that in Figure 16.5, process 1 creates relationships between store X and store Y, and process 3 creates relationships between store Y and store Z. This will cause a piece of the data schema containing stores X and Y and relationship R to be dropped into bucket A, and a piece containing stores Y and Z and relationship S to be dropped into bucket B. The results are shown in Figure 16.7.

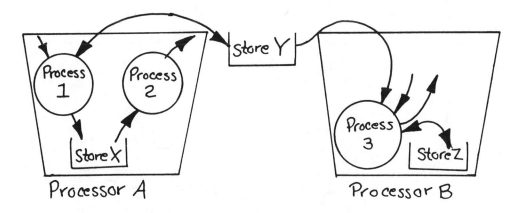

Figure 16.5. Result of a process repackaging.

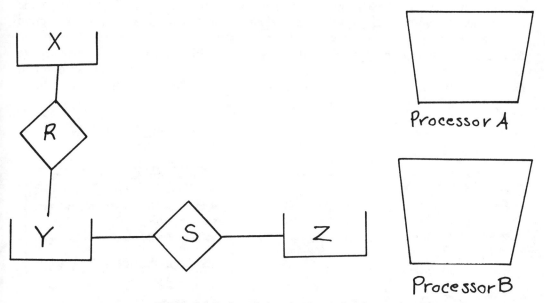

Figure 16.6. Imagining data repackaging.

The examples given in Figures 16.4 and 16.5 involved only stored data connections between processes. This would be the case if the pieces of the essential model being assigned to processors were event responses. If pieces of event responses must be split between processors, bubbles that are connected by flows rather than stores may end up being dropped into different buckets. Furthermore, if two bubbles are connected by a flow, the bubble producing the flow triggers the one receiving the flow. This means that the two processors must coordinate their activities so that when the first process produces an output, it will be sent with minimal delay to the second processor, which then must start up the second process.

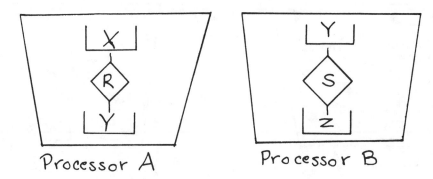

Figure 16.7. **Result of a data repackaging.**

The most extreme case of repackaging is the splitting of a single lowest-level bubble between two processors. Imagine that for some reason the income tax process represented by Figure 16.8 needed to be split between processors. The arrow on the process description reminds you that an intermediate result within a process description acts just like an internal dataflow. If the process bubble is torn in half, the process description must also be torn in half, as shown in Figure 16.9. Any intermediate results from the first half of the process description that are needed by the second half must show up as flows between the pieces of the bubble. The final result of the repackaging is illustrated in Figure 16.10.

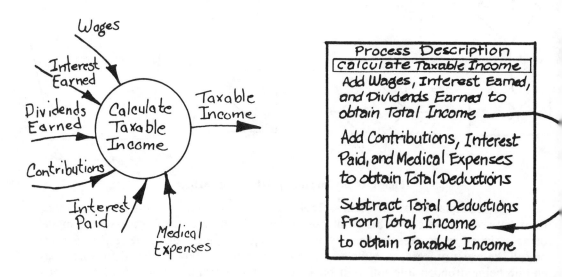

Figure 16.8. **Income tax process.**

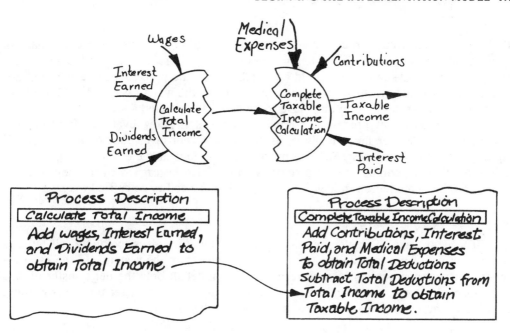

Figure 16.9. Splitting the income tax process.

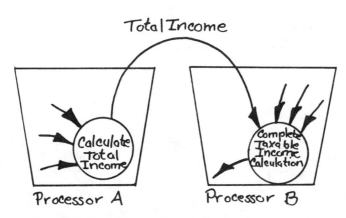

Figure 16.10. Repackaging the income tax process.

A data store must also be split in this way, if each of two processors needs a different subset of the data elements that described the original store. As in the case of a data store shared between processors, this will require some extra processes to maintain coordination between the two new stores.

The actual process of repackaging isn't quite as exotic as the imaginary description given above; it involves pencil, paper, transparent tape, and scissors rather than tennis balls and buckets. A large clean sheet of paper is used for each processor, with the processor name written at the top. Each time a piece of the essential model is assigned to a processor, the corresponding bubble is cut out and taped (or simply redrawn) on the sheet representing the processor.

The level of the essential model from which the bubble is taken depends on how much distortion the repackaging involves. If an entire system-level process is to be assigned to a single processor, the bubble is cut out of the system-level process schema. If a system-level process is to be split, the child diagram for that bubble is examined.

If the split doesn't cut through any of the child diagram's bubbles, the child diagram may be split in two and assigned to the processors. If there is a split at the subsystem level, the sub-subsystem level should be checked, and the process may be repeated until a level is reached at which no bubbles are split. In the worst case, a lower-level bubble and its process description may have to be split as illustrated above.

The reassignment process is complete when all the low-level bubbles from the essential model (either individually or as part of a higher-level bubble) have been assigned to one of the processors. The process descriptions and the flow, store, relationship, and element composition descriptions should also be carried over; they now are part of the implementation model. Definitions do not need to be carried over.

16.3 Elaboration of interfaces

The next stage of implementation model building involves looking at all bubbles that accept data from outside the system or send data from the system. In the essential model, these movements of data were not shown in detail; only the net transfer of data was modeled. It will now be necessary to describe these data transfer processes in more detail; that means deciding how these processes will be implemented.

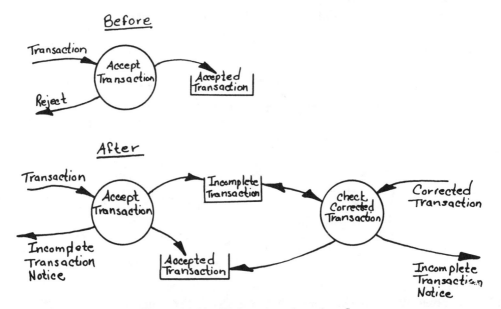

Figure 16.11. Elaboration of a reject flow.

One type of process requiring elaboration produces an output flow that was simply labeled Reject in the essential model. In order to complete this stage of the implementation model, the responses to the following questions must be added:

- What information must be provided as part of the Reject message so that the submitter of the original input can take appropriate action? (Normally, the input will be resubmitted in some form.)

- Must the entire input be resubmitted, or will the correct portions be stored and supplemented by resubmitted data?

- Is there a limit on the number of times an incorrect input may be resubmitted?

- Are subsequent errors handled in the same way as preliminary ones?

Figure 16.11 provides a before and after example of a process of this type.

Another type of process requiring additional details accepts human input interactively, normally through a data entry terminal with a screen and a keyboard. Some ways of implementing this type of process include displaying a data entry screen showing the names of the data elements to be entered and providing blank spaces for filling them in; displaying existing data element values when an update is to be made, and permitting the values to be changed; and providing help messages to guide the user in submitting correct data when an error is detected. Figure 16.12 describes the elaboration of an interactive data entry process.

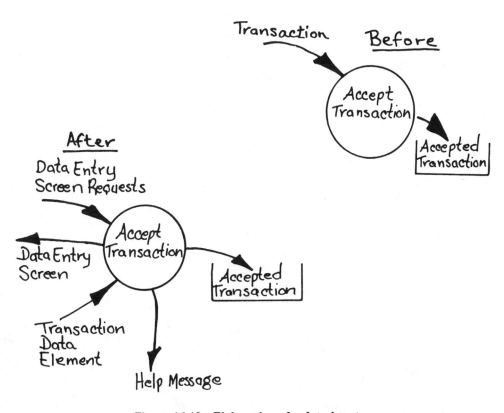

Figure 16.12. Elaboration of a data input.

In both the cases just described, modifying the process schema alone is not sufficient. It will be necessary to modify existing process descriptions, add new process descriptions, and add or modify flow and store composition descriptions to keep the model complete.

16.4 Organizing the implementation model

After assigning the essential model to processors and elaborating on the interfaces, the schematic portion of the implementation model consists of a group of large sheets of paper, each containing a collection of processes from various levels of the essential model. This model is not yet presentable and must be reorganized. The first stage in the reorganization is the creation of a system-level process schema for the implementation model. This is done by drawing on a separate sheet of paper a bubble for each processor, and connecting the net inputs and outputs for each processor diagram to the corresponding bubble. If the system is large enough, intermediate levels of process schemas should be created, and the original processor diagrams split into child diagrams of the intermediate-level schemas. The numbers on the processes that were carried over from the essential model must be changed to be consistent with the new leveling scheme. To reduce the complexity of the upper levels, lump groups of low-level flows into single higher-level flows. If this is done, composition descriptions should be added for the new flows.

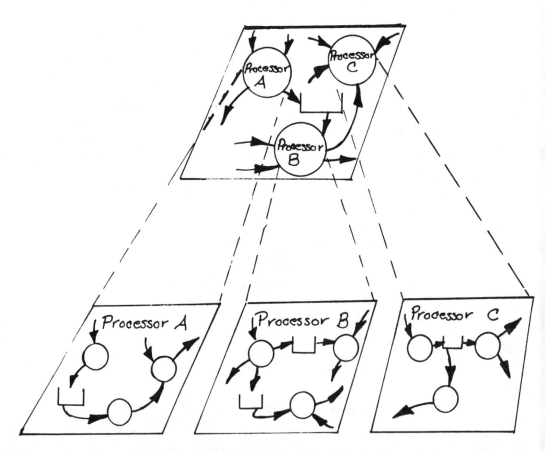

Figure 16.13. Leveling the implementation model.

After the leveling process is completed, two complete models of the system exist: the new implementation model and the original essential model. For future reference, it's important to keep track of where in the essential model a particular piece of the implementation model came from. One simple way to accomplish this is to leave the bubble numbers from the essential model as comments on the recopied processes. Another method, which will result in cleaner process schemas, is to create a separate cross-reference between essential and implementation process numbers. (It's convenient to be able to go from processes in the essential model to processes in the implementation model as well as the reverse.)

As a final organizational step, a complete balancing check should be carried out on the implementation model.

16.5 Implementation options

The completion of an implementation model is not necessarily equivalent to the selection of an implementation. The fact that the model is mechanically consistent and that it contains all the details from the essential model will not guarantee its cost-effectiveness or even its technological feasibility. In order to select the best implementation, it may be necessary to consider a variety of options. This is best accomplished by building rough models of the various possibilities, so that the details of each can be examined for advantages and disadvantages.

One method of testing a model is the playthrough described in Chapter 15. A playthrough on an implementation model might concentrate on interfaces between humans and computers. In addition to a script and a copy of the implementation model, drawings of proposed data entry screens might help people visualize system behavior.

If the interfaces are elaborate, it might be useful to build an automated simulation before making a final decision. Various commercially available software packages allow the building of a mock-up of a data entry interface, which will accept inputs and produce dummy outputs in any desired format.

16.6 Summary

Although users won't be involved in *all* the details of a system's implementation, it's critical that they be involved in *some* of these details. The guidelines for this involvement were presented in this chapter.

There are certain kinds of implementation details that can't be modeled effectively by the modeling tools presented thus far. Part IV addresses those details.

Chapter 16: Reference

1. J. Palmer and S. McMenamin, *Essential Systems Analysis* (New York: Yourdon Press, 1984).

    The authors present a description of the allocation of the essential, or logical, model to processors.

Part IV
Beyond the Basic Model

The modeling tools and techniques described in Parts II and III are sufficient to build essential models for most systems and to build high-level implementation models for many systems. However, implementations that involve complex time-dependent interactions can't be adequately modeled using the basic process schema. Chapter 17 describes some extensions of the process model to handle these complexities. Since the patterns modeled with ASML will be incorporated into computers, there are some useful things to know about computer hardware and software. Chapter 18 explains basic computer concepts in the context of systems development. We then follow the extension of the implementation model to a point where it can be turned directly into computer instructions. Chapter 19 provides this description.

17

Adding Dynamics to Process Models

In the previous section, systems were described as stimulus/response mechanisms. If you think about the systems we've used as examples in this book, you will find that they respond to stimuli in a way that doesn't change over time. When the Month of the Book Club receives an enrollment, the detailed output produced may vary (for example, some enrollments may be rejected). However, the basic behavior of the system doesn't change; the set of rules by which an enrollment is processed is always the same.

Suppose that the rules for processing did change, depending on the time of day. Perhaps, whenever the book club receives a delivery from a supplier between 10 and 11 a.m., it ignores the next ten enrollments it receives. Such behavior would be bizarre in a book club system, since it would serve no discernible purpose. However, behavior changes very similar in nature to this *do* serve purposes in many systems. System behavior that varies depending on the time is called dynamic or time-dependent behavior. This chapter will explore dynamic system behavior, and introduce some additions to the basic process model that help to describe it.

17.1 The need to model dynamics

The system represented by Figure 17.1 keeps track of activity in the international currency market. As the dollar varies against the yen, the pound against the mark, the lira against the peso, the details are recorded by the Change Buy/Sell Value process. A requester may find the minute-to-minute exchange rates by submitting a Current Rate Request to the Check Buy/Sell Value process. In addition to this, a periodic report is issued by the Perform Currency Analysis process. The report shows not individual exchange rates, but comparisons and statistics involving all the data in the Currency Exchange Activity store. This store represents a time delay; in other words, since someone may want a current rate of exchange at a time later than it's reported, the data must be maintained over time.

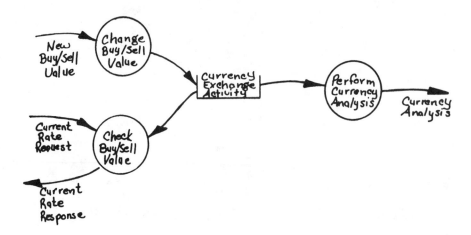

Figure 17.1. Currency exchange information system.

So far, no surprises. I'm sure you're comfortable with looking at a process schema and thinking about time with respect to the data. But what can you tell about time *as it relates to the processes?* In particular, can you tell how long it takes the processes to do their job, or whether two or even all three of the processes can be active at the same time? Don't spend a lot of time pondering these questions; the model simply doesn't provide answers. Let's attack from a different angle. Suppose you want someone to build a currency exchange information system for you. Figure 17.1 is part of your essential model for this system; it's a picture of the desired behavior of the system. How long would you like it to take between the submission of a Current Rate Request and the issuing of a Current Rate Response? I think you would answer, "No time at all!" or, more moderately, "as little time as possible." In the unlikely event that you actually wanted a delay between the submission of requests and the issuing of responses, you would have modeled the system as shown in Figure 17.2.

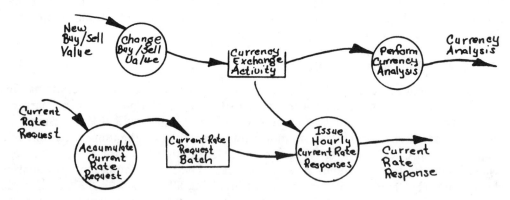

Figure 17.2. A built-in delay.

In a similar vein, I think you'd like the Check Buy/Sell Value and Change Buy/Sell Value processes to be able to operate at the same time, especially if the data being checked differs from the data being changed. We can conclude from all this that two fundamental premises apply to essential process schemas: *Processes do their jobs in as little time as possible* and *processes can be active simultaneously* (or at least, they delay each other's operation as little as possible).

Now imagine that you submit your currency exchange model to the data processing manager. After studying it, he or she informs you that the Perform Currency Analysis process, which will need to be run about once an hour, will take five minutes to do its job and that during that five minutes, the process must run through the stored data several times. In addition, the manager tells you that any changes made during that time will damage the results. Therefore, although the Check Buy/Sell Value process can operate continuously, the recording of new currency values must be suspended for five minutes out of each hour. After some initial grumbling, and after learning how much it would cost to avoid the delay, you reluctantly accept this implementation plan.

What does this mean with regard to the essential model? It means that although the implemented system will perform the *work* exactly as specified by the essential model, its time-related behavior will only approximate what you want. This kind of outcome, of course, is typical in real implementations, and I want to investigate how a situation of this kind can be modeled. In the following sections, we'll look at what needs to be done to the essential model to change it into an *accurate* implementation model; that is, one that shows the periodic suspension of the Change Buy/Sell Value process.

17.2 Control flows

Remember the light bulb example in Figure 7.13? It has Electricity as an input flow and Heat and Light as output flows. This process has all the inputs it needs to produce its output, since electricity flowing through a filament will produce heat and light. Figure 17.3 reproduces the light bulb example, with an additional input flow. The dotted arrow labeled On/Off is an example of a *control flow*. Its role in the model is described by its name; it acts as a switch to turn the light bulb on or off. When the control flow is on, electricity is permitted to enter the bubble and to produce heat and light. When the control flow is off, electricity is prohibited from entering and no outputs are produced.

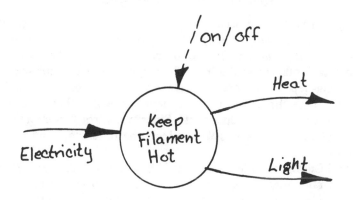

Figure 17.3. Light bulb with control flow.

The On/Off flow is different from the other input flows encountered so far. In a way, it's a dataflow, since it brings data of a sort to the process. In another way, it's not a dataflow at all: *It's not transformed into anything by the process.* Remember that the light bulb had all the inputs required to produce its output before the control flow was added. Why haven't control flows shown up in the systems described in this book? The answer lies partly in the type of model I've been describing and partly in the type of system used as an illustration. Essential models of the typical systems found in organizations can be built perfectly well without control flows. Implementation models often require control flows, but I've shown you only the first stage of a few implementation models. (Essential models of certain systems also require control flows; however, such systems are specialized and haven't been used as examples in this book.)

Control flows, as shown in the light bulb example, are used to turn processes off and on. If you look back through the essential model examples in the last few chapters, you won't find any situations in which you'd want to turn a process *off.* Most processes can be pictured as turning themselves on when they receive an input flow, and turning themselves off when they're finished transforming it.

An example of a situation in which you might want to turn a process *on* can be found in Figure 17.4, which could represent either a report generated periodically or a report generated on request. In either event, the process description can handle things adequately: It will say either "Once a day, do the following . . ." or "Upon request, do the following. . . ." The currency exchange system described earlier in the chapter is the first situation encountered so far where control flows can add something useful to the model. Specifically, the Change Buy/Sell Value process must be turned off (prohibited from accepting input flows) while the Perform Currency Analysis process is active. This could be modeled by showing an On/Off control flow as an input to the Change Buy/Sell Value process in Figure 17.1.

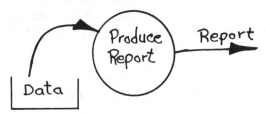

Figure 17.4. Process to be turned on.

Prohibiting a process from accepting inputs during some time period is an example of *time-dependent behavior.* Nearly all the other process schemas in this book describe *data-dependent behavior.* If the outcome of submitting data to a process depends on the data contained in the input flow or on the data contained in some store, the process has data-dependent behavior. However, if the result depends on what else is going on at the same time, or on the sequence in which things have occurred, the behavior of the process is time-dependent. Since a control flow represents something other than the data used by a process that affects the outcome, control flows and time-dependent behavior go together.

A common instance of time-dependent behavior involves the interaction of a human being with a computer using a keyboard and a display screen. Many keyboards contain special function keys in addition to the normal keys with letters of the alphabet, numbers, and punctuation marks. These keys are typically labeled F1, F2, and F3, or something equally uninformative. The keys are used to save work when extracting information from the system.

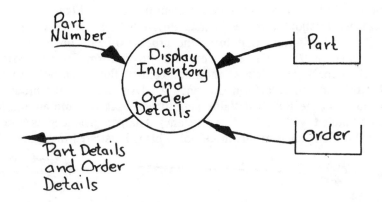

Figure 17.5. Inquiry and response process for an essential model.

Figure 17.5 shows the display of information about a part (quantity on hand, total orders) and of information about the orders for the part (customer name, quantity ordered, delivery date). Since Figure 17.5 is part of an essential model, it deliberately omits details about the form of the display. It might well describe extracting data from filing cabinets and transferring the details to a sheet of paper. Let's assume, however, that the data is to be displayed on a screen in response to a part number entered through a keyboard. Let's also assume that there's too much data about the part and the orders to display all at once. The system can be implemented so that the entry of a part number will cause the data about the part to be displayed. The subsequent depressing of the F1 key on the keyboard will cause the display of data about orders. The effect of pressing the F1 key thus depends on when it's pressed. Before a part number has been entered, pressing the key will have no effect.

On an implementation model, the pressing of the F1 key can be represented by a flow entering the system. This flow has something in common with the On/Off flow in the light bulb example; it doesn't get transformed into an output but controls the transformation of other data. The F1 key is represented as a control flow (Figure 17.6); again, control flows occur when system behavior is time-dependent.

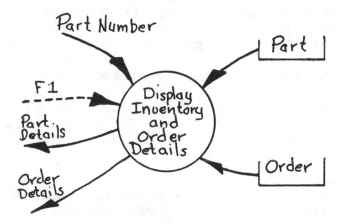

Figure 17.6. Inquiry and response process for an implementation model.

17.3 Control processes

Let's return to the currency exchange system depicted in Figure 17.1. Simply adding an On/Off control flow into the Change Buy/Sell Value process isn't too useful. The model still won't describe what turns the process off and on, or the connection between the Change Buy/Sell Value process and the Perform Currency Analysis process. A better approach is to show an input control flow that both turns Change Buy/Sell Value off and turns Perform Currency Analysis on. But the modification still doesn't show how Change Buy/Sell Value gets turned back on, and an additional control flow must be added. When Perform Currency Analysis produces its output data, it signals Change Buy/Sell Value to turn back on. This is illustrated in Figure 17.7.

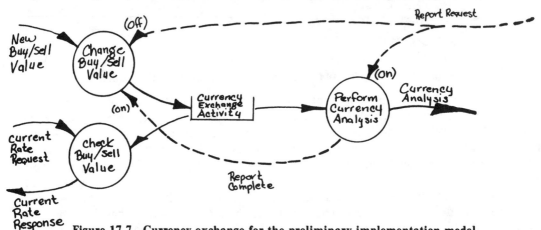

Figure 17.7. Currency exchange for the preliminary implementation model.

All the processes described so far in this book have transformed data (or sometimes material). By sending a control flow to Change Buy/Sell Value, Perform Currency Analysis has taken on a new kind of job. In addition to transforming input flows into output flows, *it controls other processes.*

Perform Currency Analysis is partly a transformation process and partly a control process. It's possible to add processes to schemas that are solely control processes, as shown in Figure 17.8. The Control Data Entry process acts as a sort of traffic officer for the process schema. Although Perform Currency Analysis needs to signal when it's done, it no longer directly controls anything. The advantage of the model in Figure 17.8 is that the control flows are all single purpose. This provides an improvement over the model depicted in Figure 17.7 in which the Report Request control flow was both an on signal and an off signal.

There are some additional aspects of Figure 17.8 worth noting:

- The control of Change Buy/Sell Value works differently from the control of Perform Currency Analysis. Change Buy/Sell Value is both turned on and off; Perform Currency Analysis is turned on but turns itself off.

- The fact that Change Buy/Sell Value is on doesn't mean that it's actually doing anything. Unlike the electricity flow, which is always available to the light bulb, the New Buy/Sell Value flows come in sporadically. The fact that Change Buy/Sell Value is on means that it will accept inputs when they appear.

- Check Buy/Sell Value is not controlled by the control process, nor is its behavior time-dependent. It's always on and will accept Current Rate Request flows and transform them into outputs whenever they occur.

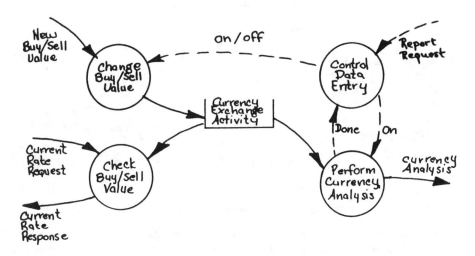

Figure 17.8. Currency exchange for the control process model.

17.4 The state transition diagram

What would the process description for Control Data Entry in Figure 17.8 look like? For this simple case, a short narrative description would suffice, as follows: When a Report Request is made, turn off Change Buy/Sell Value and turn on Perform Currency Analysis; when Perform Currency Analysis is done, turn on Change Buy/Sell Value. This description does not indicate what will happen if an additional report is requested while the first one is being produced; presumably the request would be ignored.

The state transition diagram provides a graphic method for describing what a control process does. Figure 17.9 illustrates a state transition diagram for the Control Data Entry process. The two graphic symbols used on this diagram represent *state* and *transition*. Specifically, the long narrow box with the label in it is a *state*. The two states in this system are Accepting Updates and Not Accepting Updates. The vertical arrow between states together with the horizontal line drawn at a right angle is a *transition*. There are two labels on the transition, one above the horizontal line and one below. The label above the horizontal line describes the *condition* that causes the transition, and the label below the line describes the *action(s)* taken when the condition occurs.

A state represents some high-level observable aspect of the system's behavior, which can change over the course of time. The obvious time-dependent feature of the currency exchange system is whether or not it's accepting updates to its stored data, so the states have been named accordingly. When the system changes its behavior, it's said to have made a transition from one state to another. The condition is what causes the transition to occur, and the actions are what the system needs to do to effect the change in behavior.

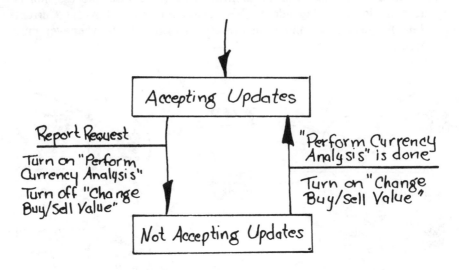

Figure 17.9. A state transition diagram.

A system may be in only one of the states on the diagram at any given time. (You can think of a light bulb glowing in one of the state boxes to tell you which state the system is in.) The fact that a system is in a state doesn't necessarily mean that anything is happening. To identify what is happening or what can happen in a state, one must look at the processes on the process schema and also at the actions that were taken when the system entered the state. In order to keep the state transition diagram from becoming overly complicated, we observe the following rule: Processes that have input dataflows are on unless turned off, and processes that have only stored data inputs are off unless turned on. Applying this rule to Figure 17.8 shows that Change Buy/Sell Value is normally on, Check Buy/Sell Value is normally on, and Perform Currency Analysis is normally off. Remember that a process isn't necessarily doing anything when it's on; it's simply prepared to accept input flows when they occur.

The unlabeled arrow into the Accepting Updates state on Figure 17.9 indicates that Accepting Updates is the *initial state* of the system. The system will be found in this state before any conditions have occurred. Using this information and the rule about bubbles being on or off, the full description of the Accepting Updates state can be derived as follows: New buy and sell values are being stored as they occur, current rate requests are being honored as they occur, and the currency analysis is not being produced.

Now let's see what happens when a Report Request control flow arrives. The Change Buy/Sell Value bubble is turned off, the Perform Currency Analysis bubble is turned on, and the state changes from Accepting Updates to Not Accepting Updates. In this new state, New Buy/Sell Values *are not being accepted,* current rate requests are being honored as they occur, and the currency analysis is being performed. The completion of the currency analysis causes another control flow to occur, which turns the Change Buy/Sell Value bubble on, and the system returns to the Accepting Updates state. Notice that this returns everything to the way it was the last time the system was in the Accepting Updates state. The Check Buy/Sell Value bubble is *state-independent.* You can verify this by looking again at the process schema; the bubble is not connected to the control process.

In addition to portraying the time-dependent behavior of the system in graphic form, Figure 17.9 answers the question of what happens if an additional report request occurs while the currency analysis is being produced. When a system is in a state, it will only respond to the conditions shown on the transition arrows leading out of the state. In other words, when the system is in the Not Accepting Updates state, it will ignore Report Request control flows.

17.5 Modeling complex dynamics

I want to make a confession to you: The application of control flows, control processes, and state transition diagrams to the currency exchange system would be a waste of time and effort. The dynamics are just too simple. The time-dependent behavior of the system could be described in a single sentence, written as a comment on the process schema: When the currency analysis is being produced, new buy/sell values will not be accepted.

This is similar to the situation described in Chapter 14. Some database systems have processes so simple and uninteresting that it's not worth building a process schema. Other systems have stored data organizations so simple it's not worth building a data schema. Still other systems have dynamics so simple it's a waste of time to add control flows, control processes, and state transition diagrams to the process model.

Modeling the dynamics of a system *is* worthwhile when its time-dependent behavior is too complex to be described by comments added to the process schema. Figure 17.10 depicts a somewhat more complex version of the inquiry and response system shown in Figure 17.5. Here there are three different kinds of stored data. Separate screen displays are needed for the part details, the details of each customer order for the part, and the sales history details for the customer who placed each order. As in the earlier example, this system will be implemented using a keyboard and display screen. The function keys on the keyboard will again be used to assist the requester in obtaining the data.

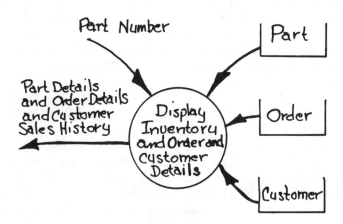

Figure 17.10. Part/order/customer display in the essential model.

The requester can initiate the display by keying in a part number and hitting the return key. This causes the system to display the data from the part store for that part. While the part data is being displayed, the requester can hit the F1 key, which will cause the details of the first customer order for the part to be displayed. The requester can also use the F3 key while part data is being displayed in order to clear the screen and allow entry of a new part number.

Once the first customer order has been displayed, the requester has various options: He or she can hit the F1 key to display the sales history for the customer who placed the order currently being displayed, hit the F2 key to display the next customer order for the part (successive hits of the key will run through all the orders for that part), or hit the F3 key to redisplay the inventory data for the part. When sales history for the customer is being displayed, the F3 key can be depressed to redisplay details of the customer order that was most recently displayed.

As you can see from this description, the time-dependent behavior of the display system is somewhat more complex than that of the currency exchange system. For example, hitting the F3 key can produce four different responses (including no action) depending on what has happened previously. In order to model this behavior graphically, we must take the following action:

- Identify the states of the system.

- Build a state transition diagram showing the conditions that will cause the system to change state, and the actions that must be carried out while changing state.

- Reorganize the process schema so that each data transformation that needs controlling is packaged in a separate bubble.

- Add a control bubble to the process schema to accept the incoming control flows (the conditions) and to send the outgoing control flows (the actions) shown on the state transition diagram. The state transition diagram is the process description for this control bubble.

The modes of behavior of the display system depend on what's being displayed on the screen: nothing, part details, order details, or customer sales history. Figure 17.11 shows a state transition diagram built around these modes of behavior. Since the creation of the Part Details, Order Details, and Customer Sales History output flows happens at different times, the process schema in Figure 17.12 has been modified to show each being produced by a separate bubble. Only the Display Part Details process actually gets a dataflow from the environment of the system (the part number). Display Order Details also needs the part number, so that it can select the appropriate orders from the order file. Since it will be run at a later time than the process that first needs the data, it has been given a time-delayed connection to Display Part Details through the Current Part Number store. Display Order Details passes the customer number of the order being displayed to Display Customer Sales History in a similar way.

Let's examine Figures 17.11 and 17.12 more closely. First, note that the action called Clear Display Screen, which is taken when the system moves from Displaying Part Details to Idle, doesn't have a corresponding bubble. Since it neither uses input data nor produces output data, adding it to the process schema doesn't provide any useful information. Next, notice that the transition with the condition F2 and the action Display (Next) Order Details is perfectly legal. It means that when the condition occurs, the system takes an action and returns to the same mode of behavior. Third, there is no reference in this model to the stopping of processes. Since no two data transformation bubbles can be active simultaneously, the bubbles are turned on by control flows, do their work, and then turn themselves off. Finally, the two figures tell us that this system requires relationships between the Part, Order, and Customer stores (which would be shown on a data schema) so that the processes can find the order details for a part and the customer details for an order.

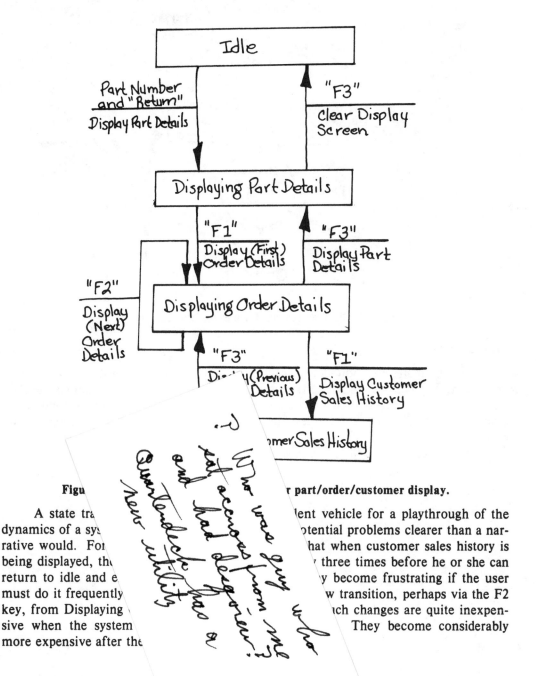

Figu ... **r part/order/customer display.**

A state tr... ...lent vehicle for a playthrough of the dynamics of a sy... ...ntential problems clearer than a narrative would. For... ...hat when customer sales history is being displayed, th... ... three times before he or she can return to idle and e... ...y become frustrating if the user must do it frequently... ...w transition, perhaps via the F2 key, from Displaying... ...ch changes are quite inexpensive when the system... ...They become considerably more expensive after th...

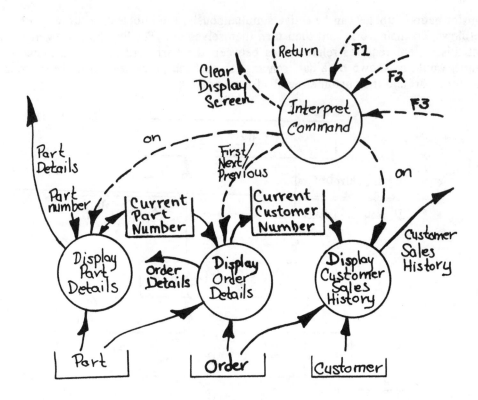

Figure 17.12. Process schema for part/order/customer display.

17.6 Summary

Certain implementation details can most conveniently be described by control flows, control processes, and state transition diagrams. This chapter describes methods for extending the process model to incorporate these features. However, extending the model in this way is not useful unless the time-dependent behavior of a system is complex.

In Chapter 18, we will look at basic computer concepts.

Chapter 17: Reference

1. P. Ward and S. Mellor, unpublished course notes for YOURDON inc.'s workshop entitled "Structured Analysis and Design for Real-Time Systems."

    The material develops use of a state transition diagram to model the dynamics of a set of processes.

18
Automated System Basics

18.1 Technological overkill

The treatment of automated systems in this chapter is deliberately quite elementary. For the reader unfamiliar with computers, it provides the needed knowledge for intelligent participation in automated systems development. For the more knowledgeable reader, it highlights the fundamental connections between the capabilities of the technology and the nature of the development process.

Bookstores today overflow with books about computers. Many of the books bombard readers with technical details in an attempt to help them understand computer hardware and software. This deluge of facts is wonderful if you happen to be a computer hobbyist, or even just someone interested in computer technology per se. However, for most organizational computer users, it's technological overkill. Facts about bits and bytes are about as helpful to the average user as facts about piston tolerances are to the average automobile driver.

Let's use the automobile analogy to explore this idea further. Put yourself in the position of a consumer about to buy or rent an automobile for your personal use. What do you need to know? My list would include knowing how to drive, knowing in general terms how automobiles work, knowing how to interpret information about automobile horsepower and fuel efficiency (to aid in selection of the most appropriate model for a particular use), and knowing how to plan a trip (for example, being able to read a map and select a route).

For a computer user, the equivalent of knowing how to drive is the ability to interact with the computer through a terminal. The user has to learn the commands that cause the system to begin communications, end communications, display information, and accept information.

The basic principles of computer technology are discussed in the next few sections of this chapter. Jargon and complexity have deliberately been kept to a minimum. I'll also discuss measurements of computer speed and storage capacity, which correspond somewhat to horsepower and fuel efficiency in autos. An understanding of these basic measurements can be useful for evaluating the costs and effectiveness of applying a particular computer to a particular task. The subject is treated in a once-over-lightly fashion, since acquiring computer hardware isn't the main focus of the book.

Finally, we come to the subject of trip planning. I hope it's clear that deciding where to go and choosing a route are what this book has been all about!

18.2 Sequences of instructions

Now let's look at the basics of computer technology. Modern computers perform an impressive variety of tasks. For example, weather bureaus use computers to digest vast numbers of facts about current climatic conditions and to predict the weather days in advance. Large manufacturers store facts about parts in their extensive inventories and recall them rapidly when needed. Or, a manager can create a memo on a television-like screen, revise words, sentences, and paragraphs with a few touches to a keyboard, and dispatch the result to people scattered all over the world without ever committing it to paper.

All of these activities are based on the carrying out of sequences of simple instructions. These instructions come in three basic types: *operations,* such as adding two numbers or retrieving a number from storage; *decisions,* such as determining whether two numbers are equal; and *jumps* to some other instruction that vary the sequence.

The power and the flexibility achievable with these simple instructions come from two factors. One is the speed and accuracy with which computers can execute instructions. The other is that the instructions can be organized in any way desired according to an externally imposed pattern.

18.3 Patterns of instructions

So that you will appreciate both the advantages and the limitations of using simple instruction sequences, I'd like you to try a short experiment. I'm going to ask you to act as a computer for me. I'll assume you can carry out simple instructions, and I'll compose a pattern of these instructions for you to carry out.

Let's start with three numbers: One will be called the first distance, one will be called the second distance, and one will be called the guess. The instructions follow:

1. Square the first distance.

2. Square the second distance.

3. Add the results of steps 1 and 2.

4. Divide the result of step 3 by the guess.

5. Add the result of step 4 to the guess.

6. Divide the result of step 5 by 2.

7. If the result of step 6 differs from the guess, start again with step 4, replacing the guess with the result of step 6. Otherwise, if the result of step 6 matches the guess, you're done.

Here's an example to verify that the instructions are clear; I'll round results to two decimal places. The first distance is 21.9, the second distance is 14.1, and the guess is 300. Step 1 is to square 21.9, giving 479.61. Step 2 is to square 14.1, giving 198.81. Step 3 is to add 479.61 and 198.81, which produces 678.42. Step 4 is to divide 678.42 by 300, resulting in 2.26. Step 5 is to add 2.26 to 300, resulting in 302.26. Step 6 is to divide 302.26 by 2, resulting in 151.13. Since this differs from 300, step 7 requires that we return to step 4. The guess is now 151.13. Step 4 is to divide 678.42 by 151.13, resulting in 4.49, after rounding to two decimal places. Is everything clear?

Now that you're warmed up, let's try it for real. The first distance is 56.01, the second distance is 25.61, and the guess is 70. Run through the set of instructions until step 7 allows you to stop. Round off your results to three decimal places to make things a little easier; you'll probably want to use a pocket calculator. I'll wait.

Finished? Your solution should have been 61.588. If you got something different, you made an arithmetic mistake somewhere. The results of the first three steps should have been 3137.120, 655.872, and 3792.992; check the rest of your calculation against this table:

Cycle	Step 4	Step 5	Step 6	Step 7
1	3792.992/70 = 54.186	70 + 54.186 = 124.186	124.186/2 = 62.093	Restart
2	3792.992/62.093 = 61.086	62.093 + 62.086 = 123.179	123.179/2 = 61.590	Restart
3	3792.992/61.590 = 61.585	61.590 + 61.585 = 123.175	123.175/2 = 61.588	Restart
4	3792.992/61.588 = 61.587	61.588 + 61.587 = 123.175	123.175/2 = 61.588	Done

Now I'll describe the problem you've just solved. Two highways cross at right angles. There's a town on the north-south highway north of the crossing, and a town on the east-west highway east of the crossing. The distances *along the highway* from the crossing to the two towns are the first and second distances. The result of the seven-step calculation is the distance "as the crow flies" between the two towns. The calculation involves finding the hypotenuse of a right triangle, and the heart of the calculation is a square-root determination (steps 4 through 7). The solution remains 61.588 no matter how many more times you repeat steps 4 through 7. The fascinating thing about this method is that you'll always come out with 61.588, no matter what guess you start with. It will simply take a few more repetitions of the instructions if your first guess at the solution is especially bad.

You didn't need to know that you were calculating a square root to get the right answer; you simply had to follow the instructions accurately. The weather bureau's computer doesn't need to know that it's forecasting the weather either. It just carries out a pattern, based on a large number of very simple instructions. Of course, neither you nor the weather bureau could have detected an error in the pattern. I could have remedied that limitation for *you* by explaining the purpose of the task; that's not possible with present-day computers.

The pattern of instructions for calculating a square root doesn't have anything special to do with computers. It was devised by ingenious mathematicians thousands of years ago. There's a very useful division of labor here: People organize simple instructions into patterns, and computers provide the speed and accuracy.

18.4 Combining instruction patterns

Let's look at two more short patterns of instructions. I'll give a name to each of the patterns so that I can refer to them later. First, here's the calculation pattern. It starts with two numbers: an amount and a count, as follows:

1. Multiply the count by 87.

2. Subtract the result of step 1 from the amount.

3. Take 94 percent of the result of step 2; this is the outcome.

This pattern is only carried out once; it doesn't need repeating. Now, here's the rearrangement pattern. It starts with a list, with each entry in the list consisting of a group of numbers. One of the numbers in each group is the index. A sample list follows:

Entry	Index	Rest of Group		
1	6	2	4	9
2	14	6	8	11
3	2	20	7	18
4	8	4	12	17

The pattern looks at a pair of entries at a time, and starts with entries 1 and 2:

1. If the index of the first entry of the pair is larger than the index of the second entry of the pair, exchange the two entries.

2. If this isn't the last pair on the list, move down one entry and repeat step 1. (In other words, if you just finished entries 2 and 3, go on to 3 and 4.)

3. If this is the last pair on the list, and if you exchanged any entries on your last pass through the list, start again at step 1 with entries 1 and 2. If you didn't exchange any entries, you're finished.

Since the rearrangement pattern is somewhat harder than the calculation pattern, let's try it on the sample list. Starting with entries 1 and 2, we *don't* do the exchange in step 1 since 6 is less than 14. Step 2 now instructs us to try step 1 on entries 2 and 3. This time, we *do* exchange the entries since 14 is larger than 2. Again, step 2 instructs us to try step 1 on entries 3 and 4. (Of course, entry 3 is now 14-6-8-11, since we did an exchange on the last pair.) We perform the exchange since 14 is larger than 8. Now we skip step 2 since we're at the end of the list. Step 3 tells us that since we performed some exchanges, we need to go back to step 1 to use entries 1 and 2.

If you're getting impatient at this point, I don't blame you. People generally don't like carrying out instructions without being told why. Humor me just a bit longer. I now want to give you one more set of instructions. This one starts with a list that has three numbers for each entry: a description, an amount, and a count. It looks like this:

Entry	Description	Amount	Count
1	1913092008	1500	2
2	1605200518	1200	1
3	0112120114	1700	4
4	1612012005	2000	3
5	2515211407	1800	1

Now here's a final pattern:

1. For each entry in the list, carry out the calculation instructions and then put the description and the outcome into a new list.

2. Carry out the rearrangement instructions on the new list, using the description as the index.

If you work your way through step 1, the new list should look like this (outcomes are rounded to whole numbers):

Entry	Description	Outcome
1	1913092008	1246
2	1605200518	1046
3	0112120114	1271
4	1612012005	1635
5	2515211407	1610

After you perform step 2, the new list should be changed to

Entry	Description	Outcome
1	0112120114	1271
2	1605200518	1046
3	1612012005	1635
4	1913092008	1246
5	2515211407	1610

What I've just given you is a computer's-eye view of a simple payroll calculation. This composite final pattern could be called List Net Pay. The calculation instructions determine the net pay (the outcome) from the gross monthly pay (the amount) and the number of exemptions (the count), assuming a $1000 yearly exemption and a tax rate of six percent. The rearrangement instructions are used to put the list into alphabetical order. (The descriptions are employee last names, encoded by substituting 01 for A, 02 for B, and so on. An employee with the last name Plate is thus encoded as 1612012005.) The final set of instructions used a nonalphabetical list (perhaps a list of employees by ID number) containing name, gross pay, and number of exemptions to create an alphabetical new list of name and net pay.

If you took the time to work through this set of instructions, you may have encountered problems keeping your place. Keeping track of which instruction you carried out last, or which entry in a list you're working on, isn't especially easy. This last exercise was harder than the square-root calculation because there was more data. The raw material for the square root calculation was three numbers and the product was a single number. The raw material for the payroll exercise was a whole list of numbers, and there were other lists as intermediate and final products. In a real-life situation, these lists would be payroll files containing data about hundreds or thousands of employees.

18.5 Hierarchies of patterns

A computer, of course, can store large numbers of instructions and large amounts of data, and retrieve a specific instruction or piece of data very quickly. In addition, a computer can keep track of which instructions and which data it is working on. Notice that this ability has nothing to do with understanding the task. You don't have to know that you're alphabetizing a list to keep track of such details as having finished a particular instruction. The patterns of instructions, the lists of data items, and the connection of a pattern of instructions with a list of data are all externally imposed.

When I gave you the last set of instructions, I referred to the calculation and rearrangement patterns. Computers perform this sort of cross-referencing by means of jump instructions. The stored instructions for the net pay list calculation could be set up as follows:

1. Get the first entry from the list.

2. Multiply the count by 87.

3. Subtract the result of step 2 from the amount.

4. Take 94 percent of the result of step 3; this is the outcome.

5. Add the description and outcome to the new list.

6. If there are still entries left in the original list, get the next entry and jump to instruction 2.

7. Get the first pair of entries from the new list.

8. Compare the indices of the two entries.

$$\vdots$$

The computer will perform these instructions in order unless one of the instructions tells it to jump. Notice that instructions 2 through 5 carry out the calculation pattern, and that the instructions beginning with 7 carry out the rearrangement pattern. If the original list had three entries, the order for carrying out instructions would be 1-2-3-4-5-6-2-3-4-5-6-2-3-4-5-6-7-8 and so on.

The mechanics of setting up these instructions are really beside the point. You can *think* of List Net Pay as a pattern containing the simpler patterns, just as you can think of a high-level bubble on a process schema as containing lower-level bubbles. Figure 18.1 illustrates such a pattern.

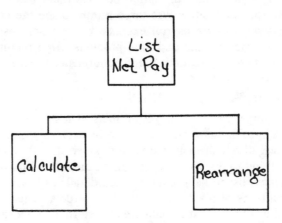

Figure 18.1. A simple hierarchy.

The List Net Pay pattern, in turn, could be incorporated into a still higher-level pattern, as in Figure 18.2. The Calculate Gross Pay and Summarize Taxes patterns are also composed from simpler patterns.

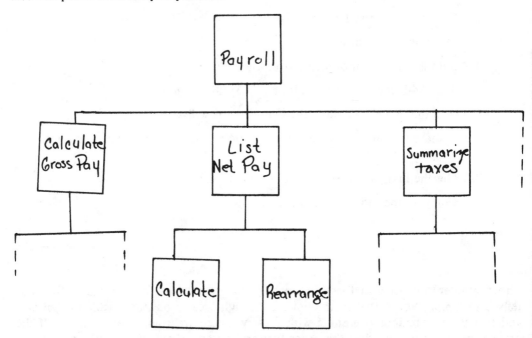

Figure 18.2. A more complex hierarchy.

This arrangement is a hierarchy, similar to the ones we've encountered in earlier chapters. The creation of hierarchies of patterns such as that shown in Figure 18.2 is what allows automated systems to perform complex tasks. The lower-level patterns in a hierarchy obviously shouldn't have to be reinvented for each new system. Computers usually come equipped with a library of patterns for common mathematical operations such as sorting, retrieving data from files, and displaying data on screens. However, the higher levels of patterns, such as Calculate Net Pay, are frequently unique to a particular organization.

In addition to standard operations, which plug in at the lower levels of patterns, computers come equipped with very high-level patterns. For example, an *operating system* such as that shown in Figure 18.3 is a management-level pattern that controls the starting and stopping of lower-level patterns such as Payroll. Operating systems for large computers typically can handle the carrying out of several lower-level patterns (for example, payroll and inventory analysis) in the same time period. The lower-level patterns are interleaved in such a way as to make maximum use of computer resources.

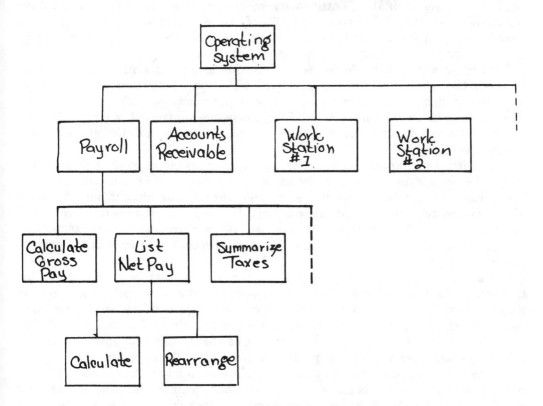

Figure 18.3. The operating system.

Computer systems that serve the needs of multiple users in an interactive fashion (for example, a system that supports the operation of a network of car rental offices) also have management-level patterns. These patterns control the low-level patterns that serve the workstations so that no user's response time is unduly prolonged.

A large, general-purpose computer system, in fact, often must simultaneously manage several batch (noninteractive) jobs like payroll while serving a number of users at interactive workstations.

18.6 Measurements of computer power

Below are four questions to be used in measuring and evaluating the capabilities of a computer and its equipment:

- How fast can instructions be carried out?

- How fast can information be stored and retrieved?

- How much information can be stored?

- How fast can information be transferred to or from other computers?

The instruction speed of a computer is typically measured in millions of instructions per second (MIPS). Contemporary medium-to-large computer systems have speeds that range from 0.5 to about 20 MIPS. These are impressive numbers. They become only slightly less impressive when we learn that what the computer folks mean by an instruction doesn't match the everyday use of the term. Adding two numbers together could consume half a dozen instructions. Retrieving or updating a record from a file might take a hundred or more. Let's say a typical payroll transaction involves reading a record, doing a couple of dozen arithmetic operations, and rewriting the record. You might conclude that since about 350 instructions are involved, a one-MIPS computer could carry out nearly 3,000 of these transactions per second. Unfortunately, you would be wrong.

The factor that limits transaction speed usually turns out to be the next measurement: the average time required to locate or change a piece of information in storage. A computer can operate at instruction speed only when dealing with the limited amount of information available in its primary memory. For large files, it must move chunks of information to or from a secondary memory, typically consisting of magnetic disk storage. Finding and extracting a randomly selected record on a large disk file might take as long as 0.1 second.

Current computer systems use multiprogramming to make better use of instruction speed. As described in Section 18.5, an operating system can set up several tasks simultaneously, and instructions for one task can be carried out while waiting for information transfer for another task. Thus, although it might take the system a half hour to do 18,000 payroll transactions, it might also be able to complete your accounts receivable job and serve a number of interactive users within the same time slot.

The storage capacity of a computer system is also an important number. The size of the *primary memory* affects the speed; a large primary memory can receive a few large transfers of information from secondary memory, rather than many small ones. The secondary memory capacity puts limits on the active (that is, readily accessible) file storage. Both primary and secondary memory for medium-to-large systems are measured in megabytes (millions of bytes). A byte corresponds to a stored character (letter of the alphabet or digit). A typical mailing list entry (name, street address, city, state, zip code) occupies about 75 bytes. One megabyte of storage could thus hold a mailing list with about 13,000 entries. Typical medium-to-large systems have primary memories in the range of 1 to 16 megabytes, and secondary memories in the hundreds or thousands of megabytes.

A final measurement of interest is the speed at which information can be transferred from one computer to another. This is becoming increasingly important as groups of computers are linked to form networks. Complex jobs can be segmented and parceled out to the individual computers in the network. Transfer rate is commonly measured in a unit called baud. Dividing the baud by eight gives an approximate transfer rate in bytes per second. Typical transfer rates are from 300 to 1,200 bytes per second, or from 4 to 16 mailing list entries per second. A computer that is processing information transferred from another computer can operate on this information no faster than the transfer rate, although it can be attending to other jobs while waiting for information to arrive.

I hope it's clear that I'm not suggesting that you negotiate a computer lease or purchase on the basis of this much information. I *am* suggesting that you have a consumer's right to understand the basics of such an evaluation, so that the selection process does not become an overwhelming mystery.

18.7 Summary

Computers carry out simple instructions very fast and very accurately. Complex tasks can be accomplished by imposing patterns on these simple instructions. These patterns are provided by the systems development process, which transforms the patterns within an organization into patterns a computer can understand. The systems development process first produces a model of the organizational pattern that contains several levels and therefore shows the pattern as a hierarchy. If the lowest level of patterns in the model can be matched with patterns available in the computer's library, an automated system matching the organizational pattern can be created.

The model created by the ASML procedures up to this point shows the processor configuration of the implementation; it typically needs more work before this matching can occur. The next chapter describes that work.

Chapter 18: Reference

1. G. McWhorter, *Understanding Digital Electronics* (Dallas: Texas Instruments Learning Center, 1978).

   This book provides an excellent introduction to the basics of automated systems technology.

19

Completing the Implementation Model

One of the major tasks in building the high-level implementation model is dividing the work of the system among the processors. In fact, the overall organization of the implementation model is determined by this allocation process; the system-level process schema has one bubble per processor.

System-level process schemas for an implementation can vary widely in complexity. At one extreme, there will be only a single automated processor. Allocation of the essential model then reduces to deciding whether any of the work inside the context bubble will be carried out manually and separating out these manual processes. At the other extreme, there may be a large, complex network of automated processors. Such a network usually results from the combination of a very large, complex set of processes and a geographically dispersed user community.

The distinction between a single automated processor and a network of processors is somewhat blurred. Many collections of electronic hardware that behave like single computers are in fact composed of two or more units, each of which can store data and carry out instructions. For example, configurations that consist of a central processing unit and a collection of interactive workstations often have small computers in each of the workstations. For our purposes, a single automated processor can be defined as some collection of hardware that acts as a unit and that is managed as a unit by its operating system. If the system builders have to address the problem of transferring data among multiple hardware units, they are dealing in a pragmatic sense with two or more processors. If they can build a system while ignoring the hardware boundaries because the operating system handles the transfer problems, they are dealing with a single processor.

A high-level implementation model can be separated into a collection of submodels, one for each processor. A submodel consists of a system-level bubble, its associated data schema, its child process schemas, and the flow, store, relationship, and data element descriptions associated with the schemas. Completing the ASML modeling procedure requires focusing individually on each submodel that represents an automated processor. The tasks involve reorganizing the lower levels of the submodel to match the technical environment within the processor, so that ultimately each lower-level piece of the model can be translated directly into computer instructions.

All of this modeling work, however, is not required for all processor submodels. The remainder of this chapter will explore the various possibilities for turning a processor submodel into a working automated system.

19.1 Purchasing an implementation

Controversies arise in many organizations over whether to build or buy an implementation. Many vendors offer software packages that can perform common organizational functions, such as payroll, accounting, inventory management, or purchasing. Some of these packages can be plugged in and can begin work immediately; others must be customized for a particular environment. In either case, the vendors claim that such a package saves time and money, and imply that an organization that creates its own implementation is reinventing the wheel.

In opposition to the vendors' arguments, users and data processing people within organizations sometimes argue that organizational patterns are too varied for a one-size-fits-all approach. They claim that purchased packages must be modified so heavily that the cost savings will be lost or that manual work patterns and other automated systems must be distorted to fit the arbitrary demands of the package. In addition, they argue that as user requirements change, the organization either will have to rely on the services of the vendor for system revisions or will have to force their own data processing personnel to tinker with unfamiliar programs.

Without attempting to resolve this controversy, I will raise a different but closely related question: What are the risks of buying a software package without first modeling the desired behavior of the system? In some cases, these risks are small. For example, there are some systems that are so simple and so well known to their users that a proposed vendor package can be evaluated almost at a glance. There are also systems that are standardized because of requirements beyond the control of an organization, for example, government-mandated accounting practices. In these cases, distorting organizational patterns so that they meet the requirements of the package is actually an advantage to the organization. Some packages of this kind offer periodic updates as the external standards change.

Unless the system in question falls into one of the categories mentioned above, buying a package without building a model first is very risky. How do you know that a purchased package will adequately support an organizational pattern if you're not clear about the details of the pattern? A study group charged with the task of comparing vendor packages and making a choice *will* end up building a model of the system to be supported by the package. The only question is whether this model will be a formal, well-organized one, or an informal one composed of sketchy narratives and verbal interchanges.

A model built using the ASML procedure is ideal for evaluating vendor packages. The investigators can work through the model systematically and compare it with a vendor's documentation. Questions that can be asked include the following:

- Where in the vendor's package is this input flow transformed into that output flow?

- Where in the vendor's storage scheme can this data element be stored?

- Does the vendor's storage scheme allow this collection of stored data to be linked with that one?

- Can the vendor's human-computer interface carry out the interaction described by this state transition diagram?

The scripts created during playthroughs of a model can also be of great value in vendor selection. If the vendor provides a working version of the package, the scripts can be applied to the actual system, and the behavior of the package can be compared with the behavior predicted by the model.

Evaluating software packages with the assistance of a model takes much of the risk out of vendor selection and can clarify whether to build or buy. It is possible to provide *specific* answers to such questions as, How much will the package have to be modified to fit the environment? or, How much will the environment have to be modified to fit the package? Decision making then becomes a matter of rational cost and benefit analysis rather than of vague philosophical arguments.

19.2 Direct implementation from the high-level model

As I noted in the first chapter of this book, computers have become increasingly accessible to the average person in recent years. Millions of people have now had the experience of writing and implementing their own computer programs. Two different trends have allowed this to happen:

- As computers became cheaper and thus appeared more frequently in schools and homes, many people decided it was worth the time and trouble to learn low-level computer languages such as BASIC.

- As software became more sophisticated and hardware more powerful, a new generation of very high-level languages emerged. These fourth-generation languages made implementing computer programs and files much simpler.

Except for the minority of computer users who are interested in technological detail for its own sake, the trend toward fourth-generation languages is clearly the more promising one, and will be discussed in the remaining paragraphs of this section.

A typical fourth-generation language is organized around display screens into which data is entered (input flows) and upon which data is displayed (output flows). A system is built by defining its display screens. Calculations (processes) may be defined relating screen inputs, screen outputs, and data stored in files. Screens may be interrelated in terms of keyboard inputs, which allow the user to move from one screen to another (state transitions). In addition to allowing calculations to put data into existing files and to retrieve data from existing files, the fourth-generation languages may also permit the user to define new files and interconnections among them (stores and relationships).

There is a very close connection between the emergence of the fourth-generation languages and the system modeling process described in this book. In the previous chapter, I pointed out that implementation becomes possible when the lowest-level details of the system model match patterns available from the computer system's basic repertoire. As the built-in patterns available in automated systems become higher level, the necessity for modeling low-level technical details will decrease.

The basic question regarding direct implementation is similar to the build-or-buy question raised in the last section about purchased software packages: Do you build an implementation yourself using a fourth-generation language, or should you buy the services of a computer professional to build one for you? The decision to buy relieves you of learning potentially burdensome technicalities, but raises questions as to whether you'll get exactly what you want.

In practical terms, the important decision is whether a processor submodel is suitable for direct implementation using a fourth-generation language. If the following criteria are met, you should be able to build the implementation yourself.

- The processes for transforming inputs into outputs and storing and retrieving data should be of low-to-moderate complexity.

- The system should store and retrieve data from existing files, or should need only simple file structures.

- All connections to the system should be through human-computer interfaces; processes that send data to or receive data from other processors should not be part of the system.

- There should be no extreme needs for computer resources (for example, extremely fast response times) or very large volumes of stored data to store or display.

Another question about direct implementation relevant to software package acquisition is, Should one attempt to implement the system without first building a model? Extravagant claims have been made for direct implementation by means of fourth-generation languages, suggesting that a user could sit down at a keyboard and make a complex system appear by some kind of magic. Very simple systems, of course, can be successfully implemented without building a model first. Beyond a certain level of complexity, however, the results of trial-and-error implementation will be similar to those of selecting a software package without sufficient study. A lot of time will be spent on an implementation that is likely to be unsatisfactory. The fact is that one simply must think out the details of a system before implementing it. The more complex the system, the greater are the benefits of using a model to organize and plan the details.

There are circumstances under which it's worth building a direct implementation of even a complex, resource-hogging system. Such an implementation is called a prototype. It is not intended to be a final implementation, but simply to permit realistic playthroughs of the system's behavior. Such prototypes are especially useful for testing complex human-computer interactions, which are difficult to visualize using a pencil-and-paper model. The costs of building prototypes can be justified in certain large development projects because of the decreased probability of postimplementation problems.

19.3 Completing the lower levels of the implementation model

Most systems of medium-to-high complexity must be implemented by data processing professionals. The ASML modeling procedure extends the modeling process, so that lower-level implementation details of complex systems can be thought out by means of the model before the system is actually built.

There are two modeling stages in addition to the high-level or *processor configuration* stage of the implementation model. The first of these is the *software configuration* stage. Building the software configuration model involves repackaging the lower levels of a processor submodel. The second stage is the *code organization* stage and is discussed later in this section. It also involves reorganizing the lower levels, in this case the lower levels of the software configuration model. Let's first examine software configuration modeling.

Nearly all automated processors come equipped with *software architectures;* these are management-level patterns of computer instructions. Such architectures can't perform calculations relating to specific applications such as accounting or inventory control, but exist to provide support services for the instructions that carry out the work of these applications. A management company that acquires an office building, rents floors to various tenants, and provides janitorial, delivery, and repair services bears the same relationship to the building and the tenants as software architecture bears to the processor and the applications.

Software architectures manage application instructions in chunks. Although these chunks are sometimes called tasks, programs, modules, or some other term, I use the term *execution unit* to refer to the chunks of application instructions managed as a unit by the software architecture. Software architectures also manage stored data in chunks. These chunks may be called files, data sets, buffers, queues, or the like, but I refer to such a chunk of stored data as a *storage unit.*

The processes and data to be managed by each processor's architecture are specified by a processor submodel. Even though a processor submodel does only a portion of the work of the original essential model, it can be thought of as a system in its own right (Figure 19.1).

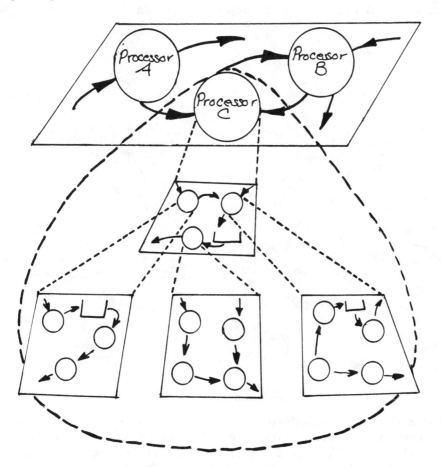

Figure 19.1. Processor submodel as system.

The lower levels of this system have no special organization; they're just pieces of the essential model, which were assigned to this processor. Building the processor configuration model involves repackaging these lower levels into execution units and storage units.

Suppose that a particular processor architecture manages applications in terms of execution units called *tasks* and storage units called *data sets.* You can imagine a bucket for each task and a bucket for each data set. Building the software configuration model involves dropping the pieces of the processor model into the appropriate bucket. This is very much like assigning pieces of the essential model to processors; it just happens one level lower.

As with repackaging of the essential model into the processor configuration model, the best strategy involves as little distortion of the original model as is consistent with technological constraints. Look back at Figure 17.11, at the F2 command, which allows the user to scan the customer orders for a part. Suppose that when the last order is reached, the next depression of the F2 key causes the first order to be redisplayed. A user who wished to carefully study the orders for a part might browse through them a number of times, revisiting each order in turn. Retrieving the order data from the file again for each pass through the orders is not efficient. It's expensive in terms of computer instructions, and might interfere with other users who wish to use the order file.

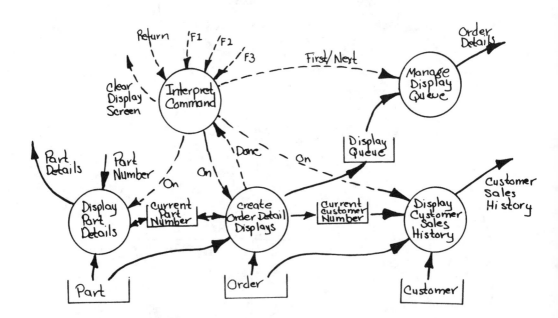

Figure 19.2. Software configuration for part/order/customer display.

Figure 19.2 shows a modification of Figure 17.12 (which should be viewed as the child schema for a processor bubble) to reflect the efficiency requirements of the software architecture. When the display of order details is first requested for a part, the Create Order Detail Displays process is turned on, creates *all* the screen displays for the orders, and stores them in the Display Queue. From that point on, the order details for the part are displayed as required by the Manage Display Queue process, which cycles through the already built screens and displays them as required. The Manage Display Queue process is part of the management software for the processor. It simply extracts data from a store and puts it on a screen; it could be displaying policy data for an insurance system just as well as order data.

The repackaging of Figure 17.12 has resulted in very little distortion of the process schema. Each of the original processes has become an execution unit. The process that created single-order detail displays now creates all the displays at once, and an extra execution unit has been added to handle the actual placing of the displays on the screen.

After the repackaging process is complete, the system-level process schema for the processor (that is, the child schema for the processor bubble) should contain one bubble for each execution unit. The lower level of each execution unit bubble contains the pieces of the original essential model that have been assigned to that execution unit. Each execution unit bubble with its lower levels can be considered a system in its own right, just as are the processor bubble and its lower levels.

This brings us to the lowest-level stage of the implementation model: the *code organization* stage.* This stage involves the reorganization of the lower levels of the execution unit to reflect the constraints of writing maintainable code. The unit of organization of the code organization level is the *module;* it is analogous to the execution unit and the processor at the higher levels. A special control relationship between two modules, known as a *call,* is of considerable importance for code organization. Figure 19.3 shows the child schema for one of the execution units on Figure 19.2, along with the process descriptions for its bubbles. Notice that both process descriptions require the conversion of a date from one form to another. Although the computer instructions for the date conversion could be written in duplicate for the two processes, a better method is to assign the date conversion to a lower-level module and to call it from both the upper-level processes.

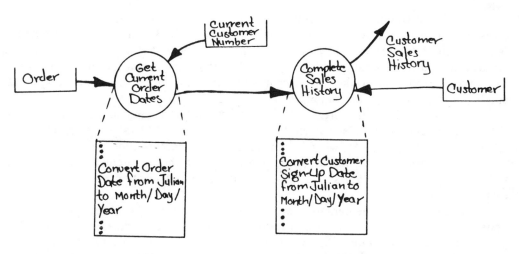

Figure 19.3. Display customer sales history.

Code is used here to mean computer instructions.

Figure 19.4 shows the representation of the call relationship. The call from Get Current Order Dates to Convert Date From Julian To Month/Day/Year can be thought of as follows:

- When Get Current Order Dates needs the date converted, it sends the date to Convert Date From Julian To Month/Day/Year, turns the lower-level module on, and turns itself off.

- When Convert Date From Julian To Month/Day/Year finishes its job, it sends the converted date to Get Current Order Dates, turns the higher-level module on, and turns itself off.

- When turned on, Get Current Order Dates picks up where it left off when it issued the call.

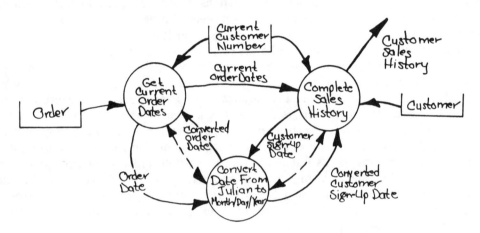

Figure 19.4. Displaying customer sales history (with call).

Pulling out common low-level pieces of work and making them called modules assures that the work will be done in a consistent fashion. It also means that the module can be placed in a library, to be used elsewhere in the current system and in other systems as needed. The creation of this type of library complements the library of standard functions provided by the processor architecture, and should make future systems building efforts for the organization progressively easier.

When the code-level reorganization of an execution unit is complete, it will consist of a hierarchy of modules connected by calls. The entire hierarchy is controlled by a high-level "boss" module, which is turned on when the execution unit is active and turns on the lower-level modules. Only one module in the hierarchy can be active at any given time. Figure 19.5 shows the completed code organization model for Display Customer Sales History.

The completed implementation model can easily be turned into computer instructions. Each module can be built and tested separately. The modules can then be integrated into execution units, the execution units tested, and so on until the entire system has been assembled and tested. At that point, the scripts created to verify the essential model can be applied as a final acceptance test.

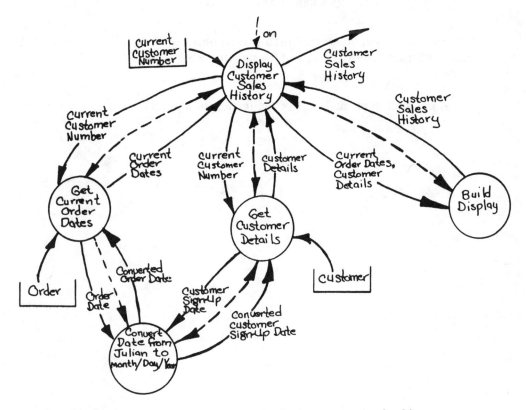

Figure 19.5. Code organization for displaying customer sales history.

19.4 Summary

A relatively simple system can be directly implemented from the processor configuration model. More complex systems will require that an implementation be purchased from a vendor or custom-built by data processing professionals. In the latter case, more modeling is desirable before the actual building begins.

In Part V, we will see how to organize the people and the tasks.

Chapter 19: Reference

1.   P. Ward and S. Mellor, unpublished course notes for YOURDON inc.'s workshop entitled "Structured Analysis and Design for Real-Time Systems."

A description of the levels of the implementation model.

Part V
Systems Development Organization

Although the models described in this book can be used informally in any kind of environment, their full benefit can be achieved only if their use is supported by the organization. In the final two chapters of the book, we cover the basic issues involved in providing that organizational support. Chapter 20 describes how to organize the people involved in systems development, and Chapter 21 describes how to organize the work of a systems development project.

20

Organizing the People

In this chapter, we give the general guidelines for the effective organization of people working on systems development. Let's first look at an instance of ineffective organization to see what we can learn from it. The company in our example is a medium-size manufacturer of mechanical devices. It purchases raw materials and components from suppliers and machine-assembles them into standard finished products. Manufacturing facilities are geographically dispersed and are specialized by product type. The finished products are stocked in regional warehouses, and are sold in small lots to customers. Customer orders are received at the warehouses by mail and by phone.

There is a computerized order filling system, which is shared by the manufacturing and distribution operations. As the company has grown and diversified, the automated system has required continual revision and enhancement. Maintenance of this system is the responsibility of a centralized information systems department.

The earlier versions of the order filling system were quite straightforward. Programmer/analysts in the information systems department obtained the requirements by interviewing manufacturing and distribution personnel, and proceeded to code and test programs to meet these requirements. Now that the growing complexities of the system have made this approach impractical, manufacturing and distribution personnel have been asked to take on more responsibility for requirements definition.

A recent system enhancement involved filtering out abnormal orders. The distribution system is set up to handle a steady stream of orders of nearly uniform size. A typical item might be manufactured in a lot of five hundred pieces once every three months. If incoming orders are steady (say, ten orders per week for an average of four units each), there will always be stock on hand to pack and ship immediately. An unusually large order will deplete the available stock drastically if packed and shipped immediately. This will disrupt service to the regular small customers while replacement stock is being manufactured.

The basic idea was simple enough. Abnormal orders were to be identified when they were entered, prevented from being packed and shipped, and reported to manufacturing for special handling. The complications involved the definition of an abnormal size, the provision of overrides at various stages of the process, and the capturing and reporting of data about the system so that its performance could be evaluated.

Each manufacturing facility determined the abnormal cutoff size for its product. Information systems department personnel combined the information from these documents with the results of extensive interviewing and research on other features to produce a system specification. This specification was to be reviewed thoroughly by the manufacturing and distribution areas before the system was built.

The overall specification had a self-contained section for each manufacturing facility, within which the changes were described on a program-by-program basis. Since the same set of programs was run for all facilities, and since most of the changes were common to all facilities, there was extensive redundancy in the specification. The final document was more than seven hundred pages long, with a minimum of one hundred pages devoted to each facility. There were a few tables, but the bulk of the document was in narrative form.

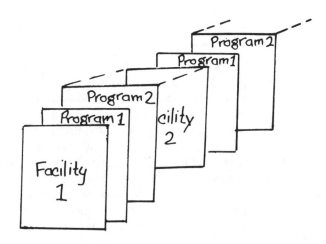

Figure 20.1. The specification layout.

The review process did not go well. Each manufacturing facility had its own section of the specification to review, and the internal divisions by program made it difficult for manufacturing people to follow the logic. The distribution people were even worse off; they had to track a feature through all the manufacturing sections to get the full story. Managers in both groups found the document so cluttered with detail that they couldn't review it for overall coherence. Finally, the information systems department personnel found the document difficult because program changes were scattered throughout the manufacturing facility sections.

The results of these difficulties were easy to predict. Deadlines for review and approval of the project were repeatedly set and then overrun. Some reviews were conducted superficially, some not at all. Finally, a high-level manager impatiently ordered that building of the system begin. When implemented, the system was denounced by both manufacturing and distribution personnel for disrupting order processing and for bearing no relation to what was wanted. Extensive revisions were made, but the system was never satisfactory.

After you have read the rest of this chapter, reread the above case study to identify the organizational features that caused the problems.

20.1 Development team organization

There is a general principle behind the guidelines given in this section; and that is that building a model of a system works best as a group activity. Unless your organization is so small that single-handed systems development efforts are unavoidable, there always should be two or more people working as a team to build the model. In fact, a team that consists of three to six members is best. There are not so many members that organization becomes a problem, nor so few that errors and incorrect assumptions can slip by unchallenged.

This does not mean that all team members must be assigned full time to systems development, nor that all members must be on the team for the entire project. Although some of the team members should be permanent, part-time and temporary members have important roles to play.

In the following paragraphs are five major guidelines for development team organization. The first three guidelines give the proper balance of team members. The fourth guideline specifies who should take responsibility for the system, and the final guideline states an important trait of project leadership.

Let us look at what our first guideline says about team members: *The interests of all affected user groups should be represented on the development team.* There are two areas of user involvement that must be considered. The first consists of people at various levels in the organization who will be affected by the implementation of the proposed system. Imagine a vertical plane, consisting of the clerk who enters data or checks output documents, the manager who is responsible for the clerks, and the vice president in whose domain the manager works. All have vested interests in some aspect of the system's operation, and anyone whose opposition or lack of cooperation can adversely affect the usefulness of the system, or whose interests are not considered in working out the model, is a potential obstacle to successful implementation. Although clerical workers and upper-level managers typically will not be active members of a systems development team, their interests should be represented by appropriate team members who act as liaison to these groups.

The second area of user interest can be thought of as existing on a horizontal plane and involves the various organizational units whose operations will be affected by the implementation. If department A must enter data into the system so that output for department B can be created, both departments must be involved in building the system model. Even more, if the proposed system will automate the making of a decision that was formerly the responsibility of some organizational unit, the cooperation of that unit must be obtained. Systems that work in theory exist in many organizations but their outputs are ignored because someone's decision making power was abrogated without permission. If the system will affect a large number of organizational units, it might not be practical to have a representative of each unit on the team, but the units that are most heavily affected should be directly represented, with one or more members-at-large given the responsibility of representing the interests of the other organizational units.

Our second guideline deals with the representation of support groups on development teams: *The interests of all affected support groups should be represented on the development team.* A support group is one that is not actively involved in the subject matter of the system, but whose resources are necessary for its creation or operation. The most obvious support group for an automated system is the data processing establishment. Clearly, it makes no sense for a development group to be modeling a system that it assumes will be implemented next year when the data processing group has three years' worth of high-priority work scheduled for completion before it can implement any new system.

In some organizations, a data administrator has responsibility for the accuracy and accessibility of all stored data within the organization. Any project with complex requirements for data storage needs cooperation from the data administrator.

A support group that is often ignored is the organization's internal auditing unit. Any system that moves money or goods needs adequate built-in controls on its operation. The internal auditors have valuable expertise to provide on this subject, and an internal auditor can sometimes block the implementation of a system built without adequate controls.

Auditors and data administration personnel are people whose participation is critical, but who can probably be temporary or part-time team members. Data processing personnel need to participate more during the building of the high-level implementation model than during the building of the essential model.

Our third guideline is that *the team should include at least one experienced analyst.* It is important to select the analyst on the basis of actual qualifications and not on the basis of job title. In many data processing establishments, the position of analyst is the next rung on the promotional ladder after senior programmer. There isn't much evidence that the skills required by a competent programmer are related to the skills required for modeling a system. Organizations that distinguish between business systems analysts and computer systems analysts are likely to find better candidates for systems development teams in the former category than in the latter, since business systems analysts are supposed to be good at defining systems, and computer systems analysts at organizing implementations. Recently, many organizations have formally or informally recognized the role of user/analyst. A user/analyst is a person whose background is in the subject area of the system (inventory control, purchasing, and so on) but who specializes in systems development.

The qualities of a good analyst are political astuteness (the ability to help people reach compromises and reconcile conflicting goals is paramount), information gathering skills (a good analyst must be able to conduct productive interviews and to extract relevant facts from masses of documentation), presentation skills (the ability to communicate complex ideas both verbally and in writing is indispensable), model building skills (the ability to organize material around a set of abstractions in order to reduce it to digestible form), and knowledge of the proposed system's subject matter. Of course, a competent analyst can learn about an unfamiliar subject quickly, but some initial familiarity will be helpful. In addition, knowledge of computer hardware and software is a useful adjunct to an analyst's skills (but is not strictly necessary).

Our fourth guideline is that *the formal responsibility for the project should lie with the users, not with the data processing group.* Many projects organized and conducted by data processing professionals have failed because the intended users never quite believe that it is their system. It is essential that the project be run by the users and viewed as their effort, which is being supported by data processing, not led by it. The team leader should be chosen from the user group with the largest stake in the project.

A final guideline is that *the actual leadership of the project team should be flexible, and should change as the project proceeds.* The person best able to direct information gathering may not be the person best able to direct model building. Whatever the formal leadership structure of the team, the day-to-day leadership role should evolve, based on the current needs of the team.

20.2 Review team organization

A system model must be reviewed by people not on the development team. Although this requirement is even more critical if the development team is very small, even fairly large teams can develop group blind spots to errors and inadequacies in the model.

The review process can take the form of a playthrough, or can be a more formal study. In the playthrough approach, the reviewers use the system model to create scripts that will uncover situations in which the model fails to predict what the system will do, or predicts undesirable behavior. The actual playthrough must be conducted jointly by the development team and the review team so that any misunderstanding of the script or of the model can be identified and corrected.

A more conventional review process requires the review team to study the model and to make proposals for additions, deletions, or changes. As with the playthrough, the review team's recommendations need to be aired and decisions made at a joint meeting of the development and review teams.

There are five guidelines for organizing the review team: First, *the role of reviewer must be formally recognized as a legitimate part of a person's job responsibilities.* Any system complex enough to be worth modeling will require a substantial amount of time to review, and management must agree that reviewing is a worthwhile activity before the process can be carried out effectively. People designated as reviewers must be given formal permission to study the model and to produce whatever review document during normal working hours.

Second, *the review process must be organized in such a way that the job can actually be done.* Review meetings must be scheduled sufficiently far in advance so that reviewers can set aside time to do the review. The reviewers must have enough time to study the model before the meeting. If major problems are encountered, a second review of the revised model must be scheduled.

Third, *the review meeting must be formally conducted as to include a moderator and a secretary.* The moderator will conduct the meeting but does not actually participate in the review process. He or she is responsible for seeing that everyone is heard, that disagreements are resolved, and that decisions are made and recorded. In addition, a secretary must keep a formal record of the meeting and distribute it to all participants.

Fourth, *an adequate follow-up procedure must be created.* One of the decisions to be made at a review meeting is whether the problems uncovered are substantial enough to require another review. If so, time must be provided for the revision of the model, and then the entire review process must be repeated. If the problems encountered are relatively small, the revised portions of the model can be circulated by mail and reviewed and initialed by the meeting participants.

Fifth, *reviewers must take responsibility for the outcome of the systems development process.* If the system is not successfully implemented because of an inadequacy in the model, the reviewers must bear part of the blame for the failure. Asking the reviewers to sign a formal document attesting to the adequacy of the model may help make this responsibility clearer.

20.3 Summary

Successful systems development requires teamwork; both the building of the system model and its review should be group activities. A team cannot function adequately unless its existence is formally recognized and supported by the organization.

Once a team has organized itself, it must organize the work to be done. The organization of work is treated in Chapter 21.

Chapter 20: Reference

1. R. Thomsett, *People & Project Management* (New York: Yourdon Press, 1980). Discussion of the need for flexible leadership on a project team.

21

Organizing the Work

The modeling tools and techniques in this book have something very important in common; they're intended to be used in an *iterative manner*. This means that you draw a model over and over again until it is right. The production of an attractive, neatly packaged final product is only a secondary end of the modeling process. Primarily, modeling is a thinking tool; it's a way to lay out your thoughts in a form that makes re-examination and refining easier. If you hesitate to draw a process schema or data schema until you've got it right in your mind, you're missing most of the value of the model. Humans are much better at improving something that already exists than at creating something entirely new. If you've got even the vaguest idea about processes and flows, make a drawing of it! No matter how off-base the resulting model is, it represents a point from which refinement can begin. This is especially important when the modeling process is conducted by a group. Your half-thought-out model may be just what one of your colleagues needs to move the process forward.

The iterative nature of modeling has some practical consequences for work organization. Models should be created using materials that can be easily modified. Paper and pencil are workable, a large chalkboard is better, and a graphics computer system is better yet. If your modeling team consists of more than two or three members, use an overhead projector and erasable markers. One of your group members then acts as a scribe, and the model is presented where everyone can see and criticize it.

Exploratory modeling, cycling, and other ideas about work organization are treated in the remaining pages of this chapter.

21.1 Exploratory modeling

The first process schemas and data schemas don't have to be built using the formalized modeling procedure described in Part III. At the beginning of a systems development project, a project team needs to explore the system's subject matter in a loose, unconstrained way. The team cannot decide what to include in a system until after it has explored the organizational environment.

Although the process schema is a useful exploratory tool, the data schema is ideal because of its abstract nature. By focusing attention on what's important rather than on what happens, the data schema discourages the exploratory modeling from getting bogged down in low-level details.

21.2 Horizontal organization: cycling

Throughout this book, I have emphasized the separation of the essential model from the implementation model. Understanding whether you are describing the essentials of a system or its implementation is important, since many systems development problems have arisen from confusing the two. However, I never meant to suggest that you should model the essentials of a system *without ever thinking about possible implementations.* For one thing, it's against human nature to investigate a problem without speculating about possible solutions. For another, completing a complex essential model before giving any thought to possible implementations can be an expensive waste of time. How do you know that some feature of the proposed system isn't impossible to implement, or would cost so much to implement that it can't be cost-justified?

Figure 21.1 presents an approach that allows the essential model and the implementation model to develop *together.* Think of the essential model and the implementation model as being side by side. Instead of completing the essential model before considering an implementation, you build the essential model one level at a time, and create the corresponding level of the implementation model before going deeper into the essential model.

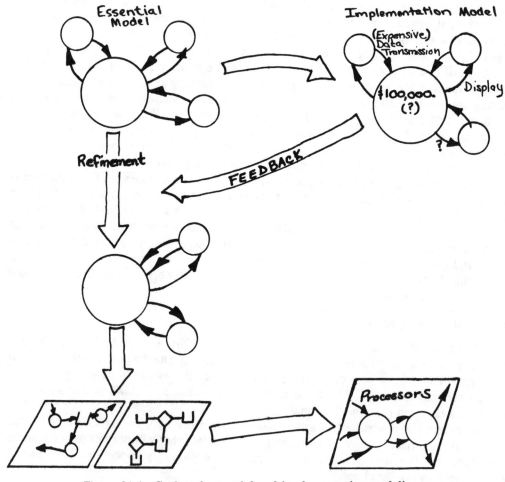

Figure 21.1. Cycles of essential and implementation modeling.

The first level of the essential model might consist of a rough context schema, a system definition, and a preliminary event list. The corresponding implementation model might consist of nothing more than some suggestions about the possible forms of interfaces, some guesses about processor packaging, and an order-of-magnitude cost estimate. These would be written as comments on a copy of the context schema.

The development team could first create the preliminary essential model and then the preliminary implementation model. Or, the models could be developed simultaneously by two different groups. In either case, before proceeding deeper into the essential model, the team considers the feedback from the preliminary implementation model and modifies the context as necessary. If the preliminary cost estimate is unexpectedly high, the scope of the system may need to be reduced. If an interface is a problem (for example, high data transmission costs from a terminator in a distant location), some alternative source of input may be sought.

Having adjusted the context schema and probably the event list on the basis of the preliminary implementation feedback, the modelers can derive the preliminary process and data schemas from the event list. These schemas are then the source of a more detailed implementation model. Perhaps a rough system-level process schema showing processor connections can now be drawn, the cost estimate refined, and some preliminary estimates of programming time made. This information is then used to make further adjustments to the essential model, and the process continues in a similar fashion.

21.3 Vertical organization: scope

As described in the previous section, implementation considerations can cause modelers to make alterations in the context schema. However, other than the estimated cost, implementation models give no feedback that can tell modelers whether the overall scope of the system is reasonable. The question of scope is the most basic one in the systems development process; this question can be worded, What pieces of existing or potential organizational patterns should be studied? or more specifically, What pieces of those patterns should be studied *now?* The questions are complex. To answer them, modelers must consider what problems with existing patterns have high priority, what new patterns are needed, how much money the project has to spend, and so on. In addition to these complexities, there are some intrinsic problems involving scope, which relate to the nature of the systems development process and to the connections between a system and its environment.

For example, there are some systems whose scope is intrinsically *too large,* as illustrated below:

A project team was told to define a system to track production in a large industrial plant. Since the finished goods were produced from raw materials, the team members decided to include the raw material receiving and storage area in their study. Since the finished goods were stored in a warehouse before shipment to customers, the team members also decided to include the warehousing operation. Furthermore, since the finished goods were produced on machines that needed periodic maintenance, they decided to incorporate the preventive maintenance. Ultimately, the team members decided to model nearly everything that happened within the walls of the plant. During the second year of the study, the development project was indefinitely suspended.

This development team ran into a common project phenomenon: If a project doesn't produce visible results regularly, it risks suspension or cancellation. Depending on the organization, the safe period can be as long as eighteen months or as short as six months.

One obvious way of reducing the scope is to carefully exclude from the system context processes that don't need automating or whose current automated versions are satisfactory. However, even if everything in the context bubble should be modeled and automated or reautomated, the scope of the system can still be larger than necessary. Project team members should consider delivering a large system piece by piece as a series of versions implemented at periodic intervals. A version might consist of any of the following:

- A working system with a set of basic functions, which will be enhanced with advanced functions in future versions.

- A system that automates part of a current manual function (perhaps the part for which computer-readable stored data is currently available) and passes the results to a human for completion. A future version will automate the entire function.

- A working model of the human-computer interface for a system involving complex interactions. While the system builders are building the insides of the final system, the users can be trying out the interface and identifying shortcomings that need correcting in the final version.

A systems development effort that produces working results at regular intervals is psychologically gratifying to the essential model builders and the implementers. It also neutralizes the enforcers of project deadlines; these typically are nervous high-level managers who worry that the modelers are *still* drawing bubbles.

Just as there are systems whose scope is intrinsically too large, there are systems whose context is intrinsically too small. Here is an example:

A manufacturing company, plagued with wildly fluctuating prices for raw materials, decided to set up an elaborate price tracking system. Part of this system was a database that was to keep three years' worth of records on quantity purchased, price paid, and vendor for each purchase of a raw material. A rather complicated program was needed to analyze this data and to produce statistics that could be used to predict future price fluctuations. When the program was completed and had been tested on sample data, it was discovered that the database couldn't be loaded with real data since *detailed records of that type simply hadn't been kept.*

This system failed because its scope was too narrow. If an event list had been created for this system, one of the events would have been "Purchasing provides data on which raw material was purchased from which vendor." This event didn't exist, since the data simply wasn't recorded. Problems with too-small scopes almost invariably result because the system modelers ignore the manual processes that must provide data to and accept data from automated systems.

One of the problems with the cycling approach described above is that the entire system must be cycled down to the lowest level of the implementation model before anything can be built. It is possible to combine the horizontal approach of cycling and the vertical approach of building versions with limited contexts, as follows:

- Use the cycling approach until the essential and implementation models are detailed enough to identify implementable versions.

- Work vertically to complete the essential and implementation models for one of the versions, build and implement it, and then repeat the process for the next version.

21.4 Organization for system maintenance

Systems development does not end with the implementation of a system. Nearly all systems require ongoing modifications as user needs change or as more powerful implementation technologies become available. The models that were built to guide the initial implementation can continue to be useful afterward.

The connection between the systems development models and the maintenance process is actually quite obvious: *The easiest way to discuss a change to the system is in terms of a change to the model.* For example, a fairly substantial change to the essentials of a system might be needed because there is a new external event to which the system must respond. The system maintainers may have to add a new data input from a terminator to the context bubble to signal the event, a new process on the process schema to respond to the event, and new stores and relationships to provide data to the process making the response. The proposed change can be formulated by noting on the essential model where the modifications must be made.

In order to make this change, of course, one of the processors that does the work of the system has to be modified to accept the new input. This change can be formulated by modifying the appropriate piece of the high-level implementation model. Ultimately, the change needs to be carried through to the lower levels of the implementation model. This modified model could guide the actual modifications to the computer instructions.

Figure 21.2 describes the maintenance process in detail. The maintenance cycle begins with either the essential model or the implementation model, depending on the type of change to be made. For example, a change in the form of an interface (such as replacing a report with a screen display containing the same data) would change the implementation model but not the essential model.

Two advantages of this approach are that the proposed change to the system can be thought out using the various models before it's actually made, and that the models are updated along with the current version of the implemented system.

21.5 Summary

Effective systems development requires an intelligent tailoring of the ASML modeling process to the specifics of the project. Such tailoring can include exploratory modeling, parallel development of essential and implementation models, and delivery of a system in versions.

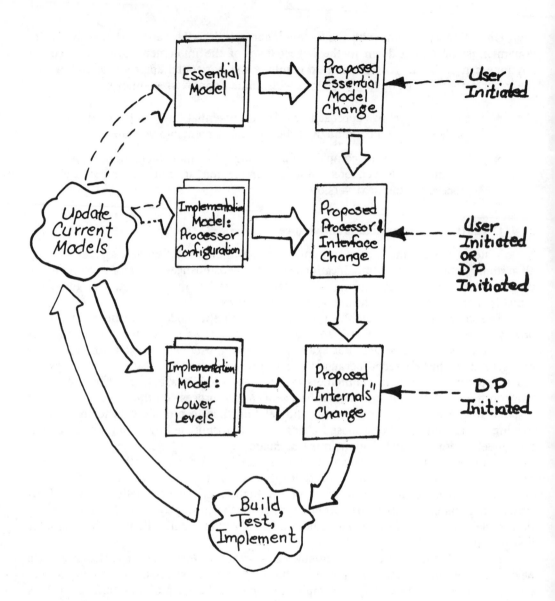

Figure 21.2. System maintenance using the models.

Chapter 21: References

1. B. Dickinson, *Developing Structured Systems* (New York: Yourdon Press, 1980).

    A detailed description of a horizontal approach to systems development.

2. T. DeMarco, *Structured Analysis and System Specification* (New York: Yourdon Press, 1978), pp. 289-92.

    A description of a formal approach for keeping a system model up-to-date.

Afterword

I am not naive enough to believe in perfect systems or in perfect systems development projects. Human beings are error-prone, and our day-to-day conduct is motivated by many factors other than allegiance to organizational goals. Our fallibilities and our mixed motivations are bound to affect the outcome of our attempts to work together, and both our manual and automated organizational patterns will inevitably be imperfect.

Nevertheless, those who have resigned themselves to misunderstanding and confusion as the natural course of a systems development project, and to an unsatisfactory, second-rate implementation as its natural outcome, have set their sights too low. Errors and conflicting motivations cannot be eliminated, but they can be reduced to manageable proportions. Most systems development problems are human communication problems — not the unwillingness or inability of people to communicate, but simply the lack of a common language for discussing complex patterns. In my work as a project manager and as a consultant, I have often seen the adoption of such a common language transform a project team's attitude from discouragement and bickering to eager cooperation. It is intellectually stimulating and emotionally satisfying to discover that most of one's work environment can be expressed in intelligible terms and flexible patterns. If I help you to experience that stimulation and satisfaction in even a modest way, my labors as an author will have been well rewarded.

Appendix

Essential Model for
The Un-College Matching System

Introduction

On the following pages you will find an essential model for The Un-College's matching system. This model is a supplement to the examples given in Chapters 12 through 15. Since the examples in these chapters are scattered throughout the text, there is no illustration of what an actual essential model would look like as organized for presentation.

The schematic section of the model is complete, and, except for some omitted data elements in the store composition descriptions, all the lower-level details of the data schema have been filled in. Although the details of the process model are not complete, one of the system-level processes (Sign-up Student) has a complete set of lower-level details.

Let me suggest two ways in which you can use this model. First, you can use the model as an exercise to test your understanding of the essential model building process. To do this, begin with the context schema, and without looking ahead attempt to develop an external event list. After you have finished, compare your results with the event list included in the model. Don't expect an exact correspondence between your results and mine; since this is an imaginary organization, your conception of how to best accomplish its purposes may be different from mine. Having completed the event list, you can then proceed to derive a process schema using the context diagram and either my event list or yours. Check your results against the process schema included in the model, and proceed with the rest of the model in a similar fashion.

The second way in which you can use the model is to practice the balancing techniques described in Chapter 11. Compare the system-level process schema with the context schema, the lower-level process schemas with the system-level process schema, and so on.

At the end of this Appendix there are some notes that discuss features of the model about which you may have questions. I suggest you work through the model and try to understand it as completely as possible before referring to the notes.

System definition

SYSTEM DEFINITION: The purpose of The Un-College Matching System is to assist students and teachers in meeting each other for purposes of learning.

External event list

Event 1: Student indicates interest in learning subject.

Event 2: Student revokes interest in learning subject.

Event 3: Teacher claims qualification to teach subject.

Event 4: Teacher revokes willingness to teach subject.

Event 5: Teacher indicates willingness to accept students in subject.

Event 6: Teacher indicates unwillingness to accept students in subject.

Event 7: Management approves proposed subject.

Event 8: Management disapproves proposed subject.

Event 9: Management approves teacher.

Event 10: Management disapproves teacher.

Event 11: No teacher has been approved for a subject for which there are a number of unmatched students.

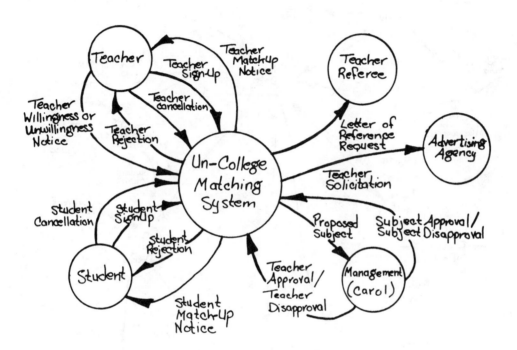

CONTEXT

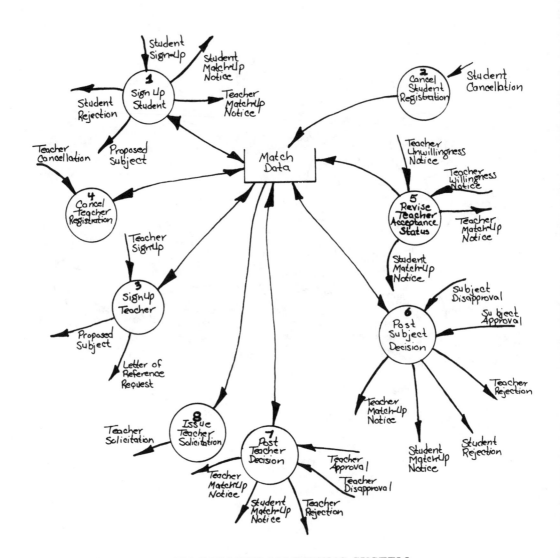

UN-COLLEGE MATCHING SYSTEM

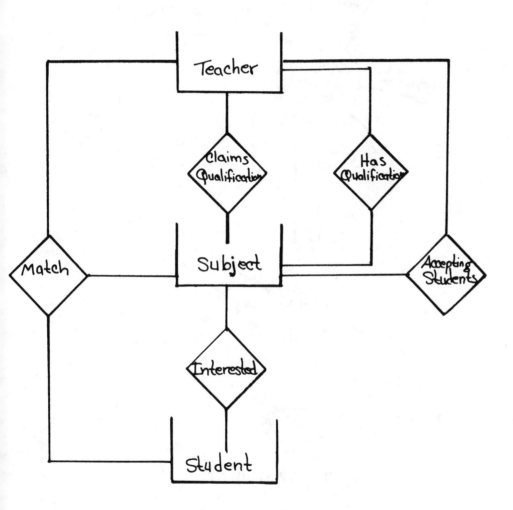

UN-COLLEGE MATCHING SYSTEM

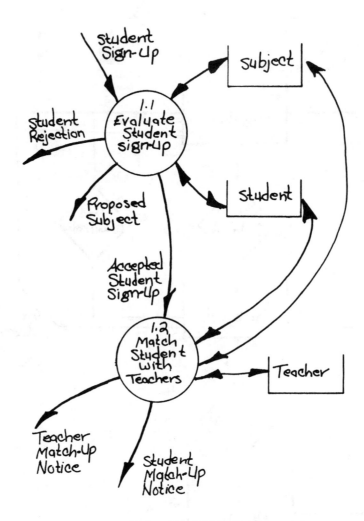

1. SIGN UP STUDENT

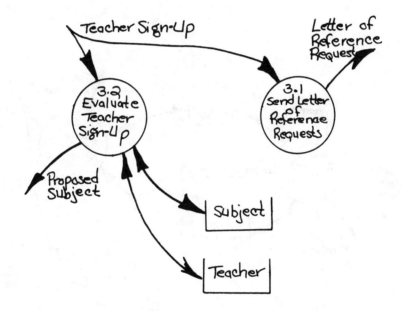

3. SIGN UP TEACHER

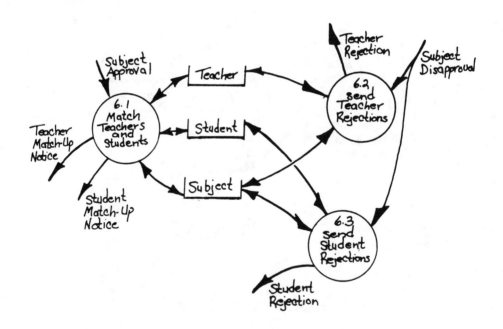

6. POST SUBJECT DECISION

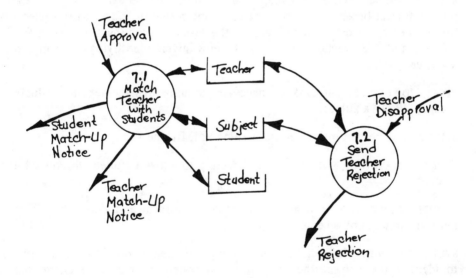

7. POST TEACHER DECISION

Definitions

ACCEPTED STUDENT SIGN-UP: Data necessary to match a student who is interested and able to learn an approved subject with a teacher.

ACCEPTING STUDENTS: An association between one teacher and one approved subject based on the teacher's willingness to accept students in the subject.

CLAIMS QUALIFICATION: An association between one teacher and one subject based on the teacher's having submitted the names of referees familiar with his or her qualifications to teach the subject.

HAS QUALIFICATION: An association between one teacher and one subject based on the teacher's referees having provided acceptable evidence of the teacher's ability to teach the subject.

INTERESTED: An association between one student and one subject based on the student wishing to learn the subject and being capable of receiving instruction in the subject.

MATCH: An association between one teacher, one student, and one approved subject based on the student being interested in learning the subject, the teacher being qualified to teach it, the teacher accepting students in the subject, and the teacher and student being given identifying information about each other.

PROPOSED SUBJECT: Information necessary to allow management to evaluate acceptability of a subject.

STUDENT: A person interested in learning at least one subject.

STUDENT MATCH-UP NOTICE: Data necessary to allow a student to contact a teacher.

STUDENT REJECTION: Information sufficient to inform a student why his or her sign-up was not accepted.

STUDENT SIGN-UP: Information necessary to maintain contact with a student, to identify the subject the student is interested in, and to evaluate the student's ability to receive instruction in the subject.

SUBJECT: An area of knowledge that may involve restrictions on potential students' ability to learn, and that must be approved by The Un-College before students and teachers may be matched.

TEACHER: A person claiming to be qualified to teach at least one subject.

TEACHER MATCH-UP NOTICE: Data necessary to allow a teacher to contact a student.

Composition descriptions

ACCEPTED STUDENT SIGN-UP consists of
      STUDENT NAME
and   STUDENT NUMBER
and   STUDENT ADDRESS
and   STUDENT HOME PHONE
and   STUDENT BUSINESS PHONE
and   SUBJECT NAME

PROPOSED SUBJECT consists of
      SUBJECT NAME

REASON FOR REJECTION
      permitted values:
      HEALTH PROBLEMS
      DISAPPROVED SUBJECT

STUDENT consists of zero or more instances; each one
is identified by STUDENT NUMBER and consists of
      STUDENT NAME
and   STUDENT ADDRESS
and   STUDENT HOME PHONE
and   STUDENT BUSINESS PHONE

      :
      :

STUDENT MATCH-UP NOTICE consists of
      STUDENT NAME
and   STUDENT ADDRESS
and   SUBJECT NAME
and   TEACHER NAME
and   TEACHER HOME PHONE

STUDENT REJECTION consists of
      STUDENT NAME
and   STUDENT ADDRESS
and   REASON FOR REJECTION

STUDENT SIGN-UP consists of
      STUDENT NAME
and   STUDENT NUMBER
and   STUDENT ADDRESS
and   STUDENT HOME PHONE
and   STUDENT BUSINESS PHONE
and   SUBJECT NAME
and optionally
      STUDENT HEALTH STATUS

SUBJECT consists of zero or more instances; each one is identified by SUBJECT NAME and consists of
   SUBJECT APPROVAL STATUS

SUBJECT APPROVAL STATUS
  permitted values:
  APPROVED
  PENDING APPROVAL

TEACHER consists of zero or more instances; each one is identified by TEACHER NUMBER and consists of
   TEACHER NAME
and TEACHER ADDRESS
and TEACHER HOME PHONE
and TEACHER BUSINESS PHONE
and TEACHER SIGN-UP DATE
and

   .
   .
   .

TEACHER MATCH-UP NOTICE consists of
   TEACHER NAME
and TEACHER ADDRESS
and SUBJECT NAME
and STUDENT NAME
and STUDENT HOME PHONE

Process descriptions

Evaluate Student Sign-Up

if the SUBJECT NAME is LION TAMING or MOUNTAIN CLIMBING or MARATHON RUNNING
then
>   if the STUDENT HEALTH STATUS is anything except OUTSTANDING
>   then
>   >   issue a STUDENT REJECTION with HEALTH PROBLEMS as the
>   >   REASON FOR REJECTION

if no STUDENT REJECTION was issued
then
>   create a new STUDENT NUMBER
>   create a new instance of STUDENT from the STUDENT SIGN-UP data
>   if there is no instance of a SUBJECT matching the SUBJECT NAME
>   on the STUDENT SIGN-UP
>   then
>   >   issue a PROPOSED SUBJECT
>   >   create an instance of SUBJECT with SUBJECT APPROVAL STATUS of
>   >   PENDING APPROVAL
>
>   record that the STUDENT is INTERESTED in the SUBJECT
>   if the SUBJECT APPROVAL STATUS is APPROVED
>   then
>   >   issue an ACCEPTED STUDENT SIGN-UP

Match Student With Teachers

if there is at least one TEACHER who both HAS QUALIFICATION and is ACCEPTING
STUDENTS in the SUBJECT
then
>   pick the TEACHER identified above with the earliest SIGN-UP DATE
>   create a STUDENT MATCH-UP NOTICE and a TEACHER MATCH-UP NOTICE from
>   the TEACHER, STUDENT, and SUBJECT data
>   record the MATCH among the STUDENT, the TEACHER, and the SUBJECT

Notes

General. The process and data descriptions shown here, although similar to the examples given in Chapters 9 and 10, aren't completely consistent with those examples. For example, the process schema for Match Student With Teacher doesn't create a new instance of Student and thus differs from the example given in Chapter 10. The differences were introduced so that the essential model forms a coherent whole.

Context Schema. The letter of reference goes from the Teacher Referee to Management. Since it doesn't cross the system boundary, it doesn't show on the schema.

External Event List. Event 1., No teacher has been approved . . . , is a time-driven event. It occurs when students have accumulated for an approved subject and no teacher has been found. The other events on the list are triggered by flows.

System-Level Process Schema. Since there are eleven external events, the preliminary process schema created from the event list has been lumped to reduce complexity. As an exercise, see if you can identify which bubbles respond to more than one event.

Process Schema for Sign-up Teacher. A teacher will not be matched with students until references have been received and evaluated. Also, if the subject to be taught hasn't been approved, management's approval must be sought. Since both teacher approval and subject approval happen outside the system and are thus time delayed, matching cannot be a direct consequence of a teacher sign-up.

Index